THE ESCAPE FROM SINGAPORE

By the same author:
SOE Singapore 1941–42

The Escape from Singapore

RICHARD GOUGH

WILLIAM KIMBER LONDON

First published in 1987 by
WILLIAM KIMBER & CO. LIMITED
100 Jermyn Street, London, SW1Y 6EE

© Richard Gough, 1987
ISBN 0–7183–0655–4

Printed in Great Britain by
Billing & Sons Limited
Worcester WR2 5JU

Contents

List of Illustrations

List of Maps

Preface

Dunkirk has an emotional appeal to those who lived through those grim war years, yet Singapore was soon forgotten and was largely ignored. Although the ultimate failure to hold Singapore must lie with successive prewar governments and their Chiefs of Staff, the disaster could have been avoided and countless lives saved.

This is not the story of the battle for Singapore, which has been well documented elsewhere, but the story of an attempt to organise an evacuation of troops from the island. This later became an unofficial escape route which saved thousands of lives.

A Dunkirk veteran, Colonel Alan Ferguson Warren, Royal Marines, head of a small war office clandestine secret unit, anticipated that in the end resourceful soldiers would try to escape rather than face capture. His unit, together with SOE, stocked desert islands with supplies and made arrangements with the Dutch to move escapers across Sumatra to the escape port of Padang. This is their story and that of the thousands of escapers and survivors from the ships lost in the last minute evacuation.

The escape route was first described to me by the late Alan Warren when he briefed me on the work of SOE's Orient Mission, described in my book *SOE Singapore 1941/42*. In 1941 he was a lieutenant-colonel in the Royal Marines responsible for creating guerrilla units to operate behind Japanese lines should war become inevitable. This story is based on conversations with him and access to his unpublished notes. Further help was given by John Davis, Boris Hembry and Frank Brewer. Both John Davis and Boris Hembry worked with Colonel Warren and SOE in Malaya before they made their separate ways to Colombo and India.

Boris Hembry returned to Sumatra by submarine and later created an intelligence organisation which infiltrated agents into the Dutch East Indies and the Malayan Peninsula. John Davis went back into Malaya and became the main link between SOE's Malayan Section and the Chinese guerrillas. Frank Brewer was less fortunate. He was with SOE and later Colonel Dalley's Dalforce in

Singapore and took part in the final battle. He was captured after a 300-mile attempted escape bid by boat.

I am also indebted to the *South Wales Echo* which helped trace some of the escapers. Amongst these were George Avery, Henry Edwards, Ivor Deare, Walter Hughes, B.L. Jenkins and A.R. Taylor who supplied me with background information and access to their unpublished notes. My thanks must also go to the TV broadcaster and writer Ian Skidmore who was kind enough to help me locate Lieutenant Lind's manuscript and to John Parker and Amy Myers for their views and advice.

A book is really not complete without photographs. So I greatly appreciated the willingness of the following to loan their material: John Davis, Boris Hembry, Jim Gavin and Frank O'Shanohun all ex-SOE, and to Doug Cuthbertson, Peter Nunn, Bush Hamilton, Walter Hughes and B. L. Jenkins and a special thanks to Colonel and Mrs Pidsley for Colonel Warren's portrait.

My very special thanks must go to my wife Rona, for her skill with the word processor and without whom writing this book at home wouldn't have been half so much fun.

Richard Gough
11 November 1986.

Why Singapore?

'Singapore' wrote Churchill in a Cabinet Paper in December 1939, 'is a fortress armed with five 15-inch guns and garrisoned by nearly 20,000 men. It could only be taken after a siege of at least 50,000 men.' Commenting on Japan's ability to mount such a siege, Churchill continued that 'Singapore is as far from Japan as Southampton is from New York. The operation of moving a Japanese Army, with all its troopships and maintaining it during a siege, which would last at least four or five months, would be liable to be interrupted, if at any time Britain chose to send a superior fleet to the scene.'

Singapore was recognised as the lynchpin of Britain's defence strategy in the Far East. Its importance lay in its recently completed, modern naval base on the Johore Strait. Beyond Singapore, a thousand miles to the east, Britain had concessions in the Treaty Ports along the north China coast. The British historic presence in both Hong Kong and Singapore played an important part in the development of these commercial interests. Singapore was also an important link between India and Australia.

Churchill's optimism in 1939 is surprising because as early as 1930 the British Government was warned in a Cabinet Paper firstly that the Japanese fleet had become the third largest in the world and secondly that it was economically impossible for Britain to maintain a permanent, large, Far East fleet.

Various prewar British governments were reluctant or simply refused to spend money on a new base until finally the High Commissioner for Australia, Mr S.M. Bruce, pointedly told the Committee for Imperial Defence in 1933 that it 'was difficult to see what could prevent Japan obtaining a complete mastery of the Pacific if it chose to go to war.'

In 1936 the Chief of the Imperial General Staff submitted a secret paper outlining the case for friendship with Japan. Alongside this on the political front Neville Chamberlain pursued a policy of appeasement. Britain was coming out of the great depression and had neither the military might nor the money to face the Japanese threat. Japan wanted a share of the trade in the Far East until now monopolized by the Western colonial powers and America. It chose China as its first victim.

As part of the appeasement policy in the early thirties the Headquarters of the Commander-in-Chief Far East moved from Hong Kong to Singapore. Faced with Japan's expansionist policies a reluctant British Government began to pump millions of pounds into the construction of a new Singapore naval base to defend India, while at the same time trying to assure Japan that its construction was purely defensive. Well aware that Japan's territorial ambitions could spill over into the China's Treaty Ports, London had a contingency plan to evacuate some 15,000 British subjects living in Peking and the Concessions dotted along the China coast. But no plans existed for Hong Kong nor Singapore.

If Japan should launch a seaborne assault on either one of these bases, the overall Eastern defence plan envisaged that Hong Kong could be defended by submarines for 40 days. This would enable the Fleet to reach the area and raise the siege. In fact Hong Kong was captured by battle-experienced soldiers who fought their way in over the mountains.

It was planned that Singapore would become a fortress, defended from a seaborne attack by the RAF together with ships sent from Britain and the new, heavy coastal guns buried deep in concrete bunkers. The army would be reinforced by units evacuated from the Treaty Ports.

Twelve months after Churchill's 1939 Cabinet Paper the British General Officer Commanding (GOC) Malaya, Lieutenant General Sir Lionel Bond, drew up a plan to hold Malaya, Singapore's back door. The popular concept of Malaya in Britain was a country of mountains and jungle; instead it had good, well metalled roads and a rail network along its west coast running from Thailand in the north to Singapore in the south. This was to be the route of Japan's thrust to Singapore.

The GOC estimated his needs to defend that route as four divisions and two tank regiments. In addition he required 582 modern fighter planes. Having lost planes, men and equipment in Norway and France, culminating with a heavy loss of aircraft during the Battle for Britain, the Chiefs of Staff replied that no warships could be spared, nor could he have tanks or anti-tank artillery. As for the planes although it was recognized that 582 aircraft may be needed they considered that 336 'would give a fair degree of security'. British troops in the Treaty Ports had already been withdrawn and absorbed in the European War.

The Chiefs of Staff's reply was in line with its Far East policy. An assessment of Singapore's military capabilities realistically pointed out that the island's sea defences were inadequate and its air force insufficient. In view of the need for all available resources to be sent to the Western Desert or kept for Home Defence, it was decided to continue the policy of appeasement and not to go to war should Japan land troops in French Indo-China.

Britain's defence of its Far East Empire was based on the assumption that Indo-China would remain French and pro-British. However, the scene had changed. France had capitulated to Germany and was about to install a Vichy-French, pro-Japanese administration in that country. The Chiefs of Staff had anticipated this occurrence.

A copy of Chiefs of Staff's secret report was sent to the GOC Malaya, carried on the SS *Autonedan* which sailed from Birkenhead on 24th September 1940. Her sole armament was a stern mounted little gun. In the Indian Ocean her skipper was called to the bridge for his view on what the second mate thought was a 'Dutchman'. The next moment a tall water spout rose high in front of the bows as the approaching vessel fired a warning shot. At the same time the coxswain saw 'the Dutchman' break out German colours. She was the German surface raider *Atlantis*.

The skipper of the *Autonedan* decided to make a fight of it and ordered the stern gun to be manned and turned his vessel's stern to the bows of the approaching raider. This not only narrowed his vessel's profile as a target but gave the stern gunner a clear view of his target. Hardly had the turn been carried out than a salvo shattered the bridge, blowing the skipper and second mate to bits. All the officers were killed and the coxswain lay badly injured among the wreckage. The only sounds seemed to be the hissing of steam and the crackle of flames. Then voices were heard as the armed German boarding party scrambled over the ship's rails.

Down below the raiders blew open the strong room door and amongst the mail bags and securities they found a heavily sealed bag of government mail. In this was a wealth of secret and confidential papers including MI6 and Naval Intelligence reports, merchant navy codes and the Chiefs of Staff Report including the all important policy paper. The latter was sent to Japan.

The Japanese Intelligence Services were overwhelmed with the windfall. A restraining factor to any military move south against Malaya and the Dutch East Indies was an assumption that the Dutch, British and Americans had an integrated defence plan for the area. They now knew that not only was that a myth but Singapore, as a fortress, was an illusion. This left them free to break out of the economic encirclement and strike south to seize the oil rich Dutch East Indies and the ricefields of Burma. In a pre-emptive strike it could neutralize the American Fleet in Pearl Harbour and eliminate the empty British naval base in Singapore.

In December 1941, only two years after Churchill gave his views on Japan's inability to mount an attack on the Malayan Barrier, Japanese troops stormed ashore in north Malaya. Despite this Churchill was still reluctant to send additional men and equipment to this new battle zone. Admitting that Malaya was low on his list of priorities, Churchill cabled the Rt Hon John Curtin, head of the Australian Labour Government, on Christmas Day 1941, that Singapore would not be strengthened at the cost of weakening Britain's position in North Africa.

Simultaneously Japan struck at Pearl Harbour, bringing the USA into the war, and bombed Singapore.

Tension had been building up between the two governments over Britain's defence policy in the Far East and Churchill's note came as a shock. The Australian Government had continually been led to believe that the Royal Navy based at the new Naval Base in Singapore, and appeasement of the Japanese, were the cornerstone of Britain's defence policy in the Far East. Now that Britain's policy of appeasement had blatantly failed, Curtin was concerned that Australia's fate must depend on adequate reinforcements, troops, planes and ships, being sent to Singapore. The Australian Government, which had given generously to the Mother Country's call for volunteers to fight the European and desert wars, now felt let down by what could be considered Churchill's cavalier attitude to Australia's security. Curtin was sufficiently upset and disappointed to announce in his New Year's message the threat that Australia looked 'towards America, free of any pangs as to our traditional links or kinship with the UK'.

Unlike Britain, the defence of Australia topped President Roosevelt's list of priorities. His memorandum on the subject in February 1942 stated that the US would take the primary responsibility for reinforcing Australia with men and materials. It was anticipated that these reinforcements would leave before 1st March. Meanwhile British reinforcements bound for the Western Desert, stopped over in Cape Town until the argument over their future was settled. As the military situation in Malaya deteriorated and the British army was rolled back by the Japanese, Curtin continued to pressure Churchill for the reinforcements to be sent to Singapore. But Churchill wasn't convinced that there was any danger and as late as 14th January 1942 implied to Curtin that Singapore could be held for some time.

However, Churchill's views received a jolt five days later when General Sir Archibald Wavell, Supreme Commander ABDA Command warned him, in a cable on the 19th, that in his opinion Singapore would not be able to withstand a siege. This arrived only five days after he had assured Curtin that Singapore could be held for some time. In a minute to the Chiefs of Staff Committee Churchill demanded to know why no one had alerted him to this defence weakness in the two years the subject had been under discussion. 'What is the use of having an island for a fortress if it is not to be made into a citadel?' he asked.

In a cable on the 20th which took away from Wavell any flexibility of action the Prime Minister wrote 'I want to make it absolutely clear that I expect every inch of ground to be defended, every scrap of material or defences to be blown to pieces to prevent capture by the enemy, and no question of surrender to be entertained until after protracted fighting among the ruins of Singapore City.'

Churchill became increasingly involved in that theatre's military affairs taking the initiative away from his commanders in the field. An anxious General Sir Alan Brooke, Chief of the Imperial General Staff, noted in his diary on 9th February that he considered it 'dangerous to interfere with a commander at a distance when you cannot be fully familiar with all aspects of the situation confronting him.' This was the situation in Malaya where Churchill bombarded Wavell with messages relating to policies that had often been overtaken by events.

It was against this political background that British reinforcements for the Western Desert, held back in Cape Town, were redirected in January to India where they embarked thousands of half-trained Indian troops for Singapore. Meanwhile although all Australia's best troops were already committed to battle in other parts of the world she nevertheless scraped the barrel and found

1,500 recently recruited volunteers as reinforcements for Singapore. With hindsight it would have been better if they had never been sent.

In Malaya each defence line crumpled, the capital Kuala Lumpur was evacuated and abandoned without a fight on 16th January 1942. The shattered and exhausted troops then withdrew 100 miles to Johore where they fell back, through the Australian lines, to a position only some fifty miles from Singapore.

Churchill now began to admit misgivings and on 21st January he urged his Chiefs of Staff to consider abandoning Singapore. The reinforcements, now on their way across the Indian Ocean, could be diverted to Burma where the Japanese were decimating the 17th Division. Alarmed by this proposal the Australian Government cabled Churchill that the evacuation of Singapore would be regarded in Australia as an inexcusable betrayal.

The War Office also had doubts about the feasibility of basing the defence of Australia on Singapore. Major-General Sir John Kennedy, the Director of Military Operations at the War Office, was of the opinion that Singapore had never been considered defensible from close attack. 'It was our opinion,' he wrote later 'that the forces at Singapore or as many as could be extracted, would be better employed holding the islands southwards than in trying to hang on to Singapore, once it had been isolated or invested.' But by this time Churchill was firmly committed to holding Singapore.

As General Arthur E. Percival, GOC Malaya, tried to extricate his men from Malaya, across the narrow, mile long causeway that linked Johore and Singapore Island, the Japanese came out of the jungle at night and overwhelmed Australian and Indian units. This move cut off and scattered thousands of recently arrived reinforcements, leaving 70 per cent of the shattered army to escape eventually across the causeway. The Argylls and the Australians, who formed the rearguard, were the last to withdraw from Malaya leaving the Royal Engineers and Royal Navy demolition experts to destroy the causeway on 1st February.

A week later, on Saturday 7th February, Churchill optimistically cabled the US President Roosevelt that Percival had the equivalent of four divisions for the 'defence of the great base'. The Japanese, he pointed out, would have 'to cross a broad moat before attacking a strong fortified and still mobile force.'

This statement was probably made for consumption in the USA.

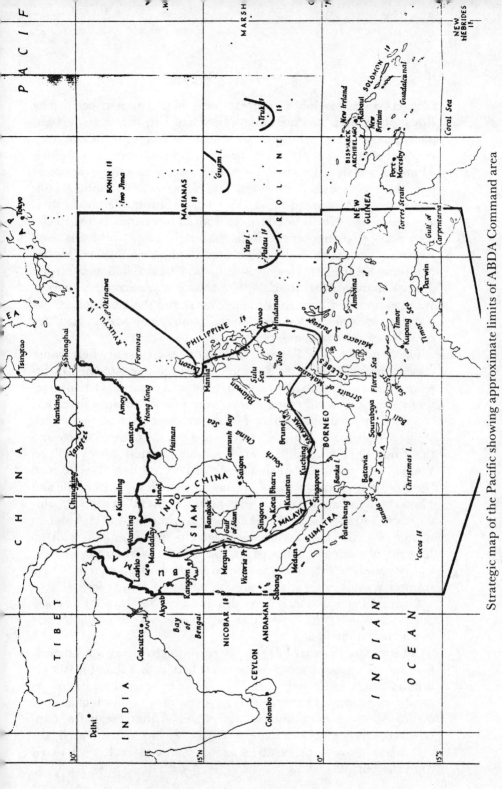

Strategic map of the Pacific showing approximate limits of ABDA Command area and the Japanese advance by mid-January 1942

Singapore was no longer a great base, if it ever had been. The Royal Navy and the Australian Navy had left; the recently completed, modern and almost unused naval base had been abandoned and destroyed; the air cover had been withdrawn and despite Churchill's instructions and Curtin's views, a selective evacuation of military personnel had begun. The island lacked suitable fortifications along its 'broad moat', the Johore Straits. Percival's divisions consisted of exhausted troops from Malaya and almost 10,000 raw reinforcements, fresh from training camps in India and Australia where some had never even used a rifle. Major-General Sir John Kennedy's view was that 'the island had never been defensible from close attack – the channel was narrow, mangrove swamps impeded the fire of the defences; and the aerodromes, the water supply and other vital installations were within artillery range from the mainland.'

On Sunday night, the 8th, little more than twenty-four hours after Churchill's signal to Roosevelt, the Japanese launched themselves across the 'broad moat'. By Tuesday morning enemy columns had successfully fought their way inland towards Percival's supply dumps around Bukit Timah, in the centre of the island. While General Percival was throwing raw, untrained troops into the front line, Churchill sent a scathing signal to Wavell on Wednesday, pointing out that General Percival had 100,000 men (in fact he had about 85,000) which included 33,000 British and 17,000 Australian troops. These must, Churchill assumed, outnumber the Japanese who had crossed over the Straits. He went on to say that 'the battle must be fought to the bitter end with no thought of saving the troops or sparing the civilian population. Commanders and senior officers should die with their troops.' He wanted Wavell to show no mercy to weakness in any form.

General Percival surrendered his army on Sunday, 15th February, after about 100 local ships had evacuated some 10,000 servicemen and civilians.

An estimated further 7,000 servicemen made their own independent bid to escape although some never fled further than the islands around Singapore's harbour. Thousands died in the attempt to escape and those who succeeded did so mainly as a result of a small dedicated group of volunteers who searched the islands for shipwrecked survivors and escapers. With the help of the Dutch, the volunteers moved the escapers across Sumatra to be evacuated from the port of Padang.

Many thousands could have been saved if the political situation had allowed the military a free hand. As this wasn't possible it was left to a small band of men to save what they could. This is the story of that evacuation and the escape route across Sumatra.

PART ONE

The Evacuation

CHAPTER ONE

The Singapore Naval Base
28th January 1942

The road from Bukit Timah to the causeway was flanked by rows and rows of rubber trees and groups of attap-roofed wooden shacks where Chinese squatters lived, recalled Colonel Warren. It was also crowded with convoys of military vehicles of every description salvaged from the debacle in Johore. In amongst the convoys were long lines of civilian cars crowded with passengers and packed high with suitcases. In the past few weeks families of the 9,000 strong British community in Malaya, businessmen, planters, mining engineers had poured into Singapore. Everything they owned was left behind as they fled from the Japanese. If they had expected some organization waiting to assist them in Sigapore, they were to be sadly disillusioned. It was every family for itself, Warren remembered.

The road from the causeway to Bukit Timah split the island roughly in half. To the west, near the causeway and in a line from north to south, was the River Kranji which poured into the Straits of Johore. A mile from Kranji creek was the new RAF airfield at Tengah and two miles south of that, the Jurong river which reached the sea six miles north of Keppel Harbour. This area, commented Warren, was 'the Australians' pigeon' (8th AIF Division) supported by the Punjabs.

Warren was on his way to the naval base which lay to the east of the causeway on the Straits of Johore. This was to be 11th Division's area and contained, apart from the naval base, two new modern RAF airfields at Seletar and Sembawang. The base and the airfields had been regularly bombed and Warren had learnt from his old friend Commander Alexander RN that the Navy were pulling out, leaving behind a lot of equipment. So Warren borrowed a lorry to go across to the base to see what he could find.

The War Office had posted Colonel Alan Ferguson Warren, Royal Marines, to Singapore ten months earlier. His job was secretly to recruit, train and infiltrate sabotage parties and armed guerrillas behind enemy lines. He had an independent role outside the Army Command structure, very much a free agent but with the strength of the War Office behind him. In the last eight weeks, he, and a small group of specially selected volunteers, had 'put-in' twelve sabotage parties and some 200 Chinese communist guerrillas. He had another thirty Chinese waiting to be infiltrated into Malaya. They had completed their training and were billeted at the SOE camp, near the estuary of the Jurong River. They were to be a thorn in the enemy's side throughout the war and a bigger one for the post-war British administration.

The driver slowed the lorry and cut across the traffic at a convenient gap, to join the Mandai/Nee Soon Road. This took him past the tall, army barrack blocks and the heavily guarded Sembawang airfield surrounded by Bofors guns, to the new naval base. This recently completed, modern base had been built on the north-east side of the island, on the Johore Straits facing the mainland.

Most of the specialist personnel at the base had been evacuated, and detachments of naval ratings were leaving daily on any available ship. The base would obviously become untenable when the Japanese arrived on the opposite bank in Johore so 'what was the point of wasting men and equipment to defend an empty, badly bombed, base?' Warren reasoned. Evidently many of his friends had similar views in 1942.

At the entrance to the base a smartly dressed, steel helmeted, young sailor stopped the car to examine his papers before passing him through the gates with a smart salute. In the base the driver turned the vehicle into the road leading to the Supply Office where Warren hoped to scrounge the equipment, weapons and boats for his planned seaborne operations. Leaving the driver to park the lorry he walked along the concrete path through the well kept lawns towards the offices.

It had been raining, he remembered, and sailors hurried past, with rain capes draped over their shoulders, head down against the wind. Huge cranes stood silhouetted, high above large hangar-like workshops; beyond them in the Straits little lighters busied themselves amongst the wharves and islands. Suddenly the air-raid sirens sounded from a low wail to a warbling pitch and the caped seamen scattered at a run. Warren glanced up and adjusted his steel helmet then walked to a nearby bunker as the first bombs crashed down amongst the buildings. The raid, which lasted six hours, was to be the worst raid the base had experienced and was to have a shattering effect on morale.

Throughout the day waves of enemy bombers in perfect V formations, oblivious of the anti-aircraft fire, flew overhead and pattern bombed all three RAF airfields and the base. The new naval base was torn apart. One bomb buried itself in the power station, exploding in a shower of fireworks, smoke and wreckage. As the flames leapt through the roof of the building, strewing debris in all directions, sailors and fireman raced along the cratered roads to deal with the inferno.

Gradually, as the electricity supply began to fail, the base died as fires raged and buildings disappeared in eruptions of smoke and explosions. The fuel tanks near the sea were ablaze and thick oily black smoke swirled into the morning air with long tongues of flame dancing and swaying amongst it. The heat was so intense that the girder supports began to melt and lean over. The most modern naval base in the world had been reduced to smoke, debris and craters.

*

One of the ships trapped in the repair yards was HMS *Kedah*, the pride of a local firm's prewar fleet, the Straits Steamship Company. Like most local vessels she was taken over by the Royal Navy in 1939. Since then she had been fitted out as an Auxiliary destroyer, armed with a pair of pom-poms, two quick firing 4-inch guns and one 3-inch high angle gun. But now, fighting one of the major battles of her life, she lay immobile with her engines in pieces and scattered around the base workshops. Nearby was another new arrival, the submarine HMS *Trusty*. She came to join the fleet of Dutch submarines operating out of Singapore but was in such a bad state of disrepair that she went straight into dry dock. While all the buildings around them seemed to explode into clouds of dust and flame, the ships' crews manned every available gun, throwing up a curtain of flak to protect their vessels.

Another caught in that raid was a P&O liner which had previously collided with the cruiser HMS *Repulse*. Since December the liner had been left to the mercy of naval fitters and native dock workers, who clambered over the vessel welding torn plates together.

One of the crew still on board the liner during this raid, was a ship's steward. He had been between decks, he recollected, and his head ached and his stomach felt queasy. Wherever his boy friend had taken him the previous night had done him 'no good at all'. He needed the toilet and the dull thud of the guns and explosions didn't improve his headache. He tried to ignore both. As he hurried along he heard the shrapnel clanging against the ship's sides. Suddenly, the lights flickered then faded and he was left in total blackness, four decks down in an almost empty ship.

Anchored off-shore was the Straits Steamship Company's SS *Relau*, a small tanker used to bunker the RN ships. She was fully loaded and shrapnel scarred after numerous near misses. The shore line was hidden from her Chinese crew by smoke, which blotted out the horizon giving the impression that the whole island was ablaze.

The skipper, who was on the small bridge, aft, waited for orders from the RN concerning his cargo. As he watched the buildings burning alongside a wharf he noticed a RN launch leave the nearby pier and approach his vessel. A young naval officer stood with his legs apart in the well of the launch. Looking up at the *Relau*'s bridge he raised his megaphone to his lips and ordered its captain to disembark his crew and evacuate to Singapore. His tone broached no argument – it was an order. 'What about my ship?' the skipper wanted to know. 'Leave her, she will be dealt with'. The launch then moved off and headed towards another vessel anchored some distance away.

The young RNVR officer in charge of the *Relau* took his Asian crew ashore and begged a lift from an RN lorry going to Keppel Harbour*.The road was congested with 11th Division's lorries full of exhausted troops rescued from the fighting in Johore. There were also ambulances full of wounded searching for a Military Hospital which had evacuated to Kallang from Johore.

The driver of the lorry, a young naval rating, dropped the crew of the *Relau* off near the company offices, where the skipper reported the position. The company executives were not amused. Next day another officer with a crew was sent to the base with strict orders to bring the ship around to the Singapore Roads. The Indian soldiers who had replaced the naval ratings guarding the gates casually

---

* Named after the British Admiral Keppel

Major Alan Ferguson Warren, as Adjutant, Royal Marine Barracks, Chatham, 1936

Cathay Buildings: Headquarters of SOE's Orient Mission and the base for Colonel Warren's operations

waved his car through as it approached the gates. Offshore the SS *Relau* was still at anchor and undamaged. With his new crew on board he cast off and took the vessel through the Straits to Clifford Pier where it anchored the following morning.

Another Straits Steamship Company vessel doing RN work that day was the HMS *Jarak* under the command of Lieutenant E.A. Hooper RNVR and former harbourmaster at Singapore. The *Jarak* too had been taken over in 1939 and had since then carried out minesweeping duties.

She had just returned from a mission behind enemy lines, one of a flotilla of small ships sent to rescue 2,000 Australian and British troops trapped at Batu Pahat in Johore. Almost as soon as she returned she was ordered to sail around to the now abandoned naval base to rescue equipment inadvertently left behind by the Navy.

As soon as darkness fell, Hooper took the *Jarak* out of the harbour, along the coast and past Changi point. The dark mass of the swamp and jungle covered island of Pulau Ubin, at the mouth of the Straits, drifted by in the darkness while ahead Hooper could see fires burning at Seletar seaplane base. Even if he had not known the landmarks he would have had no trouble in finding the base, illuminated by fierce fires burning unchecked from successive raids. When he began to close in he realized that if the enemy held the north bank of the Straits, his ship would be silhouetted against the burning buildings ashore. His fears and suspicions were confirmed when bursts of small arms fire were heard from the opposite bank. To add to his troubles he discovered that the equipment weighed three tons and he had inadequate lifting gear on board.

The *Jarak*'s officers and crew spent the next six hours ashore amongst the exploding ammunition, listening to the passage of incoming shells which whirred overhead. Having found the equipment they pushed and lifted and eventually manhandled it into a towing position behind the *Jarak*. In a race against time the ship slowly pulled her tow back along the coast.

Just after dawn the crew heard a heavy explosion and assumed an ammunition dump had gone up. Later that day the BBC announced that the battle for Malaya had ended and the battle for Singapore had now begun. The explosion was British sappers blowing apart the mile long causeway. The last unit across was the Argylls, and the last man is reputed to have been Private Hardy*,

* He escaped from Singapore with Brigadier Paris but, having survived a shipwreck in the Indian Ocean he was murdered in the lifeboat by a killer gang of soldiers.

the Commanding Officer's batman. But rumours persisted that thousands of soldiers were still in Malaya, lost behind enemy lines.

*

The Supreme Commander, General Wavell, had flown into Singapore the previous day, 30th January, to discuss the military position with the General Officer Commanding, Lieutenant-General Arthur Percival. He agreed that Percival should give up the mainland and withdraw his tired troops across the causeway to Singapore. He also ordered all aircraft to be flown out to Sumatra except eight Hurricanes and six Buffaloes which would provide local air cover for the defenders. As for the naval base, Churchill wanted it so thoroughly wrecked that it would be useless for at least eighteen months. Concerned for his troops still fighting in Johore, General Percival asked Rear Admiral Spooner not to fire the oil reserves at the base because of the effect it would have on morale.

Meanwhile Air Vice Marshal C.W.H. Pulford in command of the RAF at Singapore ordered what was left of, his diminishing air force to fly to secret airfields near American-owned, Palembang oilfields in Dutch Sumatra. This obviously saved the irreplaceable aircraft but left behind thousands of RAF ground staff and their families who would also have to be evacuated.

Apart from Tengah airfield very few demolitions were carried out by the RAF and Navy before the bases were abandoned. Eventually the army was called in to complete the job. The demolition teams, drawn mainly from Gunners and Royal Engineers from the recently arrived 55th Infantry Brigade, were called to destroy the airfields.

Fresh from training camps in Britain and a three-month sea voyage around the Cape, 55th Brigade arrived in Singapore in mid-January as reinforcements. They were immediately thrust into Johore's collapsing front line where they were almost overrun and only escaped encirclement by abandoning their guns and equipment. With the shock of the retreat still fresh in their minds they were ordered to destroy the abandoned RAF airfields.

One group from the brigade, who arrived at Sembawang airfield, jumped down from their lorries to look around the bomb-cratered base leaving their officers talking demolitions to the RAF counterparts. The runways were full of holes and debris, most of the buildings showed signs of bomb damage from recent air-raids and oily black smoke drifted across the field from burning fuel tanks. As they wandered around they were astonished at the apparent haste of the RAF departure. Cold mugs of tea were left in the workshops; offices were strewn with open files and discarded papers and the officers' mess even had the table laid for 30 places. Their most useful find were the stores packed with equipment and clothes and a car park full of vehicles left behind in good working order. The lorries were quickly loaded with equipment and clothes and driven away by smiling quartermasters from the brigade, to replace the equipment lost in the last ditch stand in Johore.

At the Seletar seaplane base a group of Royal Engineers were shown around by a RAF officer who pointed out the targets which needed attention. The Sappers decided to start with the jetty, which carried the fuel lines to the refuelling points for the flying boats and seaplane tenders. The young Sapper officer in charge, Lieutenant James Bradley, queried whether the fuel had in fact, been turned off. Reassured by his guide he and his men quickly got down to drilling holes, laying wires and finally fixing the charge. With a last look around and a warning shout for everyone to get their heads down, the charges were blown. The jetty disappeared in a tremendous roar and erupted into a black and crimson cloud of smoke which rolled and danced skywards as the fuel still trapped in the pipes caught fire and fed the flames.

In Government House the Governor, Sir Shenton Thomas, recorded in his diary later that week that the Naval Base was 'abandoned in a precipitate fashion by its staff who seemed to have left for lunch and never returned. Since the navy evacuated the base it was at the mercy of anyone in uniform'.*

The naval base had been almost stripped before the demolition teams arrived. Roving Regimental Quartermasters found the base only lightly guarded by inexperienced Indian troops fresh from training camps in India. The base was found to be packed with undamaged stores and equipment. Wandering around the bomb-damaged base, they stared in disbelief at the tons of supplies abandoned in this apparent Aladdin's cave. The godowns were crammed with tinned foods of every description; the lorry parks full of undamaged vehicles and stores full of clothing. There was also an arsenal of weapons together with some 180,000 tons of stock-piled ammunition ranging from .303 armour-piercing bullets to

---

* Diary entry 5th February

15-inch shells. Soon convoys of vehicles of every size and make converged on the base to pick the corpse clean.

*

While the RAF and Navy were busy back-loading men and equipment to Java, a convoy packed with reinforcements approached Singapore. This convoy, BM12, was the last to reach the island and had left Britain three months earlier with desert-trained troops. The ships were rerouted at Cape Town following news of the Japanese attack on Malaya. In a stop-over in India they were joined by half-trained Indian troops fresh from training camps. All the well-equipped Indian Division had been earlier sent to the Western Desert leaving only raw recruits in the training camps. It was these men who joined the East Anglian 18th Division as reinforcements. They brought with them much needed light tanks but the vehicles were so badly maintained that they were almost useless in the fast approaching final battle for Singapore.

Amongst the senior staff officers who joined the 18th Division during its stop-over in India was Colonel Andy Dillon, known to many as Dillo. He was an old Indian Army man, veteran of the North-West Frontier where he won his Military Cross. His new job was AA and QMG with the 18th Division.

The orders to reroute the convoy from the Middle East to Singapore didn't appeal to the civilian crews manning the troopships, especially on the old coal burning *Empress of Asia*. By the time she reached Sunda Straits, which separates Java from Sumatra the murmurings of discontent became an all-out strike, but with so many civilian trades amongst the troops it was an easy matter to replace the strikers.

The daily programme on the troopships varied little. On deck every morning the troops paraded for physical exercise, then firing practice and bayonet drill. Later, sitting shirtless in the sun on deck, they listened to lectures on VD and the dangers of mixing with the local women. Another useful piece of information they were given was that although the Asians may look alike, you could always recognise the Japanese because they invariably wore glasses with thick lens, had poor eyesight and buck teeth.

The soldiers on rifle-points duty kept a watchful eye open for enemy aircraft. There was a minor scare near Banka Island, off the coast of Sumatra, when they were attacked by enemy bombers, but apart from that the voyage was uneventful. The ships continued north through the Rhio Archipelago, full of small tropical islands, some just small, tree-covered rocks but others were large with a fishing village half hidden amongst the sloping palm trees.

As the convoy approached Singapore the troops noticed a brown haze above the islands which grew more dense as the convoy steamed through the Durian Straits, about thirty miles from Singapore. On board every ship the tension increased and rumours circulated that Singapore was a mass of flames. These stories seemed to be supported by the smuts which came down with the monsoon showers and the fact that the convoy's escorting destroyers appeared to be racing around more.

The occasional appearance of a Hurricane from one of the abandoned airfields in Singapore was greeted by cheers as it circled the convoy before it continued its journey to Sumatra. One of the pilots, Flight Lieutenant Arthur Donahue, an American serving with the RAF later wrote*, that as he looked down on the city for the last time it had a 'tragic mantle of smoke across the middle of Singapore island which covered and darkened the city.' There were 'huge leaping fires in the north and south parts of the city' with 'sinister curtains of black smoke which rose and towered over it like a great over-hanging cloud of doom.' He won the DFC in the Malayan Campaign but was killed later in the war.

Monday, 2nd February

On the top deck of the *Empress of Asia*, Sergeant Fred Austin watched the convoy separate into two parts as it approached the Singapore's Western Entrance, through the minefield. The old coal-burning liner lagged well behind the second group. Ahead in line were two liners packed with troops, the *City of Canterbury* and the *Felix Rousel*. With Sergeant Austin at the firing point was a detachment from his Recce Regiment with bren guns and rifles.

After scanning the skies, Fred Austin looked towards the bows and idly watched the convoy steam in line into the central channel. Suddenly there were alarm bells ringing, shouts and a general burst of activity along the decks. Then ahead, in the sky above, heading straight for them were three flights of nine silver-bodied aircraft flying in close formation. All around the ship soldiers with bren guns and rifles blazed away in unison while the escorting destroyers raced around filling the skies with dirty blue puffs of anti-aircraft fire.

* *Last Flight from Singapore* Flight Lieutenant Arthur G. Donahue

Ignoring the gunfire the planes flew on, with bomb doors open, and dive-bombed the ships. As the bombs rained down and exploded alongside the fleeing ships, the Free French liner *Felix Rousel* and the *City of Canterbury* weaved and dodged and raced for the safety of the harbour. The slow-moving *Empress of Asia* was less fortunate. Within minutes she was struck by bombs and the pungent smell of cordite, mixed with burning wood, began to drift across the decks.

At his firing point Fred Austin, with his bren-gun jammed against his hip, watched in disgust, as bullet holes traced themselves across the belly of a Japanese plane which passed overhead at almost mast height. As he glanced back astern to watch the plane, he saw a long trail of smoke marking the ship's path and more smoke drifted across the deck from somewhere amidships. Suddenly a hugh spout of dirty water cascaded over the side from another near miss soaking him to the skin. Sounds were everywhere – the tack-tack-tack of bren guns, the sharp crack of rifles, the crump of exploding shells and the drone of aircraft overhead.

The Australian destroyer HMAS *Yarra* raced past, blazing away at the aircraft with all her guns, before she disappeared again into the trailing smoke. It seemed to her crew that the old troopship was on fire from stem to stern.

At their firing point on an upper deck, Fred Austin's section had avoided most of the smoke which now swept astern and obscured the rest of the vessel. But the full extent of the fire soon became known when a ship's officer stumbled up the gangway steps with a cloth over his mouth. He stopped long enough to tell Austin to take his men to their lifeboat stations. Abandon ship had been ordered. Then he was gone, into the smoke along the deck towards the stern.

Suddenly it seemed the deck was full of soldiers who appeared from every nook and cranny which offered protection from bombs and shrapnel. There was no panic, Austin remembered, 'Everyone moved off smartly to the stations, just like a lifeboat drill.' Glancing over the side, he saw boats being lowered. Some were badly holed and began to fill with water immediately they reached the sea. Others struck by water bursts from near misses, broke loose from the davits and tipped their passengers into the sea like peas from a pod. All along the length of the deck groups of soldiers peered overboard before they climbed over the rail to drop sixty feet into the sea.

He found the head of the gangway leading to the lifeboat stations jammed with troops and thick with smoke. Following the example of the more adventurous types in his group, Fred Austin climbed over the ship's rail and slowly lowered himself down onto the deck support below. Sliding down the next ten feet to the deck he repeated the exercise until he reached the open sea deck. His arrival coincided with a surge from below decks of some of his friends, who had volunteered to replace the striking ship's stokers. For one person the meeting was brief: he didn't stop but hurdled the ship's rail at a running leap and disappeared over the side.

Some of his section joined Sergeant Austin and his stoker friends on the sloping deck of the listing ship. Not all the stokers had lifejackets, despite orders that everyone should carry it with them at all times. When the soldiers in the stokehole heard the orders to abandon ship they evacuated so quickly that the lifejackets remained behind. Now on the open deck they listened while Fred Austin canvassed for ideas on how to help them. Eventually it was decided to link arms and jump together. They all peered overboard. It was a long drop into a sea full of swimming survivors and wreckage. Someone suggested that jumping from that height without holding the lifejacket could cause it to strike the chin and break their necks. The idea was abandoned.

One of the group, anxious about the possibility of a broken neck dropped his lifejacket over the side intending to jump into the sea after it. Unfortunately the ship was still under way and he was last seen running along the deck trying to keep pace with his lifejacket in the sea below. The group began to break up and Fred Austin found himself near the bows with hundreds of other soldiers. The ship had stopped and was well alight. Whilst he was making up his mind whether to jump over the side HMAS *Yarra* slowly closed and drew in bow to bow. Even before she touched men clambered over the rails and leapt the gap, to be grabbed by sailors and hustled out of the way towards the destroyer's stern.

Those already in the sea were being bombarded by falling bodies. As they broke surface and battled for breath, the towering mass of the ship's side, with smoke pouring out of her portholes, stood menacingly above until they kicked out and tried to swim clear. The vessel had stopped and had begun to list. Those in the sea could see the destroyer *Yarra* embarking men trapped near the bows. Another destroyer, probably the Australian HMAS *Woolongong*, had pulled alongside the stern and took off more survivors. Then HMAS *Bendigo* appeared out of the smoke and began to pick up those in the water. She was joined by a local vessel, the *Darvil*, which dropped clambering nets overboard.

Later, as the survivors approached the landing stage, their first sight of Singapore was columns of smoke rising from various parts of the city. Along the waterfront, buildings were on fire and there was an overpowering smell of tar and burning oil. When they stepped ashore, the dockside felt warm against their bare feet.

Eventually they were collected by army lorries driven by sailors from the ill-fated *Prince of Wales*, which had been sunk by the Japanese on 10th December, and they were taken to various camps to be re-equipped. The casualties, including some who had swallowed oil or inhaled smoke, were driven away in ambulances. At the dock gates they passed groups of Europeans, with bulging suitcases, who hurried along in the opposite direction, to embark on the recently arrived liners. Some old regulars amongst the survivors knew the city from its better peacetime days but the first sight of the Orient for many young soldiers in that convoy was of cratered roads full of debris from collapsed houses or roped off streets with signs blandly announcing 'unexploded bomb'. Amongst the ruins rescue workers scrambled over wrecked houses with ambulances waiting nearby.

While the *Empress of Asia* fought for her life her companions, the liners *City of Canterbury* and the *Felix Rousel*, fled into harbour. The latter was a Free-French liner, well known prewar on the Orient run. She was manned by a Free-French crew with a British captain. Despite her speed and her captain's skill she didn't escape unscathed. One bomb had smashed through the decks near the bridge and destroyed the officers' mess. Another exploded against the funnel, wiping out the RASC bren-gun team on a firing-point. Although she had three funnels she was in fact a motor vessel. The rudder was damaged and bomb splinters and strafing added to the casualties.

At the beginning of the voyage to the Middle East, the OC Troops discovered that all she had to defend herself with was four old Marlin guns which were unserviceable. Later, when he realized that they were being diverted into the war zone he arranged for the armourers on board to have them repaired. He also discovered that amongst the passengers were two companies of RASC who had fourteen bren-guns. These weapons were soon rescued from the hold and appointed to firing points on the upper decks. Another unit, the 9th Northumberland Fusiliers, mounted all their Vickers guns at main points around the ship, while another 80 riflemen were detailed off to other firing points and trained to fire on a given command. It seemed they mounted sufficient fire power, when the occasion arose, to drive off the enemy planes which then chose the ill-fated *Empress of Asia* as their victim.

Against the backdrop of what seemed to be a blazing waterfront a small launch was sighted crossing the harbour towards them. It carried a group of staff officers from HQ Malaya who gave instructions that all personnel were to be disembarked that night and their places taken by airmen and large numbers of women and children who had left it almost too late to escape. The RASC bren-gunners were to remain on board to provide additional ack-ack support for the journey to Java.

'Welcome to Singapore,' one officer muttered, 'but frankly I don't know why you've been sent here.'

CHAPTER TWO

Planning the Escape
February 1st—8th

Colonel Warren stood near the office window looking out across the red tiled rooftops to the harbour. He hoped to catch a glimpse of the incoming convoy, which would be the first to enter harbour during daylight since the war started. Everywhere he looked he saw pillars of smoke rising from bomb-damaged buildings. A brown haze had drifted over the city from the burning fuel tanks at the naval base and from those near the causeway. Nearby was the Fullerton Building, which housed the General Post Office on its ground floor and government offices. These included the department dealing with supplies, a large number of Royal Navy sections and the captain of the dockyard's staff.

Beyond the commercial buildings, which lined the waterfront at that point, he could see Clifford Pier and the inner harbour. Both appeared fairly empty apart from two small steamers which were owned by the Straits Steamship Company, and a few naval launches which busily fussed around. All he could see further out was the large green expanse of Blakang Mati island across the bay and inshore, through the haze, the buildings at the Empire Docks and Keppel Harbour. No sign of the convoy that everyone was expecting, he remembered, but from the sounds he could hear, like distant thunder, he guessed the convoy was 'catching a packet'.

He walked across the office and studied the wall map of south-east Asia. The enemy sweep down the coast of Borneo had out-flanked Singapore and brought the Japanese within striking distance of oil-rich Dutch Sumatra, an island about the size of California which lay parallel to the Malayan peninsula but separated from it by the Malacca Straits. This enemy naval force would not only cut the sea route to Singapore but it could also seize the American-owned Palembang oilfield. If that happened, the only route in and out of Singapore would be a 250-mile journey across Sumatra, either along the Djambi River and closer still up the Indragiri River to Rengat.

His thoughts were interrupted by the rapid fire of nearby Bofors guns dug-in on the padang,* near St Andrew's Cathedral, followed by a series of explosions as another air raid passed overhead. He lifted his steel helmet off the hat rack near the door and having placed it firmly on his head, sat down at his desk and began to rough out his ideas for what was to become the escape route for thousands of soldiers and civilians after the fall of Singapore.

Briefly, his plan was to have two bases, one at the old pirate haunt of Bagan Siapiapi in Sumatra, almost opposite Malacca. The other would be at Rengat, about 150 miles further south, below Singapore and close to the Lingga group of islands. The town was some 100 miles up the Indragiri River, a jumping off point to the deep water port of Padang on Sumatra's west coast. He proposed to use the Bagan Siapiapi Base to infiltrate men and supplies into Malaya. The Rengat Base would, with the help of the Dutch, co-ordinate the movement of men and supplies in and out of besieged Singapore. If the unthinkable happened and the Fortress was overwhelmed then it could also become an escape route for an organised movement of disciplined groups of escapers.

Apart from the men Warren had specially selected for operations behind the lines he had also drawn to him a small band of volunteers, all expert in their own field. Major Jock Campbell was the administrator and fixer. Captain Lyon was a keen yachtsman who knew the islands and could speak Malay fluently. With him also was John Davis, a Chinese-speaking police officer and Richard Broome, a Colonial civil servant. They not only looked after the training and infiltration of the Chinese guerrillas but also had useful contacts amongst the Chinese fraternity.

The obvious choice to run the escape route was Campbell and Lyon he decided. Major H.A. (Jock) Campbell had prewar been General Manager of the Labis Rubber Estate in Johore, part of the SOCFIN Group, and was used by Warren to 'open doors' into the city's commercial world. At the outbreak of war he turned up at Warren's office where he was commissioned major in his old Territorial Unit, the King's Own Scottish Borders. Captain Ivan Lyon, on the other hand, was a regular officer in the Gordons and a cousin to the Queen's Bowes-Lyon family. He was married, but had taken the precaution of sending his pretty French wife and their baby son to England via Australia.†

* A large green or park
† The ship was intercepted by a German raider and the passengers and crew handed over to the Japanese.

Campbell had an office close by in the Cathay building but when Warren tried to find Lyon he discovered he was in Johore on a SOE operation. When Lyon saw Warren the following day he described how he had spent the previous day in Johore with SOE's Lieutenant Frank Brewer and five Chinese on a mission to infiltrate a Chinese Nationalist patrol behind enemy lines.

The attempt became a farce. The Chinese contact who was to lead them to the site for the supply dump had not kept the appointment in Johore Bahru, which meant that they wasted time looking for a suitable place themselves. They had almost been captured by enemy patrols when the front line ceased to exist and only escaped when they were warned of the danger by the crew of a bren carrier covering the retreat. They eventually reached Johore Bahru where they joined the tail of the army as it retreated across the causeway.

On his return Lyon spent the evening at a Regimental dinner in the mess and it was only later, when he returned to his room at the SOE base at Tandjong Balai, that he found a message to report to Warren the following morning, 2nd February.

As he strode into the Cathay Building, past the Indian sentries, he found the hall full of packing cases and Local Defence Volunteers. He gathered they were from a Field Survey Company and were to flash spot enemy guns from the roof of the Cathay Building. After sharing the lift with boxes and theodolites he arrived at Colonel Warren's office to find Major Campbell already there.

The three sat around a small table in Warren's office with the fan quietly humming away above their heads, sending a gentle breeze which ruffled the papers. In his briefing Warren explained that the basic plan was to open a back door into Sumatra through which supplies and men could be brought into the besieged city. He stood up and used the wall map, drawing his finger from Sumatra to Rengat to illustrate the route. As the situation developed he would also probably use the route for clandestine activities, as well as to supply his jungle-based units operating behind enemy lines.

Drawing the briefing to a close he appointed Campbell to set-up and run the route in Sumatra, while Lyon would take charge of the route across the islands from Singapore to the river. He suggested they should have a base on one of the islands, as a half-way house, with food, weapons and medical supplies. They would of course need someone with medical knowledge and Lyon recommended Corporal Morris RAMC at SOE 101 Special Training School.

Corporal 'Taffy' Morris was a Welsh ex-coal miner who had a reputation of being sturdy and reliable. He also had a great sense of humour which was to be severely tested in the next few weeks. When he heard of his new job he drew a sten gun out of the armoury and gleefully practised on the range, ignoring the fact that medical personnel shouldn't carry arms. Eventually he hitched a lift to town where accommodation had been found for him in the Union Jack Club.

The SOE's small coastal steamer, the *Hong Chuan*, was tied up alongside the quay in the Inner Harbour when Lyon arrived at the docks. She was crewed by SOE instructors who unloaded boxes of supplies from two lorries parked close by. The supplies were SOE ration packs sufficient for twelve men, made up of tins of corned beef, ship's biscuits and a bottle of whisky.

The enemy bombardment of the docks continued throughout the day and the speed at which the ship was loaded may have been in direct relation to the accuracy of the enemy's fire. The enemy guns seemed to have targeted the inner harbour and salvos of shells continually hurtled over to crash amongst the godowns or explode in huge spouts of seawater, too close for comfort, to Lyon's vessel. As soon as the last crate had been carried aboard the crew slipped her cables and Lyon took her to sea while everyone on board scanned the skies for the next bomber raid.

Off Sultan Sands the crew silently watched as the ship passed the wreck of the *Empress of Asia*, with only three funnels showing above the water. Lyon knew the islands like the back of his hand and once clear of the western entrance soon navigated the vessel off the sea route and amongst the islands to avoid enemy scout planes. By morning they were in the Tjombol Strait which separates the islands around Sumatra from the Rhio Group.

They were not the only vessel hiding amongst the islands. The disabled HMAS *Vendetta* was slowly making headway, under tow from HMAS *Stronghold*. Close by were the *Hobart*, *Tenedos* and *Maryborough* – all Australian Navy ships being taken out of reach of the Japanese bombers.

The small island of Pulau Moro had been chosen for Warren's 'half way house'. This was at the north end of the wide, cliff-lined Durian Strait, one of the sea routes from Singapore. Lyon brought the old steamer close in shore and anchored near a small beach alongside an inlet. Safely hidden from the bombers by the cliff overhang. As they began to ferry the stores ashore in a small boat rain squalls swept over the islands. The driven rain beat down soaking everyone to the skin and tall palm trees bent in the wind as the crew manhandled the crates up a muddy, narrow track, through the trees to the cliff top.

Hidden by the jungle but close enough for a grandstand view of the Strait, Ivan Lyon chose this spot for his new base. A grand title for a bamboo-framed hut, walled and roofed with attap which his crew built while others humped stores up from the beach. The boxes and crates were dumped and stacked inside its bamboo frame as the hut was built around them.

The next stop was a small fishing village, Priggi Raja, in a bay close to the mouth of the Indragiri River. The hills beyond the village were shaped like two breasts which provided escapers with a good landmark from the sea. There Campbell and Lyon persuaded the local headman to look after a supply dump and to direct any visitors up-river to Rengat.

When they returned to Singapore they found that events had moved quickly. Basil Goodfellow, head of SOE in Singapore, had closed the school and ordered the permanent staff to leave for Rangoon on the SS *Krian*, a Straits Steamship vessel. All the locally recruited service military personnel were given the choice of being returned to their old unit or transferred to a recently formed unit of Chinese volunteers called Dalforce, under the command of Colonel John Dalley.

One of the locally recruited personnel was Frank Brewer, who had been with Lyon on the abortive Johore mission. He declined to return to his old unit, the Local Defence Volunteers and opted, instead, for Dalforce.

As Goodfellow wanted the *Hong Chuan* for a secret mission Campbell, Lyon and Morris were given berths on the SS *Krian*. This would take them and more stores to Pulau Moro before going on to Rengat to land Major Campbell.

On 5th February Lieutenant Lind RNVR joined Warren's team. Before the war he worked for an insurance company in Batavia and spoke Dutch fluently and Warren wanted a Dutch-speaking naval officer for his Sumatra operation. The night the causeway was blown up, Lind remembers being given a party of armed naval ratings and told to hold a position in the Kranji Creeks. After rescuing some of the stragglers who found themselves trapped on the wrong side of the Strait, and being eaten alive by insects, he and his men were relieved by a tired platoon of Australians from the

29th Regiment of Sydney. The Australians had formed the rear-guard as the army withdrew across the Johore Strait.

As his men marched away along a muddy dirt track alongside the mangrove swamp, leaving the Australians to their fate, Lind received orders to report to 'an office at the top of the Cathay Cinema (part of the Cathay Building) and ask for a Colonel Warren'. He had been selected, he was told, to take a raiding party up the Malacca Straits. Although at the time he didn't recognise the name, he discovered later that he had worked with Warren during the Penang evacuation.

When he reported to Warren's office he found John Davis and Richard Broome there. Lind remembered Warren took him to the window overlooking the harbour and pointed across the Singapore Roads at the eastern end of the breakwater. 'See that motor tongkang?' he said. 'Do you think you could collect some naval ratings and motor mechanics and drive it?' The object he explained was to sneak up the Sumatra side of the Malacca Straits to Bagan Siapiapi. His men – he gestured towards Davis and Broome – would use this as their base. They hoped to cross the Straits in a junk and make contact with the communist guerillas they had previously put in behind enemy lines.

Another welcome, but unexpected visitor for Warren that day was Lieutenant Frank Vanrenan, an ex-planter who had volunteered to go into the jungle in north Malaya with Spencer Chapman's first stay-behind party. Three other parties were later put in but in the rapid withdrawal down the peninsula, Warren lost contact both with Spencer Chapman and the stay-behind parties. In desperation Warren even resorted to uncoded announcements over Radio Malaya asking for news of Spencer Chapman and his men but all his efforts were met with silence, until now.

Vanrenan appeared tired and had lost weight. His uniform was clean but well worn and sweat-marked. Warren handed him a whisky, told him to sit down and listened to his story.

Vanrenan reminded Warren that the stay-behind party, which had the only wireless set, had been put-in a few miles south of Slim River, the night the Japanese seized the bridge. Captain Spencer Chapman was due to join them but was ill from a bout of malaria and instead went in with number two party. Recounting his experiences, Vanrenan explained that the reason for the radio silence was that within twenty-four hours of going into the jungle all their equipment, supplies and wireless set had been stolen. They waited around in their jungle hideout for Spencer Chapman to appear but when he didn't arrive they finally decided that they should try and reach British lines again.

They soon realized that this was easier said than done. Following the Slim River debacle the British Army retreated rapidly down the peninsula, evacuated Kuala Lumpur and abandoned the State of Negri Sembilan without a fight. This left his party some 150 miles behind the lines with the gap increasing each day. After considering all the options they decided to try and reach the coast near Vanrenan's old rubber plantation where he had friends who might provide a boat. Eventually about three weeks later they reached the coast and paid a local fisherman to sail them to Sumatra. With help from the Dutch they made their way to the small RAF camp at Benkalis. From there the RAF agreed to fly them in a little two-seater Tiger Moth to Singapore which was used on the twice weekly mail run. Vanrenan was the first to arrive and the others, Ronald Graham and Boris Hembry, were to follow. Despite the failure of their mission all three were prepared to go back in again, he told Warren.

After he questioned him more about Benkalis and Bagan Siapiapi, Warren began to firm up on his plans for using the latter as a base for seaborne operations against the Malayan coastline. The fact that Vanrenan's party had survived encouraged Warren to believe that the others may still be operational and could be reached from Sumatra. The proposed base could also be used to send in a search party for Spencer Chapman and for landing armed Chinese guerrillas behind enemy lines. When Basil Goodfellow heard that Vanrenan's party had emerged from the jungle and that Warren proposed to send them back in to find Spencer Chapman, he laid claim to Boris Hembry for a seaborne operation being planned by SOE.

Warren acquired a small, 80 tons diesel driven Chinese coaster called the *Hin Leong* and it was this boat Lind had seen beyond the eastern breakwater. Warren recalled that when he boarded her she was full of sugar, rice, jars of soya bean sauce and other goods, guarded by an army of cockroaches who had free run of the ship. She smelled abominably but not so bad as the living quarters where nothing his men did could overcome the reek of years of poor sanitation.

The *Hin Leong* was brought around to Clifford Pier on Saturday, 7th February. Throughout the day a succession of lorries brought supplies, weapons and explosives to the vessel and as each lorry arrived it was hastily unloaded. All day long the enemy artillery bombarded the area and when the shells stopped coming the sky filled with formations of enemy bombers. Unconcerned about the ack-ack fire, the enemy bombers flew overhead in tight formations and pattern bombed the waterfront. All along the quay, godowns packed with rubber, food, coffee and other stocks, were on fire. Their smells, blended with burning wood, oil and rotting bodies, drifted along the waterfront.

Sunday, 8th February.
On Sunday, 8th February, the *Hin Leong* was ready, her cargo trimmed and everyone on board. She was crewed by two RNVR officers, Lieutenant Brian Passmore, an instructor from the SOE school, and Lieutenant Lind. There were also six ratings, surviviors from the *Prince of Wales* and *Repulse*, and a corporal from the Gordons to look after the engines.

During the day two lorries arrived with Warren's Chinese guer-rillas, all armed. With them were John Davis accompanied by a Malay police colleague and Richard Broome with his Chinese 'boy'. As soon as they arrived they unloaded crates of supplies and equipment from the lorries and stacked them on the *Hin Leong*. In the middle of all the activity Warren found himself involved in settling a delicate matter of command. Recalling the scene some 30 years later, John Davis remembered both RNVR officers had equal rank although Lind had more days' seniority while Passmore had more sea service. The problem was resolved by Warren who put Lind in charge of the *Hin Leong* and asked Passmore to take her to sea.

Soon after that, the launch moved away from the wharf and disappeared into the oily haze that drifted across the harbour from the countless fires. Immaculate as usual in his tropical white tunic shirt and shorts, Warren watched them go and wished he had gone with them.

Turning his back on the scene he walked across the waterfront to the Singapore Club in Fullerton Buildings. He remembered that the enemy bombardment had increased in intensity and he became aware that the island's northern defences seemed to be taking the brunt of the enemy action. He passed burning buildings and teams of Chinese firemen clinging to the nozzles of their hoses as they fought an unsuccessful battle to quell the fires. All they could hope

for was to stop the blaze spreading. Warren stepped over the
round, thick hose pipes which seemed to stretch in every direction
and avoided the telegraph poles which lay across the road with
their wires, twisted and coiled, amongst craters and debris.

At the club he met his old friend Commander Alexander RN.
Some seven weeks earlier, he and Warren had co-ordinated the
night evacuation of all the European civilians and the military
garrison from Penang, an island off the west coast of north Malaya.
Only hours later the Japanese, expecting a bitter fight, stormed
ashore only to find the defenders had vanished in the night.
Alexander was now working in Fullerton Buildings and helped to
co-ordinate the movement of ships from the harbour.

Discussing the situation Warren learnt that a small convoy had
left that week for Java with all the Army's pay records and clerks on
board. The convoy was made up of the little coal-burning HMS *Circe*
and her sister ship *Medusa* and *No 51*, a small minesweeper. All
three were local vessels taken over by the Navy. Apart from the Pay
Corps clerks, room was found for a detachment of RAF ground staff
and an Australian Motor Transport Company. The Australians
had been in the front line since the war began and were being
transferred to Palembang in Sumatra.

The last of the Australian squadron, HMAS *Ballarat* and the
Toowooma, had also left, commented Alexander, taking with them
two local vessels, HMS *Gemas* and HMS *Rahman*. He added that to
help the remaining RN personnel, all the local Asian crews were
being dismissed and replaced by sailors, mostly survivors from the
Repulse and *Prince of Wales*.

One of the major problems it seemed was the wounded, packed
into overcrowded hospitals. Naval fitters in the dockyard had fitted
out the 50-year-old, 2,672 ton *Sui Wo* with special cots to take the
wounded and had rigged up an operating theatre. She was already
embarking hundreds of wounded together with military nurses and
medical staff and the Master of the Dockyard, Captain Atkinson,
hoped to get her away under cover of darkness the next day,
Monday.

Colonel Warren later had lunch with Major Angus Rose, an
Argyll officer who had commanded the Volunteers, which formed the
rearguard during the retreat from Kuala Lumpur, and Captain
Tennant RN from the ill-fated *Repulse*. Major Rose and Warren
had taken a company of Australians on a seaborne raid behind the
lines, in a commando-type operation some six weeks earlier. With
Vanrenan and Graham acting as scouts, the raiders ambushed a

Japanese convoy and wiped out the occupants of a staff car before re-embarking without casualties.

Neither seemed very optimistic about the future, recollected Warren and from the increased level of bombardment and the number of air-raids it seemed 'old Yamashita'*, was going to make his play sooner than later. It became increasingly obvious to Warren that Singapore had become untenable as a base for raids behind the enemy lines so he began to consider the possibility of getting another boat to join Broome and Davis in Sumatra.

After lunch he waited for an air-raid to finish then walked across to Cathay Buildings. To his surprise he found Lieutenant Passmore in his office waiting for him.

It seemed that the party on the launch had spent hours in the Outer Harbour engulfed by clouds of smoke, as they searched unsuccessfully for the buoy marking the entrance to the swept channel. Not prepared to risk the minefield Passmore had returned for more information.

As Warren listened he reached a decision to leave with his men. He made a number of telephone calls. One of these was to Basil Goodfellow, his counterpart in SOE. There wasn't a lot he could do in the besieged city, Warren told him, and as his work needed freedom of movement Warren decided to move and set up a new base in Sumatra. 'Goodbye and good luck'.

Recalling that day, John Davis remembered that they couldn't find their way through the minefield and so Passmore decided to return for more information. From the launch, as it crossed the harbour, the city appeared to be covered in a thin haze and columns of smoke rose from burning buildings in various parts of the city. He remembered feeling that he might not get back to Singapore again before it fell, so when the launch moored at the quay, he went ashore with Passmore to collect his kit and personal belongings from his home. When he arrived back he found Warren had joined them and, with him in command, the *Hin Leong* put to sea once more.

By now it was Sunday evening, recalled Colonel Warren, and the night sky over the north-west sector was lit by flashes from the bombardment, almost like continuous lightning, with the noise of the guns like muted thunder. In the darkness the launch crept slowly through the swept channel of the minefield, past the *Empress*

---

* Lt-General Tomayuki Yamashita, Commander of the Japanese forces in Malaya.

of Asia's three funnels marking Sultan Sands, and headed across to hug the Sumatran coast. Most of the passengers stood on deck watching distant flashes in what they guessed to be the Australian positions. Then the Chinese became voluble and began to point to a firework display of flares and reading their message Warren realized that Yamashita had launched his Grand Slam. Some of the earlier flares were Australian SOS flares but with increasing frequency red and blue rockets began to burst in the night sky announcing that one Japanese unit after another had landed and seized their objective.

*

The third member of Vanrenan's party, Boris Hembry, arrived in Singapore too late to join Warren's operation. This almost certainly saved his life as he would have probably gone ashore, and to his death, with Vanrenan. After escaping to Bagan Siapiapi the Dutch ferried Vanrenan and his party to Benkalis. The RAF Malayan Volunteer Unit in the town agreed to fly his party, singly, to Singapore. Boris flew in on Friday, 6th February, and remembers leaving the airstrip shortly after dawn in a little Tiger Moth, a vintage, unarmed, two-seater biplane without a cockpit cover. Little realizing the complete command of the air the Japanese had, he wasn't unduly worried when the Danish pilot, Sergeant Grut, gave him strict instructions to look out for enemy aircraft.

For most of the journey they flew along the jungle-covered Sumatran coast-line. Little islands dotted the Malacca Strait and occasionally they flew over fishing communities of scattered bamboo and attap houses along the water's edge. Gradually he became aware of an increasing smoke haze on the horizon and he realized this must be from Singapore. Leaving Sumatra behind the pilot headed towards the smoke and as they drew near, it seemed to Hembry that the whole island was ablaze.

Suddenly a Japanese Zero fighter appeared, flying directly at them with its guns blazing. Bits of the plane fell away and holes appeared along the fuselage. The attacker raced past and was gone. Sergeant Grut commented later that the enemy fighter probably couldn't drop down to their speed without stalling and after one pass must have lost them.

The plane flew in low across Blakang Mati island then banked towards Changi. All the airfields had been abandoned apart from Kallang, close to the city. Using this the plane circled the 750 yard runway and came in to land. All the buildings were burning or in ruins, the runway was cratered and groups of airmen were filling in the larger holes. Near the hangars lay a number of wrecked Hurricanes. As the plane taxied close to the control tower Hembry looked around expecting to be met but no one appeared. He had been recruited in Malaya and knew no one in SOE apart from Freddy Chapman. He didn't even know where the secret organisation was based. Later as he wandered around the airfield's deserted and bomb damaged administration buildings he found a RAF officer who knew that his two friends had arrived earlier and had gone to the Cathay Building.

After he begged a lift from a passing RAF vehicle he was dropped off at Raffles Square, close to the Cathay Buildings. There he found his friends had been absorbed into Warren's proposed landings to search for Freddy Spencer Chapman. Naturally he wanted to go with them but was told that he was to join in Singapore, the Deputy Head of SOE's Orient Mission, Basil Goodfellow, who had another job in mind for him. It was then he learnt of the escape route to Rengat and Goodfellow's plans for secret unmanned food dumps south of Singapore.

On Sunday morning Hembry was given a lorry and told to drive to the supply depot at the Ford Buildings in the centre of the island. All day long the noise of gunfire could be heard from the north-west sector. Shells straddled the main roads as enemy guns ranged on the Bukit Timah supply dumps. He found the depot officers only too pleased to give away their stocks of food, clothing and fuel and by nightfall his lorry was well loaded with tinned food, water canisters and plastic explosives. He also took a bren gun for himself.

The water canisters he had collected from the supply dumps were empty so Hembry drove across to the nearby Borneo Trading Company depot where he had friends from his prewar days. As it was late afternoon he accepted an invitation to stay for dinner. He spent the rest of the evening with his friends, the first opportunity he had to relax since going into the jungle six weeks earlier. That night, over a good meal and ample whisky, he described his adventures since the outbreak of war.

Boris Hembry recalled that later that Sunday evening, after dinner, they could hear the rumble of enemy artillery and the occasional explosions. He told his friends how he had spent the day collecting supplies for SOE's secret supply dumps on islands south of Singapore. These dumps were part of an escape route if the 'whole bag of tricks fell apart'. Almost unnoticed the bombardment continued throughout the night and when Hembry left to collect the lorry in the morning he discovered it covered with dirt from a shell crater, close by, in the middle of the lawn.

No one seemed to know what was going on in the north-west of the island and Hembry left his friends soon after an early breakfast. At another supply dump an army officer told him that an announcement on the nine o'clock news reported that an enemy landing was being repulsed. In fact enemy patrols were already approaching Tengah airfield, eight miles from the supply dumps. At Bukit Timah, where the roads were jammed with military vehicles, the muffled gunfire from the battle zone sounded like rolling thunder and to add to the illusion a storm swept across bringing with it a deluge of rain.

CHAPTER THREE

Japanese Assault
Sunday, 8th February

The reinforcements that arrived in the previous week gave General Percival some 85,000 troops to hold Singapore island. This included about 15,000 in the administrative tail, 38 battalions, which included 17 Indian, 13 British, 6 Australian and 2 Malay. Although this seemed a formidable force, in fact a large number were battle-fatigued having been chased down the peninsula, or had been overwhelmed in Johore and only escaped by the skin of their teeth. Some of the reinforcements included battle-tested Dunkirk veterans. Most however were green, untried troops, fresh from a long sea voyage, like the British, or recently recruited Australian and Indian volunteers, who were largely untrained and new to discipline.

Percival anticipated that the Japanese would launch their attack east of the causeway. This area he gave to the battle-experienced 3 Corps, together with most of the beach defence material such as concrete, timber, digging equipment and barbed wire. All the native population who lived in the mile deep strip along the coast were moved out.

On its left flank were the Australians who, apart from the battle-tried brigade holding the shore-line, consisted of a large number of partly trained, undisciplined new reinforcements. One unit had looted the Sultan of Johore's palace before they retreated over the causeway and threatened an investigating officer with rifles when he began asking questions.

Nestling between the two divisions, in swampy creeks and inlets around Kranji near the causeway, was the recently created Dalforce. This consisted of two thousand Chinese volunteers with two weeks training, and some European officers and NCO's including those from SOE. The weapons to equip this new formation went down with the *Empress of Asia* off Sultan Sands, so they were equipped instead with sporting rifles and shotguns with an average of five rounds apiece.

In the Sultan of Johore's Palace, which overlooked the causeway,

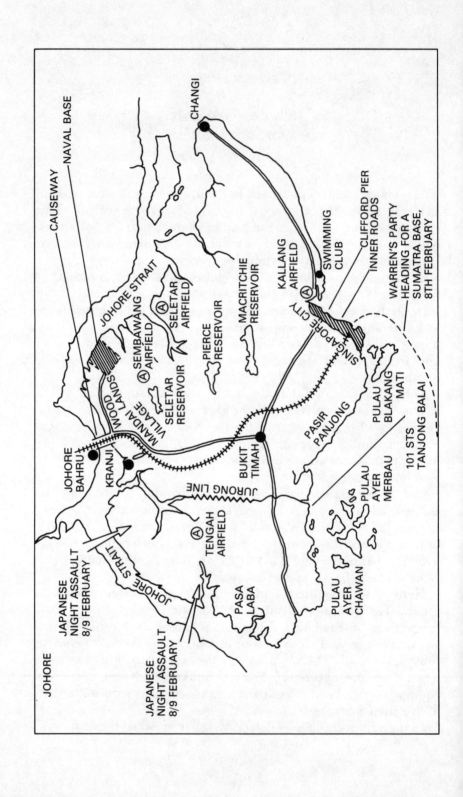

A panoramic view from the roof of Cathay Buildings

A view from Fullerton Buildings. From left to right are the Victoria Theatre, which became a casualty clearing station. To the right is the Town Hall and behind that is the high-domed supreme Court. The long building in the centre is the Municipal Offices which became the meeting place for hundreds of Australian troops who had lost their units. To the right is St. Andrew's Cathedral, also used as a reception area for the wounded. It was here that the nurses were assembled for the last official evacuation. In the foreground is the Padang and waterfront where Lt. Boris Hembry and Sgt. Lamb waited for Basil Goodfellow and Capt. Morgan.

On the occasion of General Wavell's visit to the Gordons, Singapore. From left is the Gordons' CO with General Wavell and General Percival in the foreground.

the Japanese General Yamashita, stood in the glass-domed operations room. This room, at the top of the five-storeyed observation tower, provided an ideal vantage point to watch the Australians preparing their defence positions. The room was also used by his artillery officers to locate their targets. Through his binoculars the Japanese commander could judge the ranging shots of his heavy guns at Singapore, some twenty miles away.

The General had led his men over a thousand miles to carry out a seaborne landing in Siam. In addition, in the face of a storm and against heavily defended positions, his men had carried out a seaborne assault in north Malaya. His 60,000 lightly equipped soldiers overcame all resistance and thrust some 500 miles down the Malayan Peninsula. Living off the land but mainly from supplies left behind by the British army, they arrived at the gateway of Singapore in 55 days.

The Sultan of Johore was a friend of both Count Ohtani, who planned the Japanese Malayan Campaign, and Baron Tokugawa, the paymaster for Hirohito's lethal political plots in the early 1930's. The Sultan was also a friend of the commander of the Australian 8th Division, Lieutenant-General H.G. Bennett. His men, like their Japanese counterparts, had also used the palace as their headquarters.

After the British army escaped across the Johore Straits to Singapore the Royal Engineers blew a 300ft gap in the causeway which joined the island to the peninsula. The Japanese engineers discovered that the 70ft wide link, which carried the road and rail communications, could be repaired at low tide but to do this they would need to secure both ends. The defenders opposite were Colonel Dalley's Chinese volunteers.

To have the causeway intact would have been a bonus but its destruction had been foreseen so the plan was to take Singapore Island by seaborne assault. The need for boats had also been anticipated and these were brought all the way from Indo-China and had followed the advancing army through Malaya.

To hide their assault preparations, the Japanese evicted all civilians from a twelve mile deep strip of land facing the Johore Straits. This area gradually filled up with all essentials for the task. Two divisions moved in, together with some 200 small boats. These were hidden in the rubber plantations some seven miles from the water's edge. Along the shore overlooking the Straits camped 4,000 infantry and field engineers who would form the spearhead of the initial assault against the Australian defences. Behind them were the artillery who were part of the second wave.

General Yamashita decided that the key to a successful landing would be an artillery barrage sufficient to destroy the beach defences before his men stormed ashore. To achieve this every gun left behind by the retreating British forces was ordered to be brought forward. All the way down the peninsula these guns were loaded onto trains or towed by captured British lorries over hastily repaired bridges to Johore Bahru. This trawl produced some 440 guns with 2,000 rounds of ammunition apiece to cover the initial assault. In addition larger guns and ammunition had arrived in Thailand and these were sent forward together with extra boats for the planned seaborne attack.

The planners had anticipated the British blowing the bridges and had sent an army engineer to Malaya before the war started. He drove the length of the country registering the bridges and estimating the materials and time needed for each repair, should they be destroyed. He obviously did his job well as their destruction had little effect on the Japanese advance.

From the vantage point in the Observatory, Japanese artillery officers carried out a survey of the island, revising their maps and occasionally calling for ranging shots. To their left, along the Straits, the Imperial Guards zeroed their guns on Changi searching for the heavy British 15-inch batteries deep in concrete bunkers. These had been part of the sea defences but had now been transversed, but their counter barrage did very little damage to the Japanese pieces hidden in the trees. Other enemy guns ranged down on the waterfront seeking the ships which had recently arrived in the BM12 convoy.

The Japanese also knew of plans, captured by the Germans, for the defenders to set the Johore Strait alight with burning oil which would engulf any seaborne attackers. Although the fuel would have been useful the General ordered his gunners to destroy all the oil installations on the north shore of the island held by 11th Division.

*

In Singapore, on the fateful Sunday the 8th, the churches were packed with worshippers. While army units, all over the island, held church parades, the Japanese prepared for the night attack. Amongst the trees, army engineers supervised the soldiers who manhandled the boats onto their shoulders and carried them to the forward areas. Later, in the darkness, behind the trees lining the shore, the enemy infantry began to assemble the collapsible boats while others filed past to the water's edge and boarded the launches and sampans hidden in the creeks. These local craft had been fitted with lorry engines by the engineers.

At 11pm the bombardment increased in intensity to become what was to be the greatest concentration of fire ever laid by the Japanese army. In their trenches in the north-west sector the Australians could see the trees on the opposite shore lit by the gun flashes. Then the shells began to drop in a creeping carpet of explosions up the beach, pausing briefly at the barbed wire beach defences, before moving on to the trenches where the Australians sheltered.

An hour later, at midnight, the first troop-carrying launches moved out of the creeks towards the island. The barrage lifted and moved on to concentrate on the lines of communications, to cut all forms of signals between the defenders and their HQs. In the Sultan's Palace, the Army Commander and his staff watched the successive shell bursts move over the defence perimeter. These were followed by flashes of small arms and long lines of tracer bullets arced across the water giving every indication that a fierce fight was taking place on the opposite shore. Then, at about fifteen minutes past midnight they saw the first of the blue success rockets burst in the night sky.

The returning launches emerged out of the darkness and docked alongside the quay near the palace. There they loaded up with the second wave of troops and, within minutes, turned around and sped back towards the assault beaches. The supporting artillery units moved forward and by dawn these too were ashore on the island. That night the Japanese ferried 13,000 troops across the Straits and a further 10,000 followed them next day, Monday. By dawn they had overwhelmed the Australian 22nd Brigade and moved inland.

The defenders had kept their heads down during the intense shelling but when it moved on they rose to meet the screaming Japanese infantry who raced up the beach. Amongst the craters and smashed trees they fired at point blank range, until the fire merged into scattered hand to hand clashes. These fights were bypassed by the enemy reinforcements who infiltrated into the Australians' rear areas.

The Australians' desperate defence almost destroyed their

brigade. The 2/18 Battalion with the 2/20 caught the vanguard of the assault. The latter lost 334 killed and 214 wounded. One company refused to budge and fought to the last man. The battalion's remaining surviviors began to filter back into the reserve lines that evening. This line was manned by the weak 12th Indian Brigade and another Australian battalion, made up mainly of half trained soldiers. One wit remarked that they had been recruited on a Friday and sent to Singapore on the Sunday.

The continued enemy probing supported by shell fire and air attack, confused the dazed defenders. When they found themselves separated from their flanks they began to fall back in disarray, many without their weapons and closely followed by the Japanese.

That Monday evening General Yamashita and his staff followed his men across the Straits in a small launch. When it grounded they climbed over the side, and dropped knee deep into the sea and waded ashore. The muddy beach was pitted with shell craters. Along the tree line almost every tree was a shattered stump and as they moved across the uneven ground, a brief flash from a small hand torch revealed, underfoot, rows of captured Australian soldiers bound together.

Enemy columns, led by section leaders with compasses strapped to their wrists, reached the lightly guarded Tengah airfield by Tuesday morning. The perimeter defence withdrew without making contact with the advancing Japanese leaving a small group of airmen carrying out demolition work amongst the buildings. The first news the RAF demolition team had that they were in no-man's land was when one of the airmen saw the Japanese patrols emerge from the trees bordering the airfield.

General Percival had expected the initial assault to be made against the 11th Division's north shore in the south-east sector but it was in the north-west that the enemy attacked, pressed home their advantages and captured Tengah airfield. Unless retaken it could soon be used to give close support to enemy columns advancing against Percival's second line of defence along the Jurong river. Although plans existed on paper no fortifications had been prepared along that river. It was left to the battle-weary defenders to dig trenches and map fields of fire.

CHAPTER FOUR

The First Evacuation
Monday, 9th February

The 22nd Australian Brigade was decimated in a night of fighting in which many died. Survivors, confused and lost, stumbled back in the blackness of the night. By Monday morning stragglers who had swum Tengah creek, began to filter through the 2nd Argyll and Sutherland Highlanders' position, to regroup at Bulim. Others avoided this and walked into Bukit Timah village in the centre of the island but by Monday evening groups had already reached the waterfront near the Fullerton Building. The 2/29th Regiment, which had relieved Lieutenant Lind's naval ratings in the Kranji swamps, were moved across to place themselves between the enemy and other Australian units which were falling back.

When SOE's Basil Goodfellow arrived at the Cathay Building that morning he found the pavement crowded with people hoping to pick-up fragments of information. Commander Alexander had the same experience outside Fullerton Buildings and heard later that the scene was repeated outside many public buildings that morning as people of all races searched for news.

Apart from the official communiqué which announced the landing and claimed that 'offensive action was being taken to mop up the enemy' the civilian population only had the vaguest idea what was going on. In the confusion of battle the same could be said for Headquarters Western Area Command in whose patch the Japanese had landed. It was against this background of confusion and strict censorship that rumours abounded.

The Asian population living outside the city had their own views of the situation as Boris Hembry found when he drove back to Singapore from Bukit Timah. The roads around the supply dumps were congested with military lorries and were being repeatedly shelled. Amongst the traffic jams were bullock carts, rickshaws and bicycles stacked high with personal possessions and surrounded by Chinese, Indians and Malay families from the tiny, round-eyed babies to aged elders. Lacking hard news and using their own judgement thousands of the local population were now showing their confidence in the ability of the British to contain the Japanese by voting with their feet. They saw their survival to be with family or friends on the eastern side of the island, out of the path of the expected Japanese advance.

When he reached the city Boris Hembry found the roads congested with military vehicles and he faced an almost impossible task to get through. In amongst the traffic, ambulances full of casualties from air-raids and the bombardment, struggled to negotiate the jam and reach the already overcrowded General Hospital.

In Chinatown, where 18,000 people lived jammed into 30 acres, and in other heavily populated districts the residents had no air-raid shelters or contacts outside the city to flee to. All they could do was to cower in their one-roomed homes, shared with other families, or lie panic stricken in the filthy monsoon ditches. During the indiscriminate bombing raids these areas were hit many times. The official air-raid shelter policy had been bungled and strict censorship of all news by foreign correspondents stopped the outside world from knowing the dreadful conditions suffered by civilians trapped in the city. As Tim Hudson, a divisional ARP commander, pointed out in a radio broadcast that week, 'It's no use telling people that Malta has had thousands of air raids and has stuck it out or that Chungking has had it worse than we have. They had ideal shelters not drains and the odd slit trench.'

Throughout the day and night Civil Defence volunteers, mainly Chinese, worked around the clock searching for casualties and victims amongst the bomb-damaged ruins. The continuous air-raids had brought their operations to a well organised drill. In the confused aftermath of a raid, squads would move into the devastated areas; one group would clear roads and debris to allow in vehicles and rescue workers. The rescue workers joined survivors clawing amongst the wreckage, searching for their families. The dead were laid out in rows for identification by the next-of-kin. Later the death lorries arrived to collect the unclaimed bodies which were taken away for mass burial in deep pits. For decorum's sake the races were kept apart – even in death.

The hospital admittances had reached over 2,000 a day, overwhelming both the military and civilian medical services. Unable to accommodate everyone the medical authorities took over and converted schools and large buildings. These became casualty clearing stations often manned by only a civilian volunteer nurse.

One of these was Outram Road School, close to Chinatown and the heavily bombed waterfront, manned by a young Chinese nurse and a dresser but no doctor. This temporary hospital was overwhelmed with badly wounded civilians. In the casualty packed classrooms the living and the dead lay side by side. Some of the patients hadn't been washed for days and lay in their own filth. The place stank and swarmed with flies.

In the crowded General Hospital patients lay on stretchers in the corridors. To cope with the increasing number of dead the staff dug two large pits in the lawns outside. These were sprinkled with lime and filled with unclaimed bodies.

The military hospitals were also packed with patients and, in an attempt to relieve the situation, the 50-year-old *Sui Wo*, a depot ship in the harbour, was cleaned up and converted to a hospital ship. More than a thousand patients were evacuated on Monday night together with badly needed medical staff.

Two other ships which also sailed that night were the *Kinta* and *Darvil*, two Straits Steamship Co vessels used by the Royal Navy. The latter embarked the Australian 2/3rd Reserve Motor Company for Palembang. This unit had been in action continuously throughout the campaign mainly with the Argylls. Like other vessels their Asian crews were dismissed and replaced by RN personnel. Unfortunately the naval stokers had no experience of coal-fired boilers, leaving the ships to limp along through the islands at about three knots, with their furnaces full of clinker. Behind them streamed a thick, black trail of smoke which belched from their funnels for any Japanese pilot to follow.

The liner *Phrontis* also slipped away under cover of darkness. She was crowded with a mix of both civilians and servicemen. This quiet evacuation didn't go unnoticed by the Japanese who dropped propaganda leaflets as well as bombs over the island telling everyone that ships were evacuating British and Australian troops.

In spite of the enemy landings twenty miles away and the air-raids the European social life continued unabated. Long queues of servicemen lined up to see the hit film *Blood and Sand*. In the Raffles Hotel uniformed officers rubbed shoulders with civilians in evening dress. Attractive young ladies and their mothers were in great demand. The Raffles and the Sea View Hotel were out of bounds to the other ranks who had to find their simple pleasures in the dance halls and night clubs where they were charged ten cents (less than 1d) a dance. Their partners, known as taxi dancers, and the local prostitutes had never seen so many potential customers. The breweries were also doing their bit for the war effort and worked overtime to keep up with the increased demand. Commenting on the situation later Colonel Ashmore, Royal Scots, wrote that the incidence of venereal disease was far too high and he considered this to reflect on the discipline of the troops.

Tuesday, 10th February

By Monday evening General Percival was trying to consolidate a new defence line from the River Kranji, west of the causeway, to the Jurong line which existed only on paper. This was planned to run along the banks of the Jurong River close to the now abandoned SOE School on the west coast. The cornerstone of the defence was the Australian 27th Brigade but by 7.30pm they were under heavy artillery fire which preceded fresh enemy landings.

In an attempt to capture the Singapore end of the causeway, Yamashita had launched his Guards Division across the Strait against the Australian 27th Brigade and the Chinese volunteers from Dalforce, just west of the causeway. But the attackers were thrown back with such heavy losses that he considered calling off the operation. However the Guards were ordered in again, and this time found the Australians had for some reason fallen back and left the Chinese volunteers from Dalforce, armed with their sporting rifles and shotguns, to fight it out to the end amongst the stinking mangrove swamps. This withdrawal also left 11th Division's left flank exposed.

By Tuesday morning both ends of the causeway were in enemy hands with Japanese Army Engineers already repairing the hole blasted in it by the British Army as it retreated across only nine days earlier.

General Wavell flew in that morning to see the situation first hand. Percival took him forward to see the Australian General Bennett in Bukit Timah. When they arrived the three generals were greeted by an enemy artillery barrage which severely damaged the house they were in but all three had, what General Bennett termed, 'a miraculous escape'. That afternoon reports began to come in that the Australian troops holding the centre of Jurong line had fallen back leaving a gap through which enemy patrols were infiltrating. By 4pm these patrols had advanced and threatened the supply dumps around Bukit Timah village. In their path stood fifty Argylls, all that remained of the battalion, behind a road block of motor vehicles and bullock carts.

The recently arrived Royal Bombay Sappers and Miners were ordered out of their billets, given rifles and marched in a ragged line up the Tanglin Road. These men, fresh from training camps in India and only half-trained, had never used a rifle before but were shown how to load and fire them as they marched along. The unit lacked transport, weapons and wireless equipment and when the men came to load the recently issued rifles they found that the American rimless .303 ammunition they had been given, didn't fit their rifles.

Fred Austin, who survived the sinking of the *Empress of Asia*, recalled that his unit, the Recce Regiment, was rushed to the front in lorries to protect the supply dump complex around Bukit Timah village. They debussed from lorries about, 1000 yards short of the front line and were told to collect what weapons they could find and use them. Shells were falling and exploding in every direction as they moved forward towards the sound of fierce small arms fire. He remembered that their arrival was marked by a series of earth trembling explosions as nearby fuel dumps burst skywards. As they watched, flames leapt hundreds of feet into the air, twisting in long tongues amongst the black mushroom of smoke. Caught in the breeze, it drifted towards Singapore and joined a second column of smoke from the fuel tanks destroyed at Kranji. A torrential downpour of rain which swept the battlefield brought down oily black smuts, polluted the streams and soaked everyone with oil.

In London, 10,000 miles away from the battle, Churchill chose that moment to cable Wavell that there must be 'no thought of saving the troops or sparing the population. The battle must be fought to the bitter end.' He went on to say that 'Commanders and senior officers should die with their troops. The honour of the British Empire and that of the British Army were at stake.' The cable arrived as they were about to sit down for dinner and Wavell passed it across to Percival without comment.

The Prime Minister obviously wasn't considering another Dunkirk while his new American ally was holding out in Bataan, in the Phillipines. Before claiming that any honour was at stake Churchill could have reflected that Percival's troops were paying the penalty for prewar governments' cost-cutting and 'let's be kind to the Japanese' appeasement policies. In spite of urgent requests from Percival and commanders before him, the Chiefs of Staff and Churchill refused to send adequate resources to Singapore which had been bottom of the Prime Minister's list of priorities. The troops he eventually sent Percival were largely under-trained or under-equipped and they together with the defenceless civilians, of all races, were now expected to pay the ultimate price for these decisions.

There had been some 560,000 people, of all races, living in Singapore before the Japanese thrust into Malaya and in eight weeks this figure was swollen to almost a million by refugees who fled south before the Japanese advance.

Many had lived in remote areas, in rubber estate or on tin mine concessions, and followed the course of the war on their radios. However as all news was strictly censored they were unaware of the rapid Japanese advance down the peninsula. Some of the lucky ones received telephone calls from friends or husbands in the Local Defence Volunteers. They were urged to leave in the wake of the enemy thrust as one defence line after another was given up or overwhelmed.

Some were rescued by local military units sometimes less than an hour before the area was over-run by the enemy. The first indication they received was when an army lorry, with other families on board, arrived at their isolated home and a battle-weary soldier gave them only sufficient time to pack a single suitcase before joining the women and children aboard the lorry.

Abandoning their homes and everything they owned to the inevitable looters, wives and children fled south towards Singapore by car or crammed into military organised refugee trains. At Ipoh and Taiping railway stations voluntary organisations ran a buffet of sandwiches, tea and cakes, little realising that they too would soon be refugees. By January authorities in Singapore became so alarmed at the influx of so many homeless people that instructions were sent to the British Resident of Selangor not to allow evacuees to travel to Singapore because the city couldn't cope with any more. To enforce this no railway tickets were sold except by the authorization of the area officer. Within days Kuala Lumpur and Negri Sembilan were also evacuated in nose to tail convoys.

Each day in Singapore, hundreds of women and children and families of all races emptied off the trains or poured across the causeway in private cars looking for friends or accommodation. As the Japanese fought their way through Johore, airmen and sailors drove lorries into no man's land to rescue a train load of refugees stranded on the wrong side of a demolished bridge.

Very little had been done to cope with the refugees, many almost penniless. Mothers loaded with suitcases trailed their tired children around as they trekked the streets looking for somewhere to live. Some were put up by friends but the others were faced with escalating prices as the demand for rented accommodation forced prices up. Although some may have had money in the bank, it was often in their husbands' names.

Most of the menfolk were either in the Volunteers or had attached themselves to army units as guides or advisers, where their knowledge of the country and language could be of use. In the confusion of the retreat wives and husbands lost contact with each other and neither knew whether the other was alive or dead, or even worse a prisoner. As the military refused to allow the evacuees to be billeted in empty army camps the civilian authorities were forced to issue instructions for the homeless to be billeted in hastily prepared dormitories in the Raffles College and schools.

The women and children were the governor's, Sir Shenton Thomas's, responsibility and he had been instructed by London, as early as December, to evacuate 'all useless mouths'. As a result it was decreed that there should be a flat rate cost of £120 for a passage to England, regardless of accommodation class. This seems to have been largely ignored and the shipping companies continued to charge £240 for a single ticket, which was well beyond the means of most evacuees. The shipping companies were also advised that in cases of hardship European women with children could sign for the passage. But this scheme not only put the onus for selection on to the reservation clerk but it was also not publicised in case it upset the local civilian population. Without even air-raid shelters to protect them they had no option but to stay and face the consequences of all the previous blunders by both Whitehall and the local administration.

The decision not to promote the passage-assisted scheme resulted in thousands of European women and children being trapped inside the city as the Japanese fought their way across the island. All bookings for passage from Singapore were concentrated at the P&O manager's, Frank Hammond's home, away from the city centre and the bombing. This was a large bungalow, skirted by a wide verandah with rattan shades. Along its drive from the main road women queued for hours in the blazing sun with children in their arms or young ones staying close to their skirts. The queue wound its way through the porch into a large, bare, crowded room, lined with cane chairs.

In the room were two desks. One had a card with Colombo

written on it, the other read 'UK table'. In their misery some found that the relief of reaching the desks, manned by two harassed-looking men, was premature because either the passports were out of date or the papers they needed had been left behind in their abandoned homes. One attractive young mother, with a young baby in her arms, was told that her passport was out of date as it was still in her maiden name. So she smartly stepped across to the queue at the next desk and claimed she was an unmarried mother.

In the last few hours before the causeway was destroyed, three large liners, *West Point, Wakefield* and the *Duke of Bedford* berthed in the big rectangular Empire Dock, had evacuated more than 4,000 women and children. Probably twice that many still remained in the city and the fear that Japanese troops might run amok amongst the women and girls may have concentrated the Evacuation Committee's thoughts of assembling a convoy from the ships still in the harbour.

In spite of Churchill's comments that the troops should die in close contact with the enemy, GHQ at Fort Canning decided to use the convoy to evacuate staff officers, specialists and technicians not actively involved in the city's defence. Instructions also went out for officers' wives and families to report to the docks.

Wednesday, 11th February
The enemy advance in 11th Division's north-west sector towards the Yacht Club alerted the authorities to the number of small boats and launches still berthed. Many small craft were owned by servicemen or military units. It was eventually decided to make these available to airmen with any pretensions of knowledge of sailing. The call went out on Tuesday evening and by first light on Wednesday the channel leading through the Roads was crowded with craft of all shapes, size and description all heading for the Eastern Channel. There were whalers, launches and yachts with white hulls and colourful sails, many without charts or compass, blithely heading generally south.

Initially the small boats were largely ignored by the early morning bombers which preferred to bomb the wharfs or chase after any larger ships that escaped overnight. But some were used as target practice by fighters which swooped down, almost to sea level as they raced towards the boats with guns firing. Some replied with a rifle or bren-gun but in the end the passengers leapt overboard. Those who didn't were either dead or were already so badly wounded they couldn't move. As the holed boats filled with water, and wallowed around, survivors clung to wreckage and if lucky were seen and rescued.

One of the last to leave in the small boats' evacuation was the yacht *Camiron* manned by RAF personnel. She was under the command of the RAF officer who had carried out the demolitions at Tengah and Seletar. As she approached the Eastern Channel, the horizon was black, like storm clouds. Nearby on the islands long columns of oily smoke drifted into the sky from fuel tanks destroyed by the Royal Engineers. Astern the waterfront was one mass of smoke from burning buildings and all this rolled across the bay like a fog. In amongst it weaved enemy fighters strafing any boat they could find.

From time to time during the night the crew of the *Camiron* had anxious moments when the 5hp engine coughed and spluttered. Without another craft in sight they began to feel vulnerable until just after dawn they caught-up with, what seemed to be, the tail-end of the evacuation fleet. Close to a small deserted island, anchored under the cover of overhanging trees, were the 189 ton *Rompin* (FE 14) and two vessels under tow. One was a large RAF seaplane tender from Seletar and the other a ten ton yacht, the *White Swan* which belonged to Merton Brown, manager of Thornycroft's shipyard near Kallang airfield.

*

In the city centre government departments were told to close down and evacuate their staff, that night, on the outward-bound convoy. In the Cathay Building local staff were paid off and sent home. They had remained loyal throughout, arriving for work each day despite their homes being bombed and families killed. Some departments had already destroyed the bulk of their files and papers but others, now faced with this problem, piled their files into sacks which they later threw into the burning warehouses along the dockside. Complaints from the firefighters, that they were trying to put the fires out not keep them going, were ignored.

Most of the newspapermen had already left especially when a rumour circulated that the red-haired Australian General Bennett had advised one reporter, a fellow Australian, to leave before it was too late. Those who had remained were found berths on vessels leaving that night. One enterprising reporter cycled down to the wharf, found a fisherman to take him out to a Dutch ship at anchor in the Roads and persuaded its skipper to give him passage to Java. Those who remained were searched out and told to report to Robert Scott, Director of the Far Eastern Bureau of the Ministry of Information (MoI). in the Cathay building, who was arranging berths for the newspapermen.

Boris Hembry and Sergeant Lamb with the two Chinese crewmen were on board the launch in the inner harbour. Abandoned cars from the previous evacuation cluttered the dockside and dozens of godowns were on fire along the waterfront. The swirling smoke which drifted around them gave off a distinct smell of tar and burning wood.

Later that afternoon a lorry drew up alongside the quay. Hembry recognised the driver and a passenger, who climbed down from the cab, as his boss Basil Goodfellow and Captain F.L. Morgan (nicknamed Careful Morgan) who worked in the SOE's Orient Mission's office. Morgan was a cheerful character, remembered Hembry, who had worked in Singapore before the war.

Two RNVR officers climbed out of the back of the vehicle. One was a Commander Pretty; the other he didn't know but both had worked for Straits Steamship Company. While the lorry's passengers waited for the launch to pull alongside the quay they unloaded crates, luggage and weapons from the back of the lorry then stood around while Hembry and Lamb humped them aboard the launch. One item was an airbed which Hembry decided he'd have. Both he and Lamb had lost all their kit during the retreat and all they owned they stood in. Nor did he have any money to buy replacements, recalled Hembry, the army seemed reluctant to pay him without his pay records.

They left the waterfront about 4pm and joined other small craft making for the Eastern Channel. As the old rust-stained launch got up steam and chugged across the outer harbour, a steady drone heralded the arrival of some fifty enemy bombers. Boris Hembry remembered that, 'It was as if someone had pressed a button. All the bomb doors opened and down it all came'. Near misses exploded around the ancient tin plated vessel and she was swamped with seawater leaving the occasional stunned fish floundering on the deck, to be eaten later. Several boats around them were not so fortunate' they simply disappeared in an eruption of exploding water, flame and wreckage.

*

Mavis Gully, a secretary in the Ministry of Economic War-
fare(MEW) in the Cathay Building, had been helping to burn
documents when she was ordered to leave and assemble at the
dockside. There she found a large number of radio staff from the
Malayan Broadcasting Company(MBC). The staff were allocated
berths on the *Giang Bee*, a 1,200 ton Chinese-owned, coal-burning
steamer: its captain thought differently. He refused to take the
women and only allowed the technicians on board. By the time this
news reached the Sea Transport Office on HMS *Laburnum*, the ship
had sailed and was out in the Roads before she was found, recalled
and ordered to embark a further 400 passengers. The captain's plea
that he was only licensed by the Board of Trade to take 25, and that
he did not have sufficient lifeboats for more, was ignored. Amongst
the passengers was Robert Scott, head of the Ministry of Information section, who worked his passage as a stoker.

Those who had been initially refused a berth on the *Giang Bee*
boarded the 2,500 tons *Siang Wo* anchored in the Roads. She was a
heavily camouflaged gunboat armed with a 4-inch gun and a stern
mounted machine gun. As the launches packed with passengers
approached the vessel they were caught in an air raid. The few
servicemen on board the ship who still had their weapons formed
groups at firing points to defend the ship. When the attack started,
launches and tenders swerved away and tried to escape the enemy's
target. Those which couldn't, disappeared in a mass of exploding
water and wreckage or were swamped in a tidal wave from near
misses. Some passengers having reached the comparative safety of
the ship, lay terrified on the deck or cringed in odd corners to avoid
the bomb splinters and bullets which ricocheted around.

As the momentum of the evacuation increased the Head of
Medical Service heard a rumour that all the nurses were to be
evacuated. With an increasing number of casualties from the docks
swamping his already strained resources, he was sufficiently concerned to telephone the Governor's office. He was told that the
Governor was unaware of any such plan but he would contact
General Percival. Later the assurance came back that no such
plans existed.

As far as Percival was concerned, the military nurses would stay
to the end. Their eventual evacuation was due to someone in GHQ
using his initiative.

The fruits of the Governor's lack of action to encourage the early
evacuation of civilians were reaped that day. Despite an instruction

in December from London to evacuate as many as possible he had decided to leave the evacuation on a strictly voluntary basis. This policy, confused by the strict press censorship and optimistic statements about the island's impregnability, lulled everyone into a feeling of false security, until it was too late. Those who lacked funds and learned of the opportunity to leave at the Government's expense, were now too frightened to risk the dockside carnage. The alternative, they later discovered, was a Japanese prison camp.

With the enemy at the city's gates, the volume of people trying to leave had grown into a rush as thousands of civilian evacuees streamed down to Clifford Pier and Telok Ayer Basin to search for any means of escape. The chaos increased by the hour as cars and lorries arrived packed high with luggage and crammed with passengers. In many cases after the cars were unloaded they were abandoned with keys left in the dashboard. Some owners, more aware of the regulations, drove the vehicles to the quayside, then pushed them over the edge into the sea. As the loss was deemed to be part of the military 'scorched earth policy' the owners claimed a receipt from the military to recover the cost later from the War Office.

The dockside was congested as officers and civilians brought their families to the waterfront to see them safely on board an evacuation ship. Amongst the crowds there were senior officers with orders to leave for Java and while they waited to embark, lorries drew up full of airmen. They debussed formed up along the road and filed through the throng to the ship's gangways. All around them were heart-rending scenes as families said their tearful goodbyes.

The airmen were from RAF Headquarters in Sime Road. LAC Henry Edwards from Cardiff recalled that they were ordered to destroy all the papers and smash the equipment. When this was done they set fire to the buildings and boarded their lorries for the waterfront. He found the area crowded with women, children as well as military personnel whom he presumed were under orders to leave. In fact a large number of deserters had arrived on the scene, drawn there by all the activity.

Amidst the confusion sat helpless P&O officials who tried to demand passports and boarding cards. They were often ignored as families found themselves being jostled and pushed up the canvas gangways to the liner's decks. Recalling the scene some forty years later, a lady who had been in service as a children's nanny with an officer's family, remembered that her mistress was told that all remaining officers' wives must leave immediately. They were allowed one small suitcase each and everything else was abandoned. After a very hasty pack the wife, three children and the nanny 'marched off' to the docks which they found crowded with people, just milling around. 'Every time the bombers came over we hugged the wall of a burnt-out building close to the ships.' Eventually they joined a line of civilians and servicemen filing aboard the *Empire Star*, a 10,800 tons Blue Star vessel. At the foot of the gangway an army officer strode across to the nanny and 'pushed me out of line saying that I wasn't an officer's wife'. A senior officer behind in the line, stepped forward and calling him an idiot swept him aside with his arm almost knocking him into the sea, leaving the nanny free to follow the family on board ship. 'I had no more bother and we sailed that night', she remembered.

In spite of the apparent organised confusion which seemed to exist around, the Captain of the Dockyard, Captain T.K.W. Atkinson, managed to appear unruffled as usual as he stood near the foot of the gangway. Leaning slightly on his walking stick and immaculate in his white naval uniform, he slowly straightened up and moved towards a group of bush-hatted, armed Australians moving through the crowds towards the gangway. What happened next is unclear but he confronted their leader and asked to see their orders. There was a burst of rifle fire and he was gunned down. The gang then move forward levelling their weapons at the onlookers and crew on deck as they boarded the vessel unmolested.

The *Empire Star* sailed that night with 2,000 passengers on board, including 34 children, some 150 women and an estimated 100 deserters. Another large liner which followed her across the harbour was the Blue Funnel liner *Gorgan* with 358 passengers on board.

Owing to the continual bombing a number of smaller ships were anchored out in the Roads and the harbour was busy with boats and launches which ferried passengers to these ships. Not all of them carried official passengers. One official report refers to a mass of demoralised troops looking for any means of leaving the island. They roamed the waterfront and seized the launches at gunpoint. In some cases they forced the passengers off and tried to sail the boats to Java themselves.

Another vessel ordered to leave that evening was the SS *Ipoh*, the oldest of the Straits Steamship Company ships. Her skipper was anxious about the non-arrival of his RAF passengers. She was tied-up alongside the quay, engulfed in thick smoke from the burning godowns. This probably helped the ship to escape the attention of overflying bombers which up until now had concentrated their attentions on larger vessels and those anchored in the Roads.

Most of the company's Singapore office staff were on board including the chairman, W.W Jenkins, together with Mr Crighton and Mr Gibson from the office. She was an old coal-burning ship and her age could be seen rusting through the camouflage. Her engines were in a bad state and only functioned because of the miracles performed by the ship's engineer.

That afternoon the skipper prepared the *Ipoh* for sea. Soon the engines vibrated and black smoke curled-up then belched from the funnel, signalling her imminent departure. The passengers who crowded around other vessels along the quay gradually became aware of its impending departure. Initially just one or two families asked to come aboard but soon these were lost among the large number of women and children who gathered on the quay with their luggage. As they became restless some began to clamber up the gangway and a queue formed behind them. Any crewman who tried to stop them was brushed aside. Despite pleas from the chairman and crew, they scattered around the vessel claiming berths, deck space and odd corners.

By the time 300 airmen arrived the ship was packed to capacity and the captain refused to sail unless some passengers went ashore. No one moved. The ship had by now developed a distinct list and the captain complained that she was overloaded and would be unstable at sea. Still no one moved. Below on the quay the airmen, sheltered in a nearby burnt-out godown, as well aimed shell-fire swept the waterfront.

Eventually the wing commander in charge agreed to allow his men to use the ship's hold provided they were allowed on deck in organised parties for fresh air. Although that problem solved the captain's dilemma no one was prepared to take a chance and go ashore to cast-off.

The situation resolved itself when a member of the office staff, not amongst those being evacuated, appeared on the dockside to wave them off. As he ran along the quay pulling off each hawser, 27 bombers in V formations flew overhead. The last hawser was flung clear as their bomb doors opened. On the quay, the lone figure was seen to take a running leap into a nearby slit trench. From the doubtful security of his dug-out he could hear the scream of bombs, the explosion and the whine of shrapnel. Convinced that the *Ipoh* had been hit he carefully peered over the top of the sandbags to see the ship's stern disappear through spray from near misses. Partially hidden by the belching black smoke from the funnel she headed for the Eastern Channel with 500 anxious passengers on board.

As the afternoon wore on, ships began to follow the *Ipoh*'s example and cast-off. One of the first was the *Li Sang* which sailed at about 5.30 pm. She was probably the first to reach the entrance to the minefield to find it obscured by thick black smoke from the burning fuel dumps. This blotted out almost everything, reducing the visibility to a hundred yards. Somewhere close should have been the white buoy marking the entrance through the minefield but in the gathering darkness the captain couldn't find it. Not wishing to risk hitting the mines he dropped anchor. In the darkness other ships arrived and their captains, equally confused, anchored them for the night. The irony of the situation was that amongst the specialists being evacuated were the staff responsible for replacing the navigation buoys. Their hasty evacuation probably led to the loss of thousands of lives.

The full extent of the casualties suffered by the flotilla of small boats which ferried passengers to waiting ships, was probably never appreciated, or simply ignored in the face of the greater tragedies happening at that time.

The *Mata Hari* had taken on passengers all afternoon and sailed that evening. As she got underway a waterboat approached and a young army helmsman asked the skipper, Captain Carston, whether he could take an additional 120 passengers. They had been booked onto another ship whose captain had refused to accept any more passengers. Carston agreed and the new arrivals brought the total passengers on board to 485.

Having moved off a second time the ship was again hailed but this time it was ignored. As she passed this boatload of people, and disappeared into the darkness, her stern was sprayed with a sudden burst of bren gun fire.

Eventually that Wednesday evening some 35 ships anchored at the mouth of the swept channel waiting for dawn and a race to get through before they were caught by the bombers. In the darkness the heavy guns on the nearby islands blazed away sending the last of their shells rushing overhead like the sound of an express train.

For a brief moment there was silence again, then a gigantic explosion as the guns blew up, destroyed by their own gunners. This was followed by a succession of explosions as the RN and staff of the Asiatic Petroleum Company blew the oil tanks on Pulau Bukum and Sabarok. A thick oily blast of smoke and heat swept across the anchored ships, felt more than seen, followed by a huge conflagration which sent flames roaring up 600 feet into the air turning night into day.

This illuminated four large warships which were seen to enter the harbour from the swept channel. Their sudden appearance sent a panic through the waiting ships as an enemy seaborne assault on the city was anticipated. They were, in fact, the cruiser *Durban*, and the auxiliary cruiser *Kedah* with two destroyers, *Jupiter* and *Stronghold*.

The Navy had arrived in answer to an appeal for help to evacuate the 3,000 airmen still on the island. They met the pall of smoke when they were some fifty miles away and as they approached, the familiar landmarks were hidden by the terrible oily fog, swept along by a force five wind. As the *Kedah* was a local ship she was ordered by the *Durban* to take the lead. In his report later her captain, Commander J.L. Sinclair, commented that, 'Nothing familiar could be seen only flashes, flares and fires.' Fate intervened and gave him a fix when a large ammunition dump ashore exploded revealing the three funnels of the *Empress of Asia* standing proud above the sands. The ships raced through the swept channel at about eighteen knots with visibility almost nil. Then the guns on Blakang Mati began to blaze away and for one awful moment those on board thought they had been mistaken for the enemy. This barrage was followed by explosions on Pulau Bukum which sent thousands of tons of fuel skywards lighting up the whole convoy at anchor.

In a follow-my-leader, line astern, the four ships ran toward Keppel Harbour where they found weaponless airmen and sailors from the sunken *Prince of Wales*, waiting patiently under the shelter of burnt-out godowns in Section 10. In every direction buildings were on fire and the leaping flames illuminated the embarkation. The dockside was a mess. The crews of ships which had previously refuelled had simply thrown down the feeder pipes after use, letting the oil spill everywhere. Vehicles and feet had done the rest and it was now spread all over the wharf and amongst the hundreds of abandoned suitcases, clothes and personal belongings which were scattered around the quayside. It was through this mess that the airmen formed an orderly line and filed aboard the ships covering the decks with the oil.

On the wharf was Paymaster Lieutenant B.L. Jenkins RNVR, who had been acting as assistant STO in the Ocean Buildings. He recalled that during the afternoon the Sea Transport Officer (STO) had received orders from Rear Admiral Malaya to proceed to Java with his small staff. 'Naval units would arrive at Keppel Harbour at 2200 to take them off', the message added.

Jenkins remembered that, 'The night was black with smoke and on the road to the docks we passed many fires. One spectacular blaze was the Coldbeck McGregor's bonded warehouse where vast amounts of gin and whisky disappeared in vivid blue flames.'

On the docks in Section 10, almost a thousand sailors and airmen waited patiently for the ships. 2200 hours came and went and still they waited with the noise of the battle for the dying city all about them. Less than a mile away the Japanese attacked the Malaya Brigade and the sounds of explosions and automatic fire could be clearly heard. The big guns on Pulau Blakang Mati had been traversed to face the shore and everyone instinctively ducked when their heavy shells rushed overhead.

Shortly after midnight four ships crept out of the thick oily smoke towards the wharf. 'Once berthed alongside, the embarkation was swift.' By 2 am the *Kedah* had taken 345, the *Durban* 57 and some 150 on board the other destroyers. Jenkins was aboard the *Jupiter*. When they reached the confused mass of shipping around the mouth of the channel they too had to wait for the visibility to improve with the dawn. At daylight the ships began to move, led by the *Kedah* with the *Li Sang* following. The *Durban* remained behind to cover the escape.

Lieutentant Jenkins remembered that they left just before dawn. 'It was a memorable departure and as we cleared harbour we passed through two huge pillars of fire. To the starboard were the burning oil tanks on Pulau Bukum while to port there was a mass of flames and smoke from Pulau Sambu. Looking back, away to the north were the blazing oil tanks at the now abandoned Naval Base and other tanks near the Causeway provided an impressive back-cloth' to the hundreds of fires burning along the waterfront. The first group through were some nineteen larger vessels including the *Siang Wo* with 200 passengers on board. She was fifteenth in the column. The smaller, slower vessels followed later. The missing buoy and their place in the queue to escape through the channel were to mean life or death, freedom or prison.

In the wake of the evacuation it was mayhem in the streets as civilian gangs and military stragglers looted godowns and shops. One gang of deserters broke into a motor car showroom and drove brand new cars out through the plate glass windows. Another gang tied a telegraph pole to a lorry and used it to ram down the padlocked doors of a shop full of alcohol. Close by five Australians wearing nothing but shorts sprawled on the pavement surrounded by bottles of spirits. Elsewhere a gang of armed soldiers hijacked a hospital food lorry and shared out its contents on the spot. V.G. Bowden, the Australian Government's representative in Singapore, signalled Canberra that 'the city was crowded with sullen armed deserters.' Many of these were Australians who were gathered around the now almost deserted RN offices, in the Municipal Buildings. Referring to the murder that day of Captain Atkinson, he pointed out that 'Australians and other soldiers had boarded the *Empire Star* without authority and sailed to Java'. The problem was so great that the military police couldn't handle it.

Communications had broken down and very few civilians knew what was happening, a problem shared by most military units. Even the Government official broadsheet, which substituted for the local newspaper, ceased being issued on Wednesday when the civilian editor was given two hours' notice to report with other journalists to the Cathay building for the evacuation. Rumours and speculation were rife and the hard news that did filter around to most units usually came from ambulance crews or the occasional Chinese despatch rider, a volunteer with the ARP.

The enemy artillery seemed to concentrate on the Holland Road which appeared to be under constant bombardment. The roads around the City centre were jammed with abandoned vehicles, full of craters, debris or slowing moving military convoys. Stinking piles of unclaimed, rotting bodies were everywhere and the influx of casualities to the hospitals had reached crisis level.

In another signal to the Australian Government V.G. Bowden signalled Canberra that, 'Singapore has ceased to function except as a battlefield.' General Wavell who left Singapore that afternoon reported the situation to Churchill by cable and added his fear that prolonged resistance was doubtful. The views of Brigadier J.H. Thyer, GSO1 8th Australian Division, summed up the position: did Singapore still have a strategic value to justify the sacrifice of 720,000 civilians?*

* *Percival and the Tragedy of Singapore*, page 236.

CHAPTER FIVE

The Military Evacuation
Friday, 13th February

On Thursday morning Singapore island was covered by a clear blue sky which for many people in the city, was blotted out by the smoke and haze from the burning buildings and oil tanks. In Government House overlooking the city Brigadier Ivan Simson watched 54 silver-bodied enemy bombers fly across the waterfront surrounded by brown, grey puffs of smoke from bursting anti-aircraft shells. Their destination was the Empire docks which soon disappeared behind a curtain of explosions and clouds of smoke from burning buildings. Part of Brigadier Simson's responsibilities was to ensure that the scorched earth policy, advocated by Churchill, was carried out. This had already led to a clash between Simson and the Governor, Sir Shenton Thomas, earlier in the week. When he presented the Governor with a list of the proposed works to be destroyed, the Governor deleted some forty Chinese-owned engineering works.

Sitting on the verandah of the Governor's House sipping his stengah, Shenton Thomas crossed the firms off the list commenting that, 'It would be bad for morale.' Apart from denying these facilities to the enemy he also realised that the natives would need to carry on after the surrender. It was their country and as Governor he was there to protect them, He did, however, agree that the 47 British-owned plants could be dealt with. Apart from engineering works and dockyards like Thornycroft's at Kallang, there were also vast quantities of liquor, fuel and rubber stored around the island. On Thursday it must have seemed to Simson that the Japanese were doing the job for him as the enemy launched one of the heaviest raids of the campaign.

The docks were the private domain of the Singapore Harbour Board which had godowns packed with food. Huge stocks were destroyed daily in the air-raids until Simson, who got the Governor to intervene, managed to transfer the supplies to dumps away from the high risk areas. On Thursday morning Simson had a telephone call from one of his men at the docks who was in charge of the native workers brought to the docks to empty the godowns. He was horrified to learn that all the European senior staff working for the Harbour Board had left the previous day and there was no one there to tell them what to do. Knowing the Governor's view that all senior staff should remain until the 'flag is pulled down' Simson spoke to Shenton Thomas and was told the Governor had received a cable from London with instructions to evacuate the senior Harbour Board officials if Singapore could not be held. Like the RAF and the officials at the naval base, the Harbour Board Europeans left the army and Public Works Department staff to destroy valuable machinery and equipment.

Waiting at the docks for the long gone Harbour Board staff, native workers, troops and PWD staff dived for cover amongst anything that could offer the remotest protection, as a stick of bombs straddled the godowns filled with rubber and sugar. Nearby a fuel dump exploded in a hot blast of flame and smoke which bellowed skywards, houses burst into flame from the heat and the flames leapt the road and began to spread to the timber yards and the Chinese shanty town.

The number of casualties, both military and civilian, flooding into the hospitals mounted daily. This problem was increased by General Percival's decision to reduce his perimeter and concentrate all his remaining resources for the city's defence. Patients in hospitals close to the front line were evacuated in long lines of ambulances which trailed through the bomb-shattered streets looking for hospitals to take their casualties.

While this was going on, disaster overtook the Indian Base Hospital at Tyersall. The hospital was located in the north-west sector on the outskirts of the city. Despite being clearly marked with large red crosses, the hutted hospital was a target for a wave of Japanese bombers which turned the dry, timbered huts into a raging inferno. The wounded were barbecued and roasted alive as they lay in casualty-packed wards or on stretchers in the corridors.

As an emergency measure schools and public buildings were taken over and filled with wounded, looked after by service wives and civilians whose husbands remained behind to help keep the city's services running. A hundred patients were moved into the Cricket Club and two hundred more were housed in the Victoria Club opposite. More were moved into the Raffles Hotel and St Andrew's Cathedral.

In Fullerton Buildings, Commander Alexander met an officer

(above) The *Prince of Wales*
arrives at Singapore. She was
bombed and sunk by Japanese
bombers within days of her
arrival.

(right) A large liner awaiting
repairs at the Naval Base
following a collision with a Royal
Navy ship during the arrival of
the *Prince of Wales* and *Repulse*.

Australian nurses with a General Hospital unit arriving with reinforcements for Singapore

More Australian reinforcements arriving at Singapore

from the Penang evacuation, Lieutenant Geoffrey Brooke, a survivor from the *Prince of Wales* which was sunk of Kuantan on 10th
December. He was now billeted with other survivors in the Orangji
Hotel. Some of the ratings drove lorries for the military while he
and about a dozen armed bluejackets provided a guard at HMS
Laburnum, the old hulk used as Naval Headquarters. It seemed that
the Admiral was considering putting another convoy together and
Brooke had been sent to obtain a list of all the small local steamers
still left in harbour and their locations.

In Empress Place, not far from Fullerton Buildings, Treasury
officials were burning bank notes. One of the officials was the
Acting Federal Secretary Eric Pretty who checked and noted the
numbers of each batch of notes brought from the vaults and
watched as they were thrown into the furnaces.

At Government House General Percival explained the latest
troop dispositions to the Governor. Heavy fighting had developed
along the whole front but a tank attack down the Bukit Timah
Road had been stopped. Just north of Keppel Harbour the 44th
Indian Brigade and the 1st Malayan Brigade, had thrown back a
succession of fierce enemy assaults. Meanwhile the 17th General
Hospital had been evacuated from the Changi area and the troops
were being withdrawn under cover of darkness. The big naval
guns, deep in concrete bunkers, were wired with demolition charges
and teams elsewhere were at work destroying everything that could
be of use to the enemy. With the enemy only about a mile away
from the centre of the city, Shenton Thomas agreed that the
Malayan broadcasting station should also be wrecked.

Friday the 13th.
On the east side of the island, in 11th Division's sector, Friday was
one of those beautiful mornings only the tropics can produce and
the sun, just above the horizon, was still low enough to leave the
chill of the night in the air. To the west a low, thick brown haze
hung over the city. General Gordon Bennett, the Australian Commander, remembered being driven through the city, to attend a
meeting in the battle bunker at Fort Canning. He later wrote that
the streets were cratered and awash with water from the broken
mains. Buildings blazed unattended and civilians and civil defence
workers clawed at debris frantically trying to reach people who
might still be alive. He noted in his diary that 'Rotting bodies lay in
the streets and the air smelt of smoke and cordite.'

In the Fullerton Buildings, Rear Admiral Spooner's staff spent the previous day collating information on all the ships and boats in the harbour; large and small, local steamers and launches for a proposed secret evacuation of men who had skills useful to any future war effort. On the list were coal burners, oil-fired vessels and petrol engined craft; all required to be bunkered with fuel and stocked with food and water. Many vessels needed crews especially local vessels whose Asian crews had been discharged on RN orders.

Assembly points were listed, guards arranged and boats selected to ferry passengers out to the steamers in the outer harbour. It was estimated that there would be some 3,000 berths available including room on the launches used to ferry passengers to the ships. When the ferry duty was completed the launches could make their way independently to either Java, via the Banka Strait – a long journey for overcrowded boats – or preferably steer for Warren's escape route up the Indragiri River. All this planning had been carried out in secret but by evening one major problem still remained outstanding: who should be chosen to leave?

Early on Friday morning Brigadier Simson received a telephone call to report to Fort Canning by 9 am for a conference. The room was already crowded with senior officers when he arrived including Air Vice Marshal Pulford and General Bennett. The meeting was chaired by Rear Admiral Spooner who pointed out that there were many small ships and sea-going craft, including a few armed, naval patrol vessels in the harbour. With the enemy pressing in on all sides and the reports of fighting in the suburbs, he had issued instructions for the ships to leave that night to avoid them falling into enemy hands. This exodus would provide the last opportunity for organised parties to leave Singapore. He estimated that the vessels could carry some 3,000 passengers and then began to allocate berths to the various branches of the forces. The army were allocated 1,800 places which included 100 for the Australian Division. Other places would go to naval technicians, senior officers and the remaining RAF personnel. The evacuees would be limited to hand luggage and they should report to Telok Ayer Basin by 3 pm that afternoon.

It was stressed that the evacuation must remain secret both because of morale and to avoid a last minute rush on the boats by stragglers and deserters or other servicemen who might hear of the plan. It was also emphasised that this was a military plan to save key men and it should not become a civilian evacuation of the old and sick or even women on compassionate grounds.

In most minds must have been the news of the gang rape and murder, by the Japanese soldiers, of the military nurses captured in Hong Kong. Before the meeting closed it was agreed that the nursing and medical staff should be included in the evacuation plans. Brigadier Simson was allocated three hundred passes for the civilians who remained behind to keep the city's essential services functioning including the Fire Service and ARP staff. It was now 11.30 and Simson wondered whether there was sufficient time left, for the selected evacuees to reach Clifford Pier by 4 pm. Admiral Spooner did comment, however, that if he couldn't find that many in time he could include women and children.

Later at the insistence of Lt-General Sir Lewis Heath, 3 Corps commander, General Percival called a meeting of corps and divisional commanders for 2 pm in his bunker at Fort Canning. The previous day he had ordered all units to fall back behind a new 28-mile defence perimeter encircling the built up area. This line extended from Kallang airfield in the east, took in Woodleigh water pumping station and Mac Ritchie reservoir, and extended to west Buona Vista village on the coast, north of Keppel Harbour.

Reports on his desk that morning spoke of a major Japanese offensive against the Malay Regiment, north of Keppel Harbour at Pasir Panjang. Other reports which commented on the supply position showed that there was only one small petrol dump left and sufficient food for seven days. The water supply to the native quarters had broken down because of the many breaks in the mains, in the low lying parts of the city. After briefing himself he walked into the battle bunker's conference room sat down and opened the meeting of his senior commanders.

Hardly had the meeting started than Heath, pointed out that the Japanese had driven them all down the peninsula and now stood poised for another assault, only a mile from the city centre. His troops were exhausted and dispirited and he didn't see any point in continuing the struggle.

General Bennett agreed. He had already taken the precaution of bringing all his Australians, still answering to discipline, together. He had also taken the precaution of ordering his men to create an all around defence perimeter and that all ammunition, including shells, were to be used only to defend their positions. Should the

British units, 44th Brigade, on their flank fall back, the Australians were told to stand fast and defend their square. Apart from the Australians he failed to tell anyone else of his instructions.

Percival argued that surrender was contrary to orders received from the Commander-in-Chief South-West Pacific Area, General Wavell, and in fact he (Percival) hoped to organise a counter attack shortly. Heath's view was that a counter-attack had little chance of success as no fresh troops were available. All commanders present agreed with this view and Heath went on to urge immediate surrender.

This proposal Percival could not accept and pondered on posterity's view if they surrendered the large army and valuable fortress. He also had his honour to consider. Tension had existed for some time between the two and, in a cutting reply, Heath commented that he (Percival) had lost his honour in north Malaya.*

Whatever their views Percival was not a free agent. Churchill's orders, through Wavell†, were to 'continue to inflict maximum damage on the enemy for as long as possible by house to house fighting if necessary.' Churchill had made it quite clear that he expected his senior officers to die with their men in close contact with the enemy.

*

While the conference argued about the possibility of surrender, messengers dispersed throughout the city to try and reach men chosen for the evacuation. Some officers in the front line, were actually in the midst of battle when they were confronted by a runner with a signal for them to report to the docks.

At the Municipal Buildings, Brigadier Simson briefed the chairman of the civilian evacuation committee, Mr S.M. Middlebrook and gave him 125 passes for European and Asians on the committee's list. He gave 50 more to his own deputy, Mr F.D. Bisseker, chairman of the Eastern Smelting Company and 'one of the biggest men in tin', to hand out to those businessmen who remained to keep things running. When he saw R.L. Nunn, head of Singapore's Public Works Department, he gave him 75 passes but made it quite

* Percival's Papers 43 – Notes on the Fort Canning Conferences Paragraph 3 of the Conference of 13 February 1942.
† Churchill's *The Second World War* Volume IV, page 91

clear that he should retain sufficient men in Singapore to carry out the remaining demolition work.

Although the Governor wanted heads of departments to remain until the 'flag was pulled down', the evacuation of all the Harbour Board Staff two days earlier could be considered a precedent for the PWD. Nunn was also a Group Captain in the RAF Reserve and he believed that he could do more useful work in airfield construction than rotting in a prison camp. On a more personal note, like many others who remained, his wife refused to leave without him.

When Nunn reached his office that lunchtime, he began to compile a list of staff to be evacuated. He and his wife headed the list. Two hours later there was uproar at the dock gates when armed military police refused to accept the passes. There was no mention in their orders to allow civilians to take part in this 'secret' military evacuation.

The Fire Service received about a dozen passes. One fireman, an American, was fighting a fire at the docks that afternoon when a Chinese despatch rider handed him a pass with a covering note ordering him to leave for the embarkation point. Covered in oil smuts and dirty from the smoke and rubble of the fires, he only had time to say a quick goodbye to his Chinese firecrew before he made his way along the waterfront in his high leather boots and old fashioned type fireman's helmet. At the entrance to the docks he joined the hundreds of civilians milling around pleading to be let in.

A large number of Royal Navy personnel, mainly survivors from the *Repulse* and the *Prince of Wales* were housed in the Orangji Hotel close to the waterfront. They were ordered to leave that night. They had been allocated to six ships in the harbour, the *Kung Wo*, *Ping Wo*, *Shu Kwang*, *Tien Kwang*, *Mata Hari* and the *Kuala*. The seamen were paraded in the large foyer and an officer, Lt-Commander Terry, went down the line cutting off batches with a wave of his arm. After each cut he announced in a loud voice which ship they should look for on the docks.

Terry emphasised that everyone must be at the docks by five o'clock or they would miss their chance to escape. Meanwhile, he told them, they were going to the nearby river and waterfront to commandeer all the large native boats, tonkans and sampans they could find and bring them around to HMS *Laburnum*, the old hulk being used by the RNVR as their offices. These were to be used in the evacuation.

By this time General Yamashita had brought his heavy guns across the repaired causeway and used them to steadily shell the area. As the sailors left the hotel to board lorries they scattered and flung themselves to the ground as the whirring rush of the enemy shells passed overhead to explode with a dull crump. There was noise everywhere. Overhead grey puffs of smoke marked the fire from the ack ack guns dug-in along the beach. Their bangs mingled with the sound of machine gun fire from the outskirts of the city. Planes could be heard flying overhead and the sailors felt the ground vibrate with exploding bombs. To add to their worries rumours were circulating that enemy tanks had broken through and were heading down the Bukit Timah road towards the waterfront.

Deserters and looters were now becoming a common sight and, as they drove past in their lorries, the armed sailors took little notice of the gangs of soldiers and civilians smashing their way into the shops. The Holland Road, still a target for enemy guns, was littered with abandoned vehicles including a tanker which lay almost on its side its front wheels in a monsoon ditch and petrol dripping slowly away into a water-filled crater.

At the river the naval detachments began to board some of the large number of native boats moored side by side. These were the homes of generations of Chinese and the playground for their children. Climbing down the river bank the sailors jumped down on to the decks, avoided the washing strung out amongst the rigging, and stepped from boat to boat with screaming children fleeing in front of them.

Having been on the receiving end of enemy bombs and shells the Chinese were about to be evicted from their homes by armed, steel-helmeted British sailors. Within minutes there was mayhem as the sailors stepped from one boat to another and banged on hatches with their boots and rifle butts. Frightened, crying children who had been playing on the decks fled to their mothers as the sailors, unable to speak Chinese, ordered the non-English speaking Chinese off their own boats.

Chaos erupted as the sailors fought off screaming women as pots and pans, bedding and food were dumped on the river bank. Terrified babies clung to their mothers while fathers and brothers argued with the armed sailors. The noise brought spectators including gangs of Australian soldiers who wanted to join in and help themselves to a boat. These were kept at bay by armed bluejackets.

On Kallang airfield near Changi, close to the scene of some heavy fighting, a secret RAF detachment received its orders to leave and destroy their equipment. This was a small unit of about thirty officers and men operating Radar. In the last ten days they had seen all the surviving aircraft transferred to Sumatra and watched as the remaining ground staff were evacuated on Wednesday. Apart from themselves there only seemed to be the ack-ack detachment on the airfield perimeter and the men holding the front line. The deserted airfield, cratered and with most of its buildings either on fire or burnt-out shells, was still being bombed daily so little time was lost by the men of 250 Detachment when the orders came to leave for the docks and take part in the evacuation. One of the airmen, Walter (Taffy) Hughes, remembered being ordered to destroy all their equipment with sledge hammers and smash the valves and fittings. They were then ordered to board the unit trucks and make their way to the waterfront.

Not having been in the city since the battle started, the airmen were shocked at the amount of damage. Bodies lay unclaimed in streets littered with burnt out vehicles. Buildings had collapsed blocking the road and there were fires everywhere, remembered Walter Hughes. 'When we arrived at the docks we found ourselves under continual shelling and bombing.' Overhead formations of bombers seemed to fill the sky as they pattern bombed the shoreline. Everywhere groups of civilians and military personnel crouched in doorways or amongst the ruins as bombs exploded in a line across the wharfs.

'Someone seemed to know were to go, so we followed and found a ship, the *Tien Kwang*, sailing that night for some unknown destination. This ship, and every ship, seemed to be a target for the bombers as we soon discovered in the next raid. Three flights of bombers appeared overhead then suddenly there were water fountains from the near misses exploding around the ship.' As the afternoon went by he was joined on board the *Tien Kwang* by some 350 passengers including Royal Navy personnel and some civilians.

The ship sailed after dark, he remembered, and 'the sky was brightly lit from burning oil tanks and buildings. One felt all on board were going from the frying pan into the fire.'

Not everyone enjoyed the same orderly evacuation especially men in the forward units. Last minute attempts to reach them sometimes ended in failure as messengers crawled forward to the point of combat to try and reach those selected. One officer lucky enough to be chosen was Major Bill Cowell, 18th Division Ammunition Officer. He discovered that a pass for a berth carried no guarantee. When he arrived at the basin he was told that the ship had sailed.

The same problem occurred with 38 specialists, Australians from Tanglin Barracks, under the command of Colonel Kappe, Chief Signals Officer. Their journey through the city was a nightmare. The road was under continual shell fire; they had been bombed and strafed in an air-raid and the driver needed to take many detours to bypass roads blocked with fallen masonry. After having their passes checked by the sentries they were eventually told that they were too late. The vessel had left. Instead of remaining, they returned to the barracks and eventual captivity.

A second group of Australians, under the command of Colonel Broadbent, Principal Administrative Officer with the AIF, arrived in time and left on one of the escape boats, the *Tenggaroh*. The remaining 55 Australian official escapers are believed to have missed the evacuation.

One group of British officers who arrived late were not so easily put off when they were told there were no berths available. For twelve hours they sheltered amongst the burnt-out godowns insisting something must be found for them. Eventually they were marshalled into a small launch which set out for the SOE escape route at Rengat, Sumatra.

At the 2/10 Australian Military Hospital, in a converted school, Matron Paschke interrupted a group of nurses snatching a quick lunch. She told them that a car was about to arrive to take them to the docks. Passage had been arranged on an escape ship leaving that night. Shaken by this news they protested that they couldn't leave the patients. Their pleas were ignored and they were ordered to leave. At the Outram Road dressing station nurse Janet Lim answered the telephone and was told to leave immediately. A car would soon be arriving to take her to the docks.

The civilian nurses at the General Hospital were also offered the opportunity to leave but almost all refused to go. One, who had been a nanny with an officer's family, recalled that this hospital had been one of the main reception areas for casualties from the docks and many nurses were too frightened to go there. Many nurses were wives of men who were either fighting with the army or helping to keep the city's essential services running and wouldn't leave their husbands.

The nurses that did leave were mustered in St Andrew's Cathedral, which had now become a casualty clearing station. As they sat in the pews a continual stream of wounded were carried in and laid out in rows on the far side of the church. Soon the pews began to fill with Army sisters in red capes, a few wore bush hats and some steel helmets. Others arrived in grey uniforms and some in a group from the General Hospital, arrived straight from the casualty wards, without even a change of clothing. They were followed by Australian nurses from 13 Army General Hospital and 2/4 Casualty Clearing Station.

They all talked amongst themselves but the murmuring died down when a RN officer appeared and began to go amongst them recording their names and hospitals. As they sat silently waiting they could hear the bark of ack-ack guns and the continual drone of bombers overhead. The cathedral shook with the blast from exploding bombs sending swirls of dust floating in the warm air

Eventually, late in the afternoon, the 'all-clear' sounded and the nurses began to file out to waiting lorries. These took them through streets flanked with burning buildings, crowded with an endless stream of people walking to the docks carrying what personal possessions they had left in small bulging bags or pillowcases.

Near the waterfront the congestion grew as their lorries inched past abandoned cars. A few vehicles were badly damaged but many had just been left with the keys in the ignition for anyone to drive away.

By mid-afternoon the confusion at the dock gates had become a mêlée with sentries tussling with civilians waving passes in their faces. Inside the gates were husbands or wives pleading for their spouses still barred from entry. Children lost from their parents in the tightly packed crowd at the gate had been allowed through and stood sobbing as they peered anxiously at the gates for their parents.

When Brigadier Simson, heard that the passes he issued to selected civilians were being refused he went to the docks personally to deal with the problem. He found the area congested with civilians frantically waving passes at the sentries. Shouldering people aside he pushed his way through the throng and eventually persuaded the guard commander to let them through.

At that moment the noise of the crowd was drowned by the roar of enemy bombers flying low overhead. A sea of faces watched the bomb doors open and bombs tumble loose over the godowns and crowded waterfront. One stick of bombs burst in quick repetition along the road sending the brigadier's car sky high in a sheet of flame and exploding metal, killing the driver. Nearby a young husband reeled against the dock wall clutching his baby to his chest. At his feet lay his decapitated wife. Dead and wounded lay around the entrance and survivors began to move around dealing with the casualties. The dead were pulled to one side while nurses and doctors, amongst the official evacuees, tended the injured until the ambulances arrived to take the wounded to the already over-crowded hospitals.

Inside the Basin, along the quayside, the nurses lined up patiently to wait for their launches. With them were three doctors, Dr Coates from the 2/10 AMH and two civilians, Dr Cuttwood and a lady, Dr Thompson. A drunken soldier from the Argylls had managed to breach the security and now weaved amongst them waving a bottle of whisky and offering the nurses a swig. The Argyll recalled that one nurse, who had politely refused his offer, observed 'It seems you're in more need of it than I am.'

The Argyll, who survived the war as a prisoner, had been in continuous action since north Malaya. Cut off after the Slim River disaster, his group trekked 400 miles to Johore. They were still some miles away when they heard the explosion as the causeway was blown up. About this time they ran into a Japanese column and fought their way clear. In the skirmish their officer had been badly injured in the legs and the Argyll carried him the rest of the way to the Straits of Johore. There they stole a boat and rowed across to the Naval Base at about the time it was taken by the Japanese, escaping through one gate as the Japanese entered through another.

Whatever organisation existed on the docks broke down under the strain. There was organised confusion as queues of passengers intermingled and the wrong passengers arrived at the wrong ships. To add to this, unofficial escapers took the places of casualties and others who were delayed. Heavy bombing also took its toll and those who survived the dockside faced being drowned or killed in the small boats being used to ferry the passengers to the ships.

When Lieutenant Geoffrey Brooke returned to the Orangji Hotel after commandeering the native river craft, he was told to report to the *Kung Wo*. This was an old Yangtse river boat with a straight, tall funnel amidships. She was embarking passengers near the hulk of HMS *Laburnum* he was told, but when he arrived he found the place crowded with people. Luggage, sacks of supplies and crates were strewn everywhere while alongside motor gunboats, heavily armed Fairmile motor boats and launches were crowded with passengers. Plenty of activity but the *Kung Wo* was nowhere to be found. Someone told him that she left to bunker coal at Keppel Harbour. He borrowed a car and raced across the town along roads pitted with craters and arrived at Keppel Harbour just as the *Kung Wo* finished coaling and was about to leave. He was greeted by an angry Lt-Commander Terry who demanded to know 'where the hell he had been.'

On board HMS *Jarak* in the harbour, Lieutenant Hooper was ordered to bunker his ship and prepare to take part in the evacuation. Aware of the confusion caused on Wednesday because of the missing buoy, HMS *Laburnum* ordered Lieutenant Hooper to sail on Friday afternoon and anchor at the entrance of the swept channel, where she would function as a lightship for the evacuation fleet. Shortly after the *Jarak* sailed, darkness quickly descended and emphasised the glow of fires all over the city and waterfront. It seemed to the passengers and crew that all Chinatown was on fire.

Within an hour the first ships appeared, briefly out of the smoke, then they were gone. In quick succession others passed by, some challenged nervously unable to grasp the *Jarak*'s job, half expecting it to be an enemy vessel. As the night drew on the camouflaged spectres became fewer, replaced in the early morning by the flight of the little ships. Six fast, armed, motor launches roared by flashing recognition signals; later the signalman identified an American Eureka O Class attack boat which swept past gently rocking the ship.

Rear Admiral Spooner, Air Vice Marshal Pulford and a group of officers were on the *ML310*, a fast 73 tons, Fairmiles armed motor launch, under the command of Lieutenant-Commander H.J. Bull who had taken part in some of Warren's earlier seaborne raids behind enemy lines. When General Percival said goodbye to his friend Air Officer Commanding Air Vice Marshal Pulford before he left, Pulford offered to stay behind with him but Percival turned this offer down. As he left Pulford turned to Percival and remarked that 'I suppose you and I will be held responsible for this, but God knows we did our best with what we had been given.' Unable to defend themselves, one to become a prisoner and the other to die, for him his remarks were to be prophetic.

Amongst the 44 official evacuation ships which left that night were four small vessels which kept company as they passed HMS *Jarak*. They were the little *Malacca, Sin Kheng Seng, Wo Kwang* and the *Trang*, a palm oil tanker. The latter was under the command of Commander Alexander RN.

The *Trang*'s engines had been neglected and badly maintained. Ever since she had left the Basin they had given continual trouble and, after passing through the swept channel, somewhere near St John's Island, they finally stopped for the last time.

As the sound of the engines died away the hot, tired and perspiring ship's engineer climbed slowly up the ladder from the engine room. Pausing briefly in the cool breeze that swept the deck, he glanced back at the black, thick reeking smoke from the burning oil installations, then wandered casually towards the bridge.

Alexander took the engineer's grim news with a certain amount of aplomb. Without power the ship had begun to drift towards the minefield and the order to abandon ship was given. While the ship's three boats were slung out on their davits, other crew members rushed around to open the seacocks and set the ship on fire. Thirty minutes later, with two lifeboats loaded and launched, Alexander took one last look around the burning vessel and climbed overboard. The ship settled fast as water poured in through the open valves. The two other lifeboats had disappeared into the night beyond the circle of light from the burning ship. As this last boat was about to be pushed away it was found to lack oars. Without hesitation a stoker leapt back on board the sinking vessel, which was now a mass of flames. It must have been almost an inferno below decks but despite this the stoker fought his way through the blaze and returned with two shovels. Using these the crew poled the lifeboat away from the burning ship and rapidly paddled to safety.

In the darkness they were hailed and the shape of the second lifeboat appeared through the smoke. This was under the command of Lieutenant Hollywell who had taken her some three hundred yards away then waited for Alexander, whose boat could be seen illuminated by the blaze. From this safe distance they watched as flames leapt out of the portholes. Eventually she rolled over, enveloped in a cloud of steam. Even from that distance they could hear the engines tearing themselves from their mountings and the bulkheads collapsing under the pressure of a tidal wave of water which burst through the ship. Then suddenly it was dark and nothing left but two crowded lifeboats rocking in the waves.

The third boat, commanded by Lieutenant H.T. Rigden, got safely away and made for the SOE escape route up the Indragiri River.

CHAPTER SIX

The Bitter End
Saturday and Sunday, 14th–15th February

Although he was obviously concerned at his dwindling supply of ammunition, General Yamashita ordered his big guns and tanks to join in the daily bombardment. Shells and bombs crashed down on the defenders and helpless civilians alike. To the Japanese observers on the high ground above the town, near the Mac Ritchie reservoir it must have seemed as if the whole city was an inferno. A Malay Operations Record stated that, 'Aerial bombing, artillery fire and the oil tank explosions have created a hell's port.'

In his headquarters near Bukit Timah, Yamashita ordered his troops across the rain-soaked ground in what was to be almost his final assault against the British defences. As he waited he realised that should his exhausted troops break through the defence perimeter they would be faced with a daunting street by street battle for possession of the city.

In his underground bunker in Fort Canning's battle box, General Percival read reports of continued Japanese attacks along the front line. A Japanese division had been thrown against the 2nd Malaya Brigade, on the extreme right flank close to the abandoned Kallang airfield. Further inland, around Woodleigh pumping station, his 11th Division's troops were being pushed back towards the city. Further west Yamashita's Guards Division had broken through 18th Division's front at one point and threatened to plunge down the Thomson Road into the city. This was finally stopped, by a battalion drawn from the right flank, at the cost of many casualties.

Another report brought news of a massacre at the Indian Military Hospital at Alexander. This hospital had been over-run when Japanese soldiers, who burst through the open doors, shot down medical staff and ran amok along the corridors packed with stretcher cases and into the casualty filled wards, bayoneting the screaming patients to death. What Percival didn't know was that some two hundred survivors of the massacre, patients and medical staff, had been imprisoned overnight in one of the staff bungalows and were that morning being taken out and beheaded. While he read his reports, news reached him that a fresh attack had developed against his left flank, between the Australian lines and the sea.

The 1st Malaya Brigade bore the brunt of that attack and in their trenches overlooking the brigade's positions, the Australians watched the preliminary bombardment and saw the enemy infantry move into the attack. The Australians avoided taking any offensive action and the guns remained silent. Because of a growing shortage of 25 pounder ammunition the gunners were forbidden to engage the enemy unless attacked themselves. So their guns remained silent as Japanese threw themselves against the defenders.

In spite of suffering heavy casualties from the intense enemy bombardment, the defenders stood their ground and met the Japanese in fierce hand to hand fighting. Using bayonets and rifle butts they fought back until gradually the number of Japanese trickling back to their own lines became a flood. Suddenly from above the noise of exploding shells and automatic fire came a resounding explosion. The Australians watching the battle turned to see a black and crimson cloud roll skywards as the British army's last ammunition reserves disappeared in a series of blasts.

When runners brought the news to Yamashita that his attack had failed, defeat stared the Japanese Commander in the face. His casualties had been heavy and his remaining troops were exhausted. What ammunition they had left was running out and there was little prospect of fresh supplies. All along his supply route through Malaya from the Slim River to Johore sabotage parties left behind by Warren, together with the Chinese guerrillas, were ambushing road convoys and destroying trains and track. The fresh troops Yamashita needed for the final battle were becoming involved in anti-guerrilla sweeps or absorbed in guard duties.

While General Yamashita considered the prospect of defeat, his British counterpart General Percival faced his own pressures. Winston Churchill insisted that the army should fight to the last man. On the other hand Percival was being urged by some of his senior commanders to surrender. Unknown to him the Australian commander, General Bennett, had gone as far as sending a cable to the Australian Army Headquarters in Melbourne announcing that 'If the enemy enter the city behind us we will take suitable action to avoid unnecessary sacrifices.' After the war he admitted it was his intention to surrender.

Bennett's assessment of the probable military situation was supported by the news that the Malay Brigade, between the Australians and the sea, had been finally forced back after fighting off attacks by three enemy infantry regiments. This left the Australian Division on a salient.

The Japanese, broadcasting from Penang Radio Station, left intact by civilian technicians, boasted to the world that there would be no Dunkirk for the British Army trapped in Singapore. Percival also realised the truth of these claims as he knew no further help could be expected from Java or from Churchill and his Chiefs of Staff in London. All Churchill could now offer Percival and his men was words. The honour of the British Empire and the British army was at stake – the battle must be fought to the bitter end – and commanders and senior officers should die with their troops. In political rhetoric terms it meant that Percival and his men had been abandoned.

Under orders to continue the fight General Percival had no plans to save his army but in those last hours, when it was realised that the 'bitter end' couldn't be far away, individual officers and men alike began to consider contingency plans.

On the eastern end of the front line, the 2nd Malaya Brigade broke up an enemy column trying to infiltrate along the beach. If they had succeeded they would have broken into the city and over-run the anti-aircraft battery alongside Kallang airfield. When this news reached them the shirtless gunners searched for their rifles and self-consciously fixed bayonets. As the Battery Commander, Captain Rowley-Conwy (later Lord Langford) watched his men do this he decided that when the end came he would do everything possible to avoid his men being captured.

The Argylls, now down to some fifty officers and men, stopped a column of tanks on the Bukit Timah Road with hand grenades and tommy guns. If the tanks had broken through they could have careered down the Bukit Timah Road to the gates of Fort Canning, splitting the defences wide open.

The Argylls also realised the end couldn't be far away and they too began to consider their options which included a large yacht owned by one of the officers which could probably take what was left of the battalion.

In GHQ at Fort Canning Brigadier Simson accepted an invitation to join an escape party being organised by a staff officer, Major Coode. He had a launch secreted away and canvassed selected officers to leave with him. General Bennett was also getting restless. He believed that with his anti-Japanese combat experience he would be more useful back home in Australia, where he could train others to continue the fight, rather than rotting in a Japanese prison camp.

While some made plans others took a more positive stance. When the news eventually leaked out that a secret evacuation had taken place, the armed military police at the dock gates were besieged by hundreds of deserters and stragglers, some armed, who tried to rush the dock gates. When the trouble was at its peak a petrol tanker arrived and slowly inched its way through the mob. It gently nudged forward until it stood at the gates. There it stayed while one of the passengers, from the oil refinery, tried to persuade the guards to let them through. But the guard commander knew if that gate opened he could not stem the rush which would cause a heavy loss of life. Finally the civilian turned to the mob, who were in an ugly mood, and appealed to the leaders 'to play the game' as it was essential to get the fuel into the docks. Eventually the leaders moved aside, weapons were lowered and the lorry moved through the now open gates and disappeared inside leaving the sentries to continue their 'stand-off' with the mob.

The tanker drew up alongside a launch and refuelled it. The three civilians then boarded the vessel, fired the engines, untied it from the wharf and steered a course out into the Roads, to Sumatra.

Elsewhere a lone officer disguised in native clothes, his face darkened with brown shoe polish, searched the beach for a boat. Over his shoulder he carried a canvas bag containing a change of clothing, currency, jewellery and watches.

That evening another officer, an Australian armed with a bren gun, found a rowing boat hidden near the beach but no oars. In the shadow of nearby palm trees he located a small hut, built on stilts, the type normally used by fishermen. The ladder had been drawn up so he shinned up the supports and kicked in the bolted door, covering the darkened room as he did so. On the floor in the far corner two shapes moved, one shouted at him in Chinese.

A dark-haired, attractive, sleepy-eyed young Chinese girl, sat up in bed terrified and naked; the other, presumably her husband, was older and angry. By sign language the Australian pointed to the boat, then the islands, then to the Chinese and himself. Under such conditions the boot and butt can clear up any misunderstandings and the Chinese dropped over the edge of the verandah and returned with two oars. Followed down to the beach by the Australian at a quick walk, the Chinaman pushed the boat into the sea climbed aboard and adjusted the oars. The officer, with his gun cradled in his arms took one final look at the fires burning in the distance then at the naked girl in the shadows, before wading out to the boat. Ever watchful he stepped over the side and gestured to the Chinaman to start rowing.

Near the docks a group of soldiers led by Gabby Gavin were also looking for a boat. Gavin had been seconded to the secret SOE School where agents were trained to carry out missions behind enemy lines. When the School evacuated to Java all seconded personnel were either returned to their units or offered a place in the mainly Chinese-manned Dalforce.

Gavin had opted for Dalforce. Now this too had been disbanded. The Chinese volunteers had been paid off and its officers and British other ranks were given permission to escape if they could. Companies of Chinese volunteers had arrived by lorry in the grounds of a large civilian bungalow being used as Dalforce Headquarters. After being paid they changed out of their blue uniforms into civilian clothes and disappeared in ones and twos back to their families. Some kept their weapons and joined the Communist underground who were already preparing to fight on.

After his company had been paid off and disbanded, Gabby Gavin was joined by some six fellow European NCO's and other ranks. He led these down to the docks and separated the group into two parties. One would look for supplies, while he and his friend Joe looked for a boat. The area had been well covered by previous would-be escapers and anything worth having was already gone. Nevertheless they did find a broad beamed, nine feet sampan, less its oars. Leaving Joe on guard armed with a tommy-gun, Gabby stripped off and waded into the sea. Using the burning buildings as markers he swam along the sea defences and barbed wire entanglements until he finally broke into the harbour. Fighting against a strong tide he went from boat to boat until he accumulated six paddles.

When he returned to the beach he was discovered by three very drunk soldiers who seemed confused as to why anyone would want to swim to Singapore when everyone else was trying to get away. Intrigued they followed him back to the sampan. Joe was still on guard but the others never returned to the rendezvous. Gabby Gavin waited as long as he dared for his missing companions before thrusting an oar into the hands of each bewildered drunk, who hardly seemed to know what was going on. He then got them into the boat and pushed off from the beach. On board he organised a steady paddle rhythm and navigated the sampan out to sea and through the minefields.

Sunday 15th February

Dalforce had taken over the now empty home of the Belgian Consul for Singapore as headquarters. Inside Lieutenant Frank Brewer, Local Defence Volunteers and one-time instructor with SOE, had spent the last few hours paying off the Chinese volunteers. He remembered that when each company came in they dumped their weapons, shotguns and old sporting rifles in the back of the lorry. This was driven away by a fellow officer who 'probably dumped them in the sea' he commented.

The remaining members of Dalforce Headquarters staff had moved off during the night he recalled, leaving him to pay off the men. The last party came in just before daylight, discarded their blue uniforms and threw their weapons into the back of the lorry. They signed for the pay and after wishing good luck, left. Leaving a fellow officer to drive off with the lorryload of weapons Brewer made his way to Fort Canning in another vehicle. He found his fellow officers from Dalforce digging trenches alongside a road through the open area leading to GHQ. From them he learnt that their commanding officer, Colonel John Dalley, was at the Fort looking for new orders. Brewer parked the lorry, picked up a spade and began to dig in for the last stand.

The Colonel arrived back later that morning a bit put out that 'those headquarters chaps' were organising groups of officers to get away in launches and small boats. As he spoke his officers kept ducking as salvo after salvo of enemy shells screamed in overhead to explode amongst the docks and the nearby Holland Road. In a brief discussion everyone seemed to think that GHQ's plan was a good idea and pointed out that if they had a boat they could reach Sumatra and join Warren at his guerrilla base in Bagan Siapiapi. Warren was a friend of Dalley's and had used his home in Kuala Lumpur as his office when Warren and Spencer Chapman planned and organised the placing of sabotage parties behind enemy lines.

Suitably satisfied about the ethics of leaving, Dalley returned to Fort Canning's battle bunker. As a contingency Frank Brewer left to search for a boat along the waterfront and Telok Ayer Basin.

The road to the Basin and Empire Docks was pitted with bomb craters and the roadside shops were being looted by civilians and soldiers alike. Above in the clear blue sky the usual formation of 27 bombers passed overhead. Just ahead of the lorry near the beach, an ack-ack battery with steel helmeted gunners, stripped to the waist, disappeared behind a line of bomb explosions.

The attempt to get some officers away may have been the result of a signal General Percival had received that morning from General Wavell. It seemed that now when it was too late to save or salvage anything from the mess Churchill had relented. Conveying the Prime Minister's views, Wavell urged Percival to fight on and inflict losses and damage but more important he gave him discretion to surrender. The signal concluded by saying, 'Just before final cessation of fighting, opportunity should be given to any determined bodies of men or individuals to try and effect escape by any means possible. They must be armed.'

About the time Frank Brewer arrived at GHQ General Percival, who had just returned from morning service, called an urgent meeting for all of his senior commanders for 9.30 to discuss the proposal to recapture the Bukit Timah supply dumps. His commanders thought differently and argued that their troops were exhausted, they were running short of 25 pounder and Bofors ammunition and the water supply had broken down. General Bennett listened with interest to the debate across the conference table, on whether or not to surrender. He had already cabled his Prime Minister in Canberra, without telling Percival, that he proposed to negotiate an independent surrender should formations around him fall back on to the city.

The conference lasted barely twenty minutes and Bennett noted in his diary that, 'Silently and sadly we decided to surrender.' This decision was followed by an order to all units to destroy codes and secret material. Units were told to cease fire at 4 pm but retain their personal weapons in case the Japanese refused to stop fighting.

At 11.30 three men, Brigadier T.K. Newbiggins, Percival's adminstrative officer, Hugh Fraser, the Colonial Secretary and a Japanese-speaking officer from 3 Corps, Captain Cyril Wild, left Fort Canning in an open car with a white flag in the back, and drove towards the Japanese lines.

In spite of this apparent last minute change of policy to allow determined bodies of men or individuals to escape, very little was done by GHQ to ferry large numbers of men away from the island. Instead as news of the impending surrender spread, it was left to unit commanders to use their own initiative and allow their men the opportunity to avoid capture. One of these was the Commanding Officer of the Recce Regiment, which arrived on the ill-fated *Empress of Asia* two weeks previously.

Three days earlier the regiment had been rushed in to seal a gap in the front line near Bukit Timah; now the CO called his officers together to break the news that a cease fire was ordered for 4 pm. This seemed to confirm rumours of an impending surrender. Although the men were given the option to escape if they could find a boat, almost all of them just wanted to fall into an exhausted sleep. While the quartermaster searched nearby supply dumps for food and stocks of clothes, other men began to equip themselves with items useful in prison camp, like wire cutters, spanners, compasses and maps. Fred Austin who had stood on the burning deck of the sinking troopship watching the Japanese bombers flying overhead, remembers one soldier 'with an Italian sounding name' getting permission to leave. He reached the docks and managed to find a place on an escape boat. After this boat was wrecked he made his way by island hopping to Sumatra and where he eventually reached Padang and was captured. He was sent to work on the Burma end of the railway from where he escaped a second time.

Another shipwreck survivor trapped in Singapore, was Stoker George Avery RN. He had been on the Prince of Wales when she was bombed and sunk. He remembered that on the Sunday when Singapore surrendered he was acting as a runner, carrying messages between the Argylls and the Australians. 'We worked in pairs with a native as a guide.' The guide kept talking about the surrender, Avery remembered, and at first they thought the 'Aussies had packed in and that we were cut off'. He reflected that 'in fact the whole lot had gone. When we realised this we got him to take us to a friend of his with a boat.' They pooled all their money and gave it to the boatman 'to get us away. We left in the early hours of Monday morning and by evening we were amongst dozens of small islands. Suddenly out of the darkness came a British submarine. She had been stuck in Singapore under repair but at the last moment she escaped but could only travel on the surface and not submerge.' Neither was she under full power and this caused her to crawl along on the surface by night and hide during

the day. 'She came alongside and picked us up leaving the fisherman behind on his boat.' The submarine eventually reached Java.*

In Fort Canning the Australian representative Mr Bowden,
accepted an offer to escape in a small ten-seater launch, the *Osprey*,
only if his two assistants could go with him. The launch was
moored in the Basin.

Bowden sent his last message to Canberra from a small hand-set
near the water's edge, manned by a Royal Signals wireless operator.
'Our work is completed. We will telegraph from another place at
present unknown.' The Australian Government had expected him
to remain and be interned so that arrangements could be made
later, for him to be included in an exchange of Japanese and
Australian Diplomatic staff.

When his party reached the quayside they joined the group of
officers from Dalforce and others from GHQ. This brought the
numbers of escaper to 38. On the quayside they were also joined by
a large group of deserters who tried to seize the launch. 'We were
not going to have that,' commented Frank Brewer, 'so we sent them
packing.'

The sea was covered with a thick oily haze, Brewer remembered,
and fountains of water erupted as enemy guns still continued to
bombard the waterfront. After a couple of naval officers had packed
the 38 officers into the ten seater launch *Osprey*, they took her out of
the Basin and eventually drew alongside a 40-foot larger vessel, the
diesel-engined *Mary Rose*. While a number of passengers hauled
themselves up its side, the *Osprey*'s engine ticked over and gently
rocked the boat. One moment it was a gently rock then a shudder
and the engines began to scream. The *Mary Rose* shuddered and
began to buck, raising shouts of alarm from those on board both
boats. Someone rushed to the *Osprey*'s engine and switched it off.
Looking up, Brewer could see the entire length of the *Mary Rose*
guard rail lined with passengers looking down at the men still in the
launch. From the stern came a shout that the propeller had fouled
the larger vessel's mooring rope. After many attempts to free her it
was decided that all the passengers remaining on the *Osprey* should
join the *Mary Rose*. The mooring rope was slashed and the launch
moved out into the outer harbour leaving the deserted *Osprey* to
drift away in the darkness.

* George Avery believes it was HMS *Rover* but it may have been HMS *Trusty* which
was under repair at that time.

After the *Mary Rose* party had left Fort Canning, Brigadier Simson rechecked his small escape pack, and looked at his watch. The surrender was planned for about 4.30 and now it was nearly 6 pm and Percival had still not returned from the Ford factory near Bukit Timah where he had been meeting with his Japanese counterpart General Yamashita. Simson had earlier mentioned to Percival that a GHQ officer, Major Coode, had arranged for a group of selected officers to escape in a launch soon after the surrender was announced. Percival had made no objection. As Coode's launch was due to leave the waterfront at 7 pm Simson was anxious to be away but didn't want to leave without saying goodbye to his commander, General Percival.

Soon after six he was told that Percival's car had returned and hurried along the corridor to the office. Pausing briefly, he knocked and entered. Percival was sitting behind his desk. The Brigadier smiled, saluted and held out his hand to say good-bye. Percival looked up at the Brigadier, ignored the outstretched hand and refused him permission to escape. He commented that 'officers should stay with their units'. Taken aback Simson reminded his commander that he had no units. This was brushed aside and Percival indicated that their conversation had finished by picking up and examining papers on the desk.

The Australian Commander General Bennett had already made his plans to leave and didn't make the mistake of seeking Percival's permission. When it became obvious that the end was not far away many officers and men in his division were openly discussing the possibility of trying to escape. However Bennett seemed concerned that any disorganised mass escape by individuals and small groups would court disaster and possibly lead to needless deaths. Enemy fire against his sector during Sunday had been sporadic and when the news arrived of the cease-fire he issued instructions that all Australian units were to stay at their posts until 8.30 the following morning. They would then assemble at Tanglin Barracks where every man would be issued with new clothing and rations. He pointed out that 'all precautions must be taken to ensure that the spirit of the cease fire is not destroyed by foolish action'.

Having done this he left with two of his officers for the docks to find a boat. Driving into the city that evening the skyline was lit by the dull red glow of fires, reflected against the black pall of smoke blocking out the night sky. The news of the impending surrender was now sweeping the city. In the streets they passed groups of recently arrived Indian soldiers tying strips of white cloth around their hats; some had sewn little Japanese flags to their tunics having hidden them for just such an occasion. Looters were breaking into shops and warehouses and carrying away their loot in handcarts, baskets and even stacked high on rickshaws. Weaving around the craters and burnt-out vehicles, the camouflaged lorry bumped over obstacles and empty hose pipes. The burning buildings alongside the road had been left to burn themselves out when the water supply failed. In the dancing shadows a gang of soldiers walked by with their arms full of beer bottles. Eventually near the waterfront General Bennett and his party abandoned their car and began their search for a boat.

A group of Volunteer gunners were also prowling around the waterfront that evening. They were led by Lance Bombardier M.C. Hays, prewar Inspector of Mines. Their unit had taken part in the retreat and formed the rear guard down the peninsula. It had also taken part in some of the bloodiest fighting for the city. When the company commander offered them the opportunity to escape, Hays and his friends left the front-line and walked into Singapore to the waterfront.

As they moved along a wharf in the flickering light of the burning buildings they saw the dark shapes of armed soldiers standing at a landing stage looking down at a small boat. Disturbed by some noise the men looked in their direction and challenged them. As they drew close they recognised the soldiers as Australians, all officers and one was a General.

General Bennett's party had found a sampan and the General's plan was to sail it to Malacca where he intended to make contact with his friend the Sultan of Johore. From there he hoped to reach Sumatra with the Sultan's help. Although they listened with interest Hays and his friends had other plans. They intended to steal one of the larger sea-going junks anchored in the Roads and sail it to the Dutch East Indies. Bennett preferred their plan and decided to join them.

Hays discovered that the sampan lacked oars but these were soon found following a quick search by the Volunteers. Another problem was that the sampan was too small to carry everyone at once, so the Volunteers agreed that Hays would ferry the Australians out first, then return for his friends.

Looking back towards the shoreline, as the little boat was conned out into the oily haze, it seemed that the entire city was in flames.

There were buildings on fire all along the waterfront and, above the rooftops towards Singapore River, the dark red glow of the fires in Chinatown could be seen reflected against the black oil clouds. The view was soon lost as they became enveloped in the thick smoke rolling across the sea. After a while a large native boat loomed out of the murk and Hays drew the sampan alongside. The boat was empty. After Hays helped the Australians to board the junk and he was about to push away and row back for his friends, Bennett tried to persuade him to stay and leave with the Australians. In disgust, Hays told Bennett to keep the boat and he and his friends would find another. At this point the General's British ADC interjected and recommended that they should all stay together and that the Australian officers should wait for the rest of the Volunteers.

Another vessel at sea that night was a medium-sized yacht, the *Cecilia*, with Brigadier Paris on board together with some of his Argylls.

At Kallang Airfield, Captain Rowley-Conwy, Royal Artillery, battery commander of the anti-aircraft unit alongside Kallang airfield, was with his men waiting for the next air-raid when he was called to a meeting at Fort Canning. When he was told, at the meeting, that a party was going forward with a white flag to negotiate surrender terms he left, not waiting for the end, and drove back to Kallang.

He had earlier 'found' a small launch, the *Joan*, in the nearby Thornycroft boatyard and while his men were destroying their guns he took a sergeant and an armed party with him on the launch to commandeer one of the large junks anchored out in the Outer Roads. The journey out took about an hour and when the launch drew alongside a junk he led his men, all armed, up and over the ship's side, ready for action. It was deserted and it stank.

Having commandeered the vessel the young 21-year-old captain sent an NCO back with the empty launch to collect the rest of his battery. By nightfall all his men were aboard. Then the junk, with the Gunners trying to master the cumbersome craft, sailed away with a gentle breeze filling her sails. Followed on behind were more Gunners packed in the launch.

In the darkness near Clifford Pier, was a group of about two dozen officers and men. The party had originally been only nine Gunner officers and NCOs selected as official escapers. When they reported to control point at the Basin on Friday evening they were told that there were no more berths available. After spending

The locally built MML 311 shortly after she was taken over by the Royal Navy

An unnamed Royal Navy vessel, probably a river gun-boat class, practising seaborne landings in Johore. The lifeboat under tow is packed with Indian troops

(Above) An unarmed Tiger Moth biplane. Lieutenant Hembry was flown from Sumatra into besieged Singapore in a Tiger Moth only days before the Garrison surrendered.

(Left) Lieutenant Boris Hembry, Special Operations Executive (SOE)

Friday night sheltering amongst the ruined godowns the Gunners were told that the evacuation scheme had finished so they were now on their own. It was everyone for themselves. The Royal Navy STO and the Harbour Board employees had all left.

On Sunday morning the officers found an abandoned lifeboat anchored offshore, which swimmers amongst them brought in. By now their numbers were swollen by stragglers who wanted to join any group which appeared organised.

One of the officers had assumed command of the group and, when oars were found, he crowded everyone aboard the lifeboat. After a brief period of tangled oars and rowers catching crabs, the oarsmen became more disciplined and the boat gradually moved away from the burning waterfront.

That night and Monday a wave of escapers abandoned Singapore in small boats of every description, some with only a vague idea of which direction to steer. The situation can best be described by the experience of Captain Ernest Gordon. He had been wounded in the shoulder in Malaya and hospitalized in Singapore. When he was discharged he rejoined the Argylls at Tyersall Camp where he was given 30 men and sent down to the docks to help get some of the evacuation ships away. Having survived the continuous shelling and bombing he was then ordered to carry-out a seaborne landing behind enemy lines with a company of Indian troops. These troops were stationed on one of the offshore islands but when he arrived to collect them he was told that the mission had been cancelled and he should return to Singapore. That was Friday evening.

The next morning he learnt that a small palm oil tanker the *Sir Hugh Frazer*, under the command of a Sergeant Major MacLaren had docked overnight. Its profile was not unlike a landing barge. This would take him back but to have attempted it during daylight would have been suicidal. Later they tried to sneak back under the cover of darkness but were picked out in the beams of captured searchlights, sweeping the sea for any escape ships. The enemy artillery then opened up, scoring near misses, which were sufficiently close enough to make them change their minds and retire out of range.

They finally dropped anchor off a large island to discuss their next move. The ship had hardly anchored, when out of the wafting smoke which swirled around the vessel, came a hail, followed by a bump alongside and the ship was boarded by a group of escapers.

Their delight in having found it after hours of rowing must have soon disappeared when they learnt that MacLaran was trying to get the vessel back to Singapore. Throughout Saturday night the little tanker filled up with exhausted and hungry escapers, deserters and stragglers. They came in all manner of crafts, junks, sampans launches, boats of all shapes and sizes including canoes and even baulks of timber.

Finally when one party of four in a hull from the Singapore Rowing Club, brought the first definite news that the fighting had stopped, Gordon ordered Sergeant MacLaren to head for Sumatra. During the next 24 hours they continued to rescue escapers, either from unseaworthy boats or stranded on the many islands.

PART TWO

The Fate of the Evacuation Ships

CHAPTER SEVEN

The Escape Route

A Dutch fighter pilot flying over the islands south of Singapore on Monday morning described the assortment of little boats and yachts with colourful sails, packed with escapers fleeing from Singapore, as a regatta. But a large number of the boats' crews lacked both charts and even the most basic knowledge of seamanship. Many soon found this out when they ran their boats aground or became marooned on islands less than twelve miles from Singapore. Some boats ripped their bottoms open on reefs leaving their passengers to drown or starve to death on desert islands.

No plans existed in General Wavell's headquarters in Java, to mount any form of search and rescue operation despite his signal to Percival that 'opportunities should be given to determined bodies of men, with their weapons to try and effect an escape'. If any thoughts had been given to this problem they were quickly over-shadowed by air reconnaissance reports which told Wavell that the large enemy fleet which had been at anchor off the coast of Malaya, in the China Sea, had now merged with a second one from Indo-China.

This new combined force, with many troop transports and warships including cruisers, was under the command of the Japanese Vice-Admiral Jisaburo Ozawa. When the fleet was off the coast of Borneo, on Saturday 14th February, General Wavell ordered the Dutch Naval Commander, Admiral Doorman, to assemble what naval units he had left and engage the enemy.

As this Allied fleet sped north to intercept the Japanese, now known to be approaching Banka Strait, the Dutch warship *Van Ghent* ripped her bottom open on an uncharted reef and sank. A second Dutch ship stopped to pick up survivors and the remainder, which had raced ahead, came under heavy air attack as they approached Banka Island. These Borneo-based enemy bombers scattered Doorman's ships and used up most of fleet's ammunition. Assessing the situation Doorman believed he had no option but to retire.

It was left to one of the escape ships, a Royal Navy auxiliary vessel, HMS *Li Wo*, to carry out the only surface attack on the enemy invasion fleet. She was a paddle boat converted at the outbreak of war to a minesweeper. On Saturday morning, she and two other escape ships, the *Ping Wo* and the *Vyner Brooke*, were making a final dash for the Banka Strait. Converging, on the same course but still over the horizon was the Japanese fleet also headed for the Banka Strait. The leading ship of the three evacuation vessels was the *Ping Wo* which fled through the Strait less than an hour before the Japanese arrived. The second vessel was the *Li Wo* which was in open water about ten miles from the Strait when her crew sighted the first of the Japanese ships. They were at first mistaken for British warships, but when it was realised what they were the *Li Wo* tried to race them to the Strait. Pounding along at about four knots she was quickly overtaken. With the Japanese ships only about a mile away the *Li Wo*'s captain decided to engage the enemy. The surprised enemy look-outs saw the White Ensign break out from the paddle steamer's mast as she turned towards the fleet. While her four-pounder gun pumped shell after shell at the enemy warships, supported by rifle and bren gun fire, the paddle steamer rammed and badly damaged one of the troop transports. As she pulled clear, leaving a gaping hole in the victim's side, military passengers on the *Li Wo*'s deck racked the enemy vessel with small arms fire including a passenger on deck who banged away with a pistol.

As the *Li Wo* pulled clear she was set upon by destroyers which raced to the scene firing salvo after salvo. Shuddering from successive hits and on fire she broke up and sank. A few miles away enemy bombers, who now preceded the convoy, caught the *Vyner Brooke* only five miles off the Banka Strait. Packed with women, children and nurses, she was bombed and sunk within minutes.

The Japanese captured Banka Island on the 15th and found three of the ships which sailed from Singapore on Wednesday, beached near the harbour, at Muntok. They were either casualties of enemy bombers or had engine trouble and managed to get as far as Muntok. Some three hundred evacuees from Singapore were rounded up and imprisoned. Survivors from the *Vyner Brooke* who reached Banka were bayoneted to death on the beach.

By the 15th, Admiral Ozawa's ships occupied the northern end of the Strait which effectively cut the sea route from Singapore. Dozens of ships and small craft trying to escape through Banka Strait were captured but when Japanese air patrols reported that Admiral Doorman's Allied fleet had been sighted approaching east of Banka island Ozawa took measures to save his fleet. He ordered his troops up Moesi river to give support to paratroopers dropped around the Palembang oilfields the previous day. His destroyers were sent north to hide amongst the islands to avoid battle while he, with his heavy naval units, stood fast and prepared to fight.

This move sent his destroyer screen amongst the unarmed or slightly armed ships packed with evacuees from Singapore. Some of the small slower ships, which were last through the minefield at dawn on Thursday morning, were now close to the Japanese-occupied Strait. It was these ships the Japanese navy found first.

As the enemy warships raced north their crews were on full alert and prepared for a fight as they sweated in oven like gun turrets or fed-up ammunition from the magazine below. A light cruiser and three destroyers which moved up the Sumatran side of the coast, spotted the unarmed SS *Redang*. From a distance of half a mile the destroyers fired salvo after salvo. The *Redang* disappeared in fountains of water and sank within minutes, taking with her 58 escaping servicemen and crew. The enemy force then moved away leaving some 31 survivors clinging to wreckage.

Another victim was the *Giang Bee*, with 300 passengers on board. She hoved to when the enemy ships were sighted and on this occasion the enemy gunners held their fire while the officers scanned the vessel's deck with their binoculars. The captain of the *Giang Bee*, anxious to show that the ship was simply a passenger ship, ordered all the women and children on deck but as she was flying the White Ensign the Japanese may have suspected a trick. For some hours the warships played a game of cat and mouse with the ship while their victim repeatedly signalled for instructions. Eventually the captain ordered everyone into the boats and to abandon ship but as she had insufficient lifeboats about a hundred passengers and crew were still on the deck when she was blown apart by the Japanese gunners.

The four-year-old Yangtse river boat HMS *Scorpion* had passed

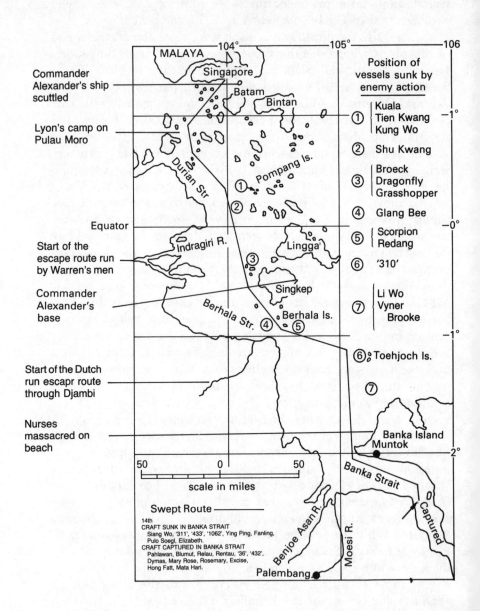

Commander Alexander's ship scuttled

Lyon's camp on Pulau Moro

Equator

Start of the escape route run by Warren's men

Commander Alexander's base

Start of the Dutch run escapr route through Djambi

Nurses massacred on beach

MALAYA

104°   105°   106

Singapore

Batam

Bintan

Durian Str.

Pompang Is.

Indragiri R.

Lingga

Singkep

Berhala Str.

Berhala Is.

Toehjoch Is.

Banka Island
Muntok

Banka Strait

Captured

Benjoe Asan R.

Moesi R.

Palembang

Position of vessels sunk by enemy action

① Kuala
   Tien Kwang
   Kung Wo

② Shu Kwang

③ Broeck
   Dragonfly
   Grasshopper

④ Glang Bee

⑤ Scorpion
   Redang

⑥ '310'

⑦ Li Wo
   Vyner
   Brooke

-1°

-0°

-1°

-2°

50   0   50
scale in miles

Swept Route ————

14th
CRAFT SUNK IN BANKA STRAIT
  Siang Wo, '311', '433', '1062', Ying Ping, Fanling,
  Pulo Soegl, Elizabeth.
CRAFT CAPTURED IN BANKA STRAIT
  Pahlawan, Blumut, Relau, Rentau, '36', '432',
  Dymas, Mary Rose, Rosemary, Excise,
  Hong Fatt, Mata Hari.

through the Berhala Straits on the last leg of her journey to Banka when she too was intercepted by the four enemy ships. All five ships fired simultaneously but within minutes she was ablaze from stem to stern and sank. Her crew managed to launch three Carley floats and twenty survivors on floats were rescued by the Japanese. About twelve hours later the *Mata Hari* sailed through the stream of wreckage and found six more survivors, while a further 29 are believed to have reached Dabo. That brief engagement accounted for 100 passengers and crew.

The enemy warships sighted the heavily laden *Tanjong Pinang*, a small Dutch palm oil tanker, low in the water. She was returning to Dabo having rescued survivors marooned on Pom Pom. Some were on deck but many casualties were crowded into her hold. A brief salvo from the warships' guns straddled the vessel which sank within minutes after a shell exploded in the survivor-packed hold.

Those ships which escaped the destroyers' dragnet often found themselves caught by enemy bombers flying from Malaya and Borneo. Amongst their victims were the *Scorpion*'s sister ships HMS *Dragonfly* and *Grasshopper*. These two gunboats acted as escorts for two paddle steamers and a tug boat. Led by HMS *Grasshopper* under the command of Commander Hoffman, the little convoy entered the Berhala Strait, line astern and steered for the Sumatran side of the channel.

The ship's decks were crowded with a motley collection of passengers, women, children, servicemen, PWD employers and nurses. Only twelve hours earlier they had sheltered alongside the waterfront amongst the burning warehouses, being bombed and shelled, and now – the morning was calm: the sun had risen in the early morning sky leaving some of the coves and hills on the islands, hidden in shadow. The sea was unruffled apart from the ship's wakes, churned up by the paddles and propellors.

The ship's cook on the *Dragonfly* had managed to produce coffee and corned beef sandwiches for breakfast. These supplies had been looted by the crew from the abandoned warehouses along the quayside.

The previous night must have seemed like a nightmare from Dante's inferno, with tenders and launches ferreting around the smoke-filled harbour looking for any ships' captain willing to take passengers. Some boats simply disappeared in waterspout soups of wreckage and bodies. Passengers who clambered aboard the *Grasshopper* may have expected to be safe but they were cut down by

shrapnel and bullets as they scrambled and clawed their way into
any nook or cranny that could offer even the least amount of cover.
The dead were dumped overboard to make way for the living and
the wounded lay around the ship, tucked into any odd protective
corners. The carnage was illuminated by huge fires ashore with
some flames dancing 600 feet into the night sky.

But the fears and horrors of Wednesday were gone and Singapore was now seventy miles astern. In two days they should be off
Banka Island and halfway to the journey's end. All shipping had
been warned to sail only at night and hide amongst the islands
during the day to avoid enemy air attack. Daylight had only just
broken when Hoffman tried to lead his little, slow moving convoy
to the shelter of the nearby islands.

The first attack came about nine o'clock when a single plane
swooped, out of the sun. His target was the *Grasshopper*. Despite a
barrage of rifle and bren-gun fire, supported by the ships, two,
three pounders which banged away at the plane, three bombs
crashed through the decks and exploded. The attack was over as
quickly as it began leaving the First Officer checking between decks
for bomb damage. About mid-morning the ships were found by a
formation of 27 silver bodied bombers, flying in groups of nine. The
convoy was close to an island with the *Grasshopper* less than 600
yards from the beach.

As plane after plane attacked the ship her passengers scattered
across the decks and ran for cover. On deck the gunners tried to
defend the vessels with the three-pounders while the servicemen
gave support with small arms fire. Ignoring the anti-aircraft fire the
enemy planes pressed home their attack and the gun-boat was soon
surrounded by near misses which shook the vessel and popped her
rivets. About a half a mile away one of the paddle steamers had
stopped and its passengers and crew could be seen leaping overboard. This may have been the *Changteh*. The tug disappeared in an
explosion of steam and wreckage after a direct hit and in the tail of
the convoy another gun-boat, HMS *Dragonfly*, was seen to take a
number of hits. Burning fiercely and out of control she veered
sideways and suddenly capsized. She sank in three minutes.

The *Grasshopper* was now the only ship still afloat despite receiving eleven hits. With the beach only some three hundreds yards
away her skipper, Captain Hoffman, decided to beach her. As she
headed for the beach her crew struggled to unfasten the floats and
throw them overboard. The floats were followed by passengers who

leapt into the sea after them. Others ignored the floats and swam for the beach and once ashore ran and stumbled across the hot, soft sand and flung themselves into the shelter of the jungle which fringed the beach. The planes, having dropped their bombs, now turned their attention to the survivors in the water and on shore.

Flying low they strafed the swimmers and those clinging to the wreckage. Some lifeboats, which had landed survivors on the beach, risked the bombing to return to the *Grasshopper* to ferry more passengers ashore. Hoffman, and a gunner, who had manned the gun through out the attack, were the last to leave.

When the two reached the beach and began to wade ashore Hoffman stumbled and fell. Seeing this, some of the crew raced across the sand, dragged and half carried him up to the protection of the trees where they found he had been badly wounded in the leg.

Later, when the raid was over, Hoffman made camp in a clearing close to the beach, and began to plan their escape. The convoy had carried an estimated 400 passengers and crews but only two dozen had reached his survivors' camp. As he hoped some had managed to get ashore in other coves, he sent a party of six marines to check the rest of the island for both water and survivors. Near where he lay the nurses cleared the area and set-up a dressing station. Apart from the nurses, marines and some of his crew the others included Frank Brewer, a journalist, three Dutch women, one blind and two in an advanced state of pregnancy, and some young children.

Hoping that the island may have villagers who could give assistance Hoffman detailed some of his crew to take the undamaged whaler, pulled up on the beach, and circumvent the island and search for any inhabitants. Neither the Marines nor the boat party, which returned later that evening, found water or any signs of life. Next day Hoffman selected a group to sail the whaler to Dabo, the main town in the Group. Shortly after the whaler left another lifeboat was seen making for the island. This contained some twenty survivors from the *Dragonfly* who had been washed ashore on a neighbouring island.

Pom Pom

The three ships, the *Kuala*, *Kung Wo* and the *Tien Kwang*, escaped from Singapore on Friday the 13th. Between them they carried more than a thousand passengers. On Saturday morning the *Tien Kwang* reached the small uninhabited island of Pom Pom, some 70 miles from Singapore. Sumatra was 30 miles to the west. In the early morning Walter Hughes, the nineteen-year-old airman with 250 AMES (Radar) unit saw the jungle-covered island bathed in sunshine and shadow. It rose some 300 feet above the sea and was almost inaccessible, apart from two small beaches. Although no one lived there it was occasionally used by local Malay fishermen who had built a bamboo and attap hut close to a small spring in the centre of the island.

Hughes recalled that he fell asleep from sheer exhaustion soon after boarding the *Tien Kwang* in Singapore. Later on deck at first light, his friends commented that the skipper had trouble with the ship's engines all night and now intended to anchor close in to hide his ship from preying aircraft.

'The word soon went around that the skipper wanted volunteers to go ashore and cut foliage to camouflage the ship,' remembered Hughes, 'so I volunteered with a few others. While waiting to clamber down the Jacob's ladder which a member of the crew had dropped down the ship's side I saw a larger vessel some two miles away, well down by the stern close to another island.' Before he could dwell on the fate of her passengers and crew he was ordered over the side. When everyone was in the ship's boat the airmen pulled for the shore against strong currents which swept around the island.

While they rowed ashore a third vessel appeared. This was recognised as the *Kuala*, which prewar had traded in and out of most ports in the area as far afield as China. Her skipper had also chosen Pom Pom to hide by during the day because of the deep water close inshore. The *Kuala* had sailed the previous evening under cover of darkness with some 450 passengers on board. These were largely Public Works Department staff and servicemen but also included about fifty women. Both ships were anchored in a small bay close to the island.

While Walter Hughes and his companions rowed hard against the currents a fast launch approached the ships from the direction of the wreck. It first called at the *Tien Kwang*. On board was the young naval officer Lieutenant Geoffrey Brooke. He boarded the *Tien Kwang* using the ship's Jacob's ladder and recalled that people were lying all around the decks and passageways completely unprepared for enemy action.

He had come from the wreck of the *Kung Wo*, which had been bombed and badly damaged some hours earlier. He hoped that the two new arrivals could find room to embark some of the survivors who had got ashore on nearby island of Dankau. Chatting to the ship's officers, he related how after the enemy air attack about two-thirds of the *Kung Wo's* passengers and crew had managed to reach the nearby island of Dankau. He believed the remainder had either been washed away or killed in the raid. Although the survivors had two ship's boats with them, both were badly holed by bullets and shrapnel and were being patched up on the beach. The launch, he explained, belonged to a Dutch planter who simply happened to be passing the island when he saw the wreck and came ashore to investigate.

On his return journey, after visiting the *Kuala*, Brooke suddenly saw the *Kung Wo* disappear behind a curtain of water from a string of near misses alongside the ship. Above him was a formation of nine bombers, almost wing-tip to wing-tip whose noisy approach had been drowned by the launch's engine. He watched as they flew overhead, turned and started a second bombing run. She again disappeared behind fountains of sea water and as he watched the sea welled up around her and she slid away and sank with a surge of waves and steam.

On Pom Pom, Walter Hughes saw the launch move away from the *Kuala* as he scrambled over the sharp volcanic rocks and began to climb the steep hillside. At that moment he became aware of the roar of aircraft and looking up over his shoulder he saw three enemy bombers fly overhead, at tree top height, clearing the island and disappear.

'At first I thought they had not seen us but out of sight behind the island they turned and came around from its side and dropped a salvo of bombs on the ship we had just left. From the rocks we saw all hell break loose as men and women jumped into the sea or slid down ropes alongside the ship. Most were swept away by the strong currents and others in the water were killed by near misses which exploded amongst them. The bombing was so intense that we could do nothing to save them. Then the planes swept over the island bombing and strafing those who had managed to get ashore.'

Walter Hughes was struck in several places in the chest and knees before friends pulled him amongst the trees and shrubs for protection.

On the *Kuala* four hospital matrons were having a discussion in a cabin when the attack developed. As the alarm sounded the first bombs rained down and near misses rocked the ship. One struck the vessel, pierced the deck and exploded in the matrons' cabin. All around the stricken vessel gushers of sea water swept over the decks and the blast and bomb splinters tore huge chunks of wood from the deck and sent them hurtling across the deck like spears.

Suddenly the regular thump of the engines ceased and the new silence was broken by screams and the roar of escaping steam. Above the noise came the sound of long bursts of bren-gun fire and the crack of rifles. More explosions shook the vessel and the patter of bullets and shrapnel on the deck could be heard throughout the ship. Then she began to list and the smell of smoke drifted below decks.

With the help of some passengers a ship's officer, who survived the attack unharmed, immediately tackled the fires. All her regular native crew, drilled in firefighting at sea, had been dismissed on the orders of the RN and replaced by RN sailors unfamiliar with the vessel. While soundings were being made to assess the ship's seaworthiness, the medical staff amongst the passengers dealt with the wounded. The ship, which was soon down by the stern, had become a drifting hulk being carried along in a strong current until the anchors held her.

The deck seemed full of wounded and dying and rushing passengers as RN crewmen tried to lower the badly damaged lifeboats and pitch rafts overboard. Anything that could float was also flung over the side. The sea around the crippled ships was littered with deck chairs, mattresses, tables and wreckage. Down below a sailor from the *Prince of Wales*, his face covered in blood, lurched along the companionway urging everyone on deck with their lifejackets. Clouds of smoke bellowed through the ship and water had begun to lap around people's feet as they left their cabins and rooms.

Near the entrance to the deck stood a group of Chinese nurses terrified to step out because of the explosions and flying shrapnel. Other nurses in grey uniforms pushed past, head down, and lurched across the tilting deck to pull wounded passengers under cover. The sky seemed to be full of circling planes which weaved and swooped, some down to mast height firing the guns.

Passengers scrambling up from below saw the island close by. Some leapt overboard to swim the short distance but the current just whirled them away. One of the passengers sheltering on deck was a young Chinese mother with two frightened children aged two and six years old. All the lifeboats had gone and the ship began to list. Realising she must attempt to save herself and the children, she gripped them as tightly as possible, climbed over the ship's rails and dropped into the sea. With the little two year old pulling her blouse and hair in terror, she hurtled down into the water, deafened by their screams. Under the water she clung to the struggling children with both arms while all time she kicked out with her feet towards the surface.

They emerged near a large piece of wreckage onto which she managed to push her six-year-old girl, Patsy, before it was swirled away from her hands. She tried to keep afloat with one hand and with the other clung to her terrified second daughter, Lottie. The shouts and screams from other passengers drifted into the distance as she lost sight of the ship and the island. They floated for some hours under the blazing sun before being seen by other survivors in a lifeboat but as she was dragged aboard, the unconscious child slipped from her grip and disappeared. Six-year-old Patsy was also nowhere to be seen.

The swimmers around the ship found themselves in strong currents which swept them past the island and out to sea. Others in the water were carried towards the disabled *Tien Kwang* which was also under attack. With all three ships on fire or sinking the enemy pilots turned their attentions to the survivors who were machine-gunned in the water and on the beach as they staggered ashore. Other planes made bombing runs which cratered the island and uprooted trees.

Throughout the raid survivors risked their lives standing on the rocks to pull exhausted swimmers ashore and drag them to the doubtful cover of the trees. Amid the screams of the wounded and the cries of those being swept away a soldier and a civilian named Ross, a PWD employee, who had been ashore to cut branches to camouflage the *Kuala*, launched a lifeboat and tried to reach the swimmers. One rowed while the other pulled people aboard. This boat disappeared. Other boats were launched from the beach and these soon became encircled by people clinging to their sides. With life-rafts in tow the rowers strained to bring the unwieldy and heavy tows ashore.

On the island groups of soldiers scrambled along the water's edge and rescued exhausted survivors, who simply clung to the rocks unable to go further to save themselves. They also found one boat with only women on board. They had rowed their heavy boat around to the other side of the island, away from the bombing, and found a beach to run aground on.

The military nurses had small medical packs with them and these were torn open and used on the casualties. A shortage of bandages was overcome by the nurses and women who tore their dresses and underclothes into strips for bandages.

Some women, including the nurses who had been below when the raid started, reached the island with only their bra and knickers on. Others who came ashore naked were given shirts or other items of clothing by the soldiers. They had been asleep below decks when the attack came and didn't have time to retrieve their clothes before their ship sank.

Soon after the attack the launch used by the *Kung Wo* survivors returned with bearded Lt-Commander Terry on board. He brought with him medical orderlies from amongst his men, who scrambled ashore over the rocks and began to treat the wounded, recalled Walter Hughes, whose shrapnel wounds were cleaned and dressed by one of the sailors.

The next morning, Monday, three Malay fisherman reached the island with coconuts and some freshly caught fish for the survivors. The disturbing news they brought was that Singapore had surrendered and that Japanese ships were now moving around the islands. They advised Nunn, who had taken charge, to try and reach Senajang where survivors from other sunken ships were being looked after. Before the Malays left they showed Nunn where they had hidden a large outrigger canoe and left him directions how to reach Senajang.

Nunn, a First World War veteran, was of medium height with receding hair, a lean man, about 40 years old with a neatly trimmed moustache. After that war he joined the Colonial Service and served in Trinidad and British Guiana. As head of the Public Works Department in Singapore, he played a key role in keeping the city's essential services running and remained at his post after some senior staff had left, including many in the Harbour Board. His escape from Singapore is controversial and some, who remained, believed he should have stayed 'until the flag came down.' One problem he had was that his attractive wife, who had given up a successful stage career to join him in Singapore, refused to leave his side despite the dangers. The Japanese troops' record of rape and debauchery must have been uppermost in his mind when he decided to leave with his wife.

After the fisherman left he selected a nine man party, made up of both servicemen and PWD staff, to try and reach Senajang in the dug-out canoe. They took with them a small supply of food fresh water and coconuts. The following day Nunn examined the possibility of refloating the *Tien Kwang*, which was badly damaged but still afloat, close to the island. A section of Royal Engineers together with PWD staff went out to examine her and they found that she was leaking badly and the engines wouldn't start.

He must have realised that the canoe, gone to fetch help, may simply disappear or be captured by the Japanese. This would leave the survivors marooned on the island without adequate resources, so he ordered the ship to be stripped of everything serviceable and portable to be brought ashore. When this was done, she was scuttled to avoid attracting a fresh wave of bombers. Her seacocks were opened and she settled in shallow water with only her mast above the sea to mark her grave.

All this failed to save them from attack as within 36 hours the bombers returned and again attacked the island causing more casualties. To avoid a similar loss of life Nunn separated the hundreds of survivors into three large groups and allocated them their own camping areas. Walter Hughes recalled that he with other RAF personnel were moved to the other side of the island where they found a spring of fresh water near the low tide mark. The rations were broken open and each man was issued with a slice of bully beef.

By the end of the second day food supplies were running short and everyone was rationed to a cup of water and one and a half ship's biscuits a day. On the second or third days he remembered a barge arrived, manned by Royal Navy ratings, which took off a large number of casualties. This may have been the *Hung Jao*. Unknown to Walter Hughes, a Dutch trader, the *Tanjong Pinang*, had arrived the previous day and taken off some 320 women, children, nurses and the seriously injured. Nunn's plan was to evacuate the women and children first, then the other civilians then the servicemen.

On about the third day the first rescue boats from Rengat arrived. This rescue mission was co-ordinated by Major Campbell. The first boat was skippered by Bill Reynolds, a tall Australian with horn-rimmed glasses. A prewar mining engineer in the tin industry, he remained in Singapore and used his launch to help to ferry evacuees to the escape ships. His vessel was probably the last to leave following the surrender.

He made two trips to Pom Pom. On the first he embarked some 50 people, mainly women and children and fifteen casualties. On the second voyage he brought off over 80 survivors. Another rescue boat from Rengat that reached the scene was the *Numbing*, under the command of the Gunner officer from the Kallang Battery, Captain Rowley-Conwy. He took off another 60 people. Other vessels sent by Campbell embarked a further 200 leaving about the same number marooned on Pom Pom.

It was days before the next rescue boat appeared and morale on the island dropped as the shipwrecked survivors began to wonder whether they would ever be rescued. Rations were down to a ship's biscuit per person and half a cup of water from the spring which threatened to run dry. Some nine days after the sinking a Harbour Board barge, the *Heather*, crept around the island crewed by two soldiers under the command of Lieutenant Canty. Canty 'found' the barge in Singapore, packed it with escapers and sailed her to Djambi. When they arrived the Dutch Controller persuaded him to try and reach the island to rescue as many as possible. Before he left the Dutch equipped the barge with cots for the injured, blankets, food and water and a large tarpaulin to drag across the open barge to protect the survivors from the weather.

Many of the survivors were in a bad state suffering from exposure and starvation. Some 170 people were finally embarked including David Miller, director of the Chartered Bank. Despite her husband's pleas Mrs Nunn insisted on staying with him so reluctantly he gave up his leadership role and helped his wife aboard the barge. Most of those who now remained were servicemen and their thoughts, as they watched the barge's low silhouette disappear into the darkness may only be guessed at.

What little food was left on the island was shared out and the bits and pieces, clothes, soiled bandages, a knife and anything that seemed remotely useful were collected together.

Not all the survivors from the two ships reached Pom Pom. A large number of the passengers who leapt in the sea were swept away in lifejackets. They survived in wretched conditions in a slick of wreckage and flotsam, some two miles long. Amongst them was a young Chinese nurse who had dropped into the sea to swim ashore but was caught in the strong current and swept away. For a while she clung to a mattress then wreckage but this slipped from her hands and she just drifted, kept afloat by her lifejacket. Her face became sore and blistered in the sun and she lost track of time. She was found by what she described as a warship, but might have been one of the motor launches with servicemen on board.

Less fortunate was a family, a father, mother and their young daughter in lifejackets who clung to each other as they were swept along in the strong current past the many islands. They eventually died, one by one from thirst, sunstroke and exhaustion. The tragedy was repeated continually as children amongst the survivors in the sea were lifted onto life rafts by their mothers who then clung to the ropes alongside. Eventually the parents went into a coma and lost their grip, to float away and drown. Groups were formed by individuals who shared bits of wreckage or met as they drifted along in lifejackets. They clung to one another forming clusters which seemed to have a life of their own as those who died drifted away, leaving room for others to join the group.

One group lasted for two days by which time most were in a semi-coma or suffering from thirst and heat stroke. Then one evening as the sun set a sampan slid across the water and in an apparent dream they were all lifted out and dumped on a hard deck. This became warm soft sand and cool fresh water replaced the brine on their swollen and cracked lips.

Their Malay rescuers carried them to a larger vessel, a small junk with a lean-to shelter of bamboo and attap on the deck to protect them from the sun. On its journey to Senajang the boat was intercepted by a launch manned by a mixed crew of Chinese, Europeans and Malays. This was the rescue boat, *Florence Nightingale*, searching for any survivors on the islands. The sampan's passengers were transferred and the launch headed for Senajang where the Amir began to realise the enormity of the disaster.

About ten people managed to reach a small desert island. They arrived separately over a period of some two days. There was no water on the island and the palm trees lacked fruit. They just sat in the shade near the beach hoping for rescue. One day a seagoing junk was sighted and everyone rushed onto the sand shouting and waving trying to attract the attention of its crew. The Chinese owner sculled across in a small sampan and agreed to take everyone off but the total cost of the passage would be 300 Malay dollars. The few soldiers amongst the survivors were penniless and most of the civilians were destitute after losing everything in the shipwreck. This demand, after the relief and excitement of the apparent rescue, was a blow. While they were still trying to grasp the owner's demands one of the survivors, a Chinese mother with two small children by her side, produced the money from a body belt inside her blouse and paid the ferryman.

Singkep

Commander Alexander reached Singkep on about 19th February and took charge of hundreds of survivors and escapers who had reached the town. When the SS *Trang* sank some twelve miles off Pulau Batam, the survivors in the gently rocking lifeboats stared at flickering fires all around them. Fuel tanks and supply dumps on the islands near Singapore were burning and exploding while on Singapore itself the whole city seemed ablaze with a dull orange glow against the night sky. No one spoke for what seemed hours but was probably only five minutes. Eventually Alexander said, 'Well we can't stay here' and ordered the crew to put up a sail.

The two lifeboats set out for the town of Muntok on Banka Island and although this was a daunting 250 mile journey it was home waters for the RNVR officers on board who were mainly Straits Steamship Company staff. Two islands immediately barred their way, Pulau Batam and Pulau Bintan, and beyond them were hundreds of smaller islands and uncharted reefs.

When daylight came the two boats navigated the Tjombol Strait and kept the islands in the Rhio Archipelago to the east. To the west were miles of open sea and beyond that, Sumatra, thinly populated and full of jungle and mountains. Despite the occasional squalls which sent the waves breaking over their boats the journey was uneventful. Sometimes they drifted through slicks of wreckage made up of deckchairs, bedding and luggage, all mixed in with oil, wood and bloated bodies. As the days went by one of the passengers or crew would identify an island, Petong or Pom Pom or Tjempa, all covered in thick foliage and sometimes a thin streak of smoke drifting above their trees. Four days later they saw on the horizon, a long low island – Singkep in the Lingga Group. Someone who seemed to know where they were steered the boat for Dabo, the main town on the island.

As they crossed the bay, Alexander saw the small town near the water's edge surrounded by jungle and mountains. As they drew near he saw that the large wooden buildings alongside the quay were warehouses. The main street ran off the quay towards a large market square. The two boats, drew alongside a worm-eaten wooden pier and tied up. As they stepped ashore the crews were met by a native Dutch policeman in a green tunic and breeches who led them to the office of the Dutch Controlleour, a type of District Commissioner in the Dutch Colonial Service. After Commander Alexander introduced himself and explained their circumstances the Controlleour, a Dutchman, told him that his town was crammed with Europeans from Singapore, men women, children, civilian and military personnel. Alexander had already noticed the many dishevelled Europeans near the quay and groups just standing around, almost blocking the narrow streets. The Japanese had been shelling and bombing the escape vessels and many survivors had made their way to his town, the Dutchman explained.

Food was a big problem and in the market square the traders did a brisk business. The influx of some 500 people had forced the market prices up and out of reach of the local people which made them restless. Many of the survivors were penniless and so could only barter their jewellery, watches and rings for food. But the soldiers, some armed, had been given food. He told Alexander that many shipwrecked people had been rescued and transferred to boats from Rengat and Djambi but boat owners were becoming increasingly reluctant to do the voyage with the Japanese ships patrolling the waters.

That wasn't the only problem. He estimated that there could be up to 2,000 shipwrecked survivors marooned amongst the islands hoping for rescue. A Dutch captain of a little trader, the *Tanjong Pinang*, had left for Pom Pom island three days ago but as the ship had not returned, he pondered whether the captain had taken the survivors to Sumatra. The *Florence Nightingale*, a Red Cross launch with medical staff on board, had stayed to search the islands and each day fishermen brought in more survivors they had rescued from the sea or found washed up on the beaches. While he spoke the police brought in a group of seamen and marines from the old Yangtse gunboat HMS *Dragonfly*. They had rowed the ship's whaler to the town to get help to rescue soldiers and civilians, including pregnant women, who managed to reach an island after the gunboat was bombed and sunk.

Before he left the Controlleour's office Alexander agreed to remain behind and help the Dutchman evacuate everyone to Sumatra where he knew Warren's men manned an escape route up the Indragiri River. When Alexander learnt that the Dutchman had converted one of the large wooden buildings in the town into billets for the survivors he decided to tour the town to assess the conditions. The servicemen's building boasted a wide verandah running its length. As he approached he saw a number of people lounging around dressed in the bits of native clothing or parts of uniforms. He was watched with curiosity as he walked across the dirt road and up the half dozen steps into the building, replying to the occasional salute as he did so.

At the edge of town beyond the dormitory, he found the 'hospital' which was actually just a dispensary for the large tin mine nearby. The conditions were terrible and one survivor who passed through it later described it as a charnel-house. The small brick building with tin roof was never designed to cope with either the numbers or medical conditions the Chinese dresser faced. There was no doctor and all he had for broken limbs, bullet wounds, burns and dysentery was aspirins. The place stank of wounds, bodies and patients who had fouled themselves. At night in the ward the still air was filled with groans or cries of someone reliving a nightmare; in the morning the dead were taken away leaving space for a new arrival. Volunteers amongst the survivors gave the Chinaman some help and as each day went by they were joined by shipwrecked nurses and civilian doctors. One of these was a tall thin man who Alexander learnt was Dr Cuttwood from St Andrew's Mission Hospital in Singapore.

The doctor had often given lectures at St Andrew's to the nursing staff under training and one point he frequently made was that patients did have feelings. So before acting without thought, the nurses should try to put themselves in the patient's place and ask themselves what would they want? Now without even the most basic medical resources all he could offer the wounded was his skill, sympathy and patience as he operated on them with kitchen knives, without anaesthetics.

At their daily meetings the Controlleour brought Commander Alexander up to date with any news. Although Alexander wasn't too surprised to learn that Singapore had fallen, he was however shocked to learn that Wavell had abandoned Sumatra. This followed the seizure of the Banka Strait by the Japanese Navy and the capture of the Palembang oilfields by enemy airborne troops. The Controlleour reasoned that this had effectively cut the sea route to Java and it would only be a matter of time before Japanese columns raced north, through Sumatra, to close the remaining escape routes which terminated at Padang. During the conversation Alexander discovered that the Controlleour used a two-way radio to keep in touch with Java some 400 miles away. The obvious thing to do was to use the wireless transmitter to get help from military HQ in Java but even before Alexander finished outlining his idea the Dutchman's face became serious. He explained that both the mine workings and his radio set had been destroyed when he learnt that Sumatra was lost.

Commander Alexander was the senior British officer on the island and he gradually drew around him, from amongst the escapers and survivors, a team of mainly naval personnel to deal with the rescue and reception of survivors and their transfer to the mainland. One of these was a Malay-speaking RNVR officer, Sub-Lieutenant Cunningham-Reid, a fair-haired, jaunty character dressed in a khaki shirt, shorts and a naval cap. He knew how to sail native boats and volunteered to carry out on a search of the nearby islands for survivors. Two Engine Room Artificers, probably survivors from the *Prince of Wales* or the *Repulse*, joined him as crew and the Controlleour found them a boat.

The local Amir Silalahi of Senajang also agreed to help and sent a message to all his people in fishing villages on the islands to search for survivors. As a result hundreds of shipwrecked people now began to filter in through Senajang to Dabo. More arrived each day from the islands. Survivors' stories constantly praised the islanders who searched the beaches or lit bonfires to guide rafts ashore. Fishermen launched their boats to rescue people as they were swept past the islands in strong currents and boats full of exhausted and starving women and children were found and taken in tow. The survivors were brought ashore by the Malay fishermen who fed and cared for them until they were strong enough to be ferried to Dabo or Senajang.

With the help of the *Florence Nightingale* and some local fishing boats, Alexander and the Controlleour evacuated approximately 1,500 survivors to the town of Djambi, on the Djambi River or through to Tambilahan on the Indragiri River. The operation seemed to be going reasonably well until the crew of a junk brought news that enemy destroyers were anchored off the mouth of the Indragiri River, blocking access to Warren's escape route. That night the *Florence Nightingale* also disappeared and everyone feared the worst. In fact the destroyers had moved on but the launch had gone aground on a mud-bank off the mouth of one of the tributaries of the Indragiri. The boat was crowded, with stretcher cases, walking wounded and women and children but despite efforts by able-bodied passengers and crew, she remained aground for two nights. When darkness fell everyone tried to protect themselves and the wounded from the hungry mosquitoes which swarmed over the vessel in a whirring cloud from the nearby swamps. Eventually the

Florence Nightingale lifted clear on a morning tide and the launch limped her way up river with a badly damaged propeller shaft.

On about the 20th, Alexander was alerted to the news that a launch and a large junk were disembarking more survivors at the quay. The launch belonged to a Dutch planter who, with the Chinese crew of the junk, had rescued some sixty naval personnel from the island of Dankau and forty more from Pom Pom, many of whom were badly wounded women. A large, fair-haired, naval officer with a beard strode into Alexander's office to announce their arrival and Alexander was delighted to recognise Lieutenant-Commander A.H. Terry. They had worked together in Singapore. Terry who had already survived the sinking of the *Prince of Wales*, now brought the news that his ship, the *Kung Wo*, and two other vessels, had been sunk near Pom Pom. He had with him 60 sailors, all from the *Kung Wo*, and a group of civilians including Government Information Department staff from the Cathay Building.

One was an attractive Chinese girl, Doris Lim, who had already escaped from Japanese in North China and later Shanghai. As a one time British agent in China she was on the Japanese wanted list. Room was found for her and a small number of survivors on a launch which arrived that day from Singapore with escapers on board. This later reached Java, having presumably avoided the Banka Strait. The others were ferried in fishing boats to Djambi where the Dutch provided lorries which took them to Padang.

With the Controlleour's help Alexander hired four large, Chinese crewed, sea-going junks to sail to Pom Pom and bring off as many as possible. While he was doing this Terry refuelled the Dutch planter's launch and returned to Dankau to rescue more of his men. Dankau and Pom Pom were less than 50 miles away and could be reached in one day but it was safer to travel at night to avoid enemy aircraft and shipping. Four boats sailed the following evening with Cunningham-Reid in his tonkan. By morning all the vessels were anchored off Pom Pom. Leaving the junks at anchor Cunningham-Reid coasted around the nearby islands and found Lieutenant Geoffrey Brooke and 60 sailors still marooned on Dankau.

Unable to believe their good fortune the sailors on Dankau watched the boat creep inshore towards the beach. Cunningham-Reid told Brooke that he wasn't stopping as he was trying to locate more marooned survivors on other islands. He had with him, however, four junks which were anchored off Pom Pom. He offered to give Lieutenant Brooke a lift out to one of these vessels so he could then return on that boat to the island for his men. Having accepted the offer, Brooke was taken out to Pom Pom where he boarded a 40-foot, two-masted junk. Armed with a pistol he persuaded the Chinese crew of three to sail across to Dankau to collect his men.

The sailors on the beach watched the boat creep towards the island then stop, as the Chinese were reluctant to bring the boat too close inshore in case she went aground. As it was too deep to wade out, the sailors manhandled the damaged lifeboat across the beach to the water's edge. Despite their previous efforts the boat still leaked like a sieve. Undaunted they launched it, and bailing furiously, they repeatedly made trips to the junk until the beach was empty. Each trip was a race against time between the bailers and the rising water in the boat. Brooke's boat and two from Pom Pom reached Dabo, the fourth diverted to Rengat leaving the island empty apart from the graves.

At Dabo, Brooke reported to Alexander and wrote later (in his book *Alarm Starboard*) that when he arrived he found 'morose Europeans sitting on the verandah or standing around in groups outside'. As he approached the door Alexander came out to meet him. 'Good heavens, Brooke again! We always seem to meet in adverse circumstances; and how did you get here?'

By about the 22nd the number of survivors arriving daily at Dabo was beginning to decline and most had been transferred to Sumatra. The only exceptions were the wounded and some recent arrivals, including those from Pom Pom and Dankau. The wounded concerned Alexander. They not only slowed down the embarkation but also occupied twice as much space on the boats. The able-bodied could travel quicker and could, in the main, look after themselves. After talking the problem out with the medical staff he decided to move the wounded last.

The threat of air attacks and enemy warships had the effect of keeping local trading vessels tied up and hidden from prying enemy eyes. The news that the Japanese had opened a seaplane base some 30 miles away on the island of Chempa was a further disincentive. On about the 25th Alexander called a meeting of his team and told them that he intended to evacuate the island. He had a launch and he had also bribed, with opium, the Chinese owners of three seagoing junks to take everyone to the escape route, up the

Indragiri River, a journey of some 100 miles. The owners of two of the boats agreed to make a second journey with the wounded. The evacuation was to start that evening as soon as darkness fell which was about 7 pm. 'Any questions?'

The journey took two days remembered Geoffrey Brooke in his book *Alarm Starboard*. In that time enemy bombers flew overhead but ignored them and even the small fighter planes which flew by had more important business to perform while below some forty people hid and waited for the attack. They also passed the wrecked hulk of a Yangtse river gunboat, the *Grasshopper*, which had been bombed and sunk in the escape bid from Singapore. Another wreck was a large merchant vessel aground near a reef. This may have been the *Loch Ranza* bombed and sunk early in February when she was back-loading cypher and secret communications equipment to Java.

On the second day they reached the estuary. After avoiding the mud-banks, which had taken toll on the *Florence Nightingale*, the junk slide alongside the 'rickety pier' at Priggi Raja. This village was the first of Major Campbell's river staging posts. Campbell had arranged for the headman to supply food and help to all escapers and survivors. He had also pinned to the wall of a hut instructions on how to reach the next staging post, Tambilahan.

The final evacuation took place on about the 26th when Alexander and the Controlleour arranged for volunteers to carry the wounded to the quayside. A single-seater enemy plane flew overhead each day, in a wide circle to check they were behaving themselves before flying off across the island. To avoid detection the move took place as darkness swept across the sea in its usual quick fashion. Pools of light from the shops on the main street lit up the dirt road and the occasional group of bandaged figures who shuffled past. The parade of stretcher cases and destitute Europeans was watched in silence by the mainly Chinese residents of the town who stood on the pavement and in the entrances of coffee shops as the wounded filed past, shepherded by nurses and medical staff to the quayside.

The volunteers that remained helped the civilians, mainly women and children, to board the native junks. The launch Alexander kept for the more serious medical cases. They were joined by the medical staff, nurses and volunteers who had remained behind and given up the chance of escape to help the injured. The launch set out for Djambi, but somewhere near the mouth of the river she developed engine trouble so it was decided to return to Dabo rather than face the river's swift currents. As she approached Singkep she was intercepted by an enemy destroyer and captured.

Two naval officers, Dickinson and Monroe, had volunteered to remain with Commander Alexander and each was in charge of one of the junks. The casualties who had been brought on board first were crowded into every corner and square foot of the deck. Lying on their backs, they watched the junk's masts rock back and fore across the night sky, one moment pointing to a star then across to the moon which was occasionally hidden by fast moving squall clouds. Standing on the quay with the Dutch Controlleour, Alexander watched the embarkation until Monroe came across, saluted and quietly mentioned that the vessels were ready to leave.

From the deck of both boats, the passengers watched as the two lonely figures on the quayside exchanged last minute comments. Then a brief shake of hands, a salute before Alexander walked quickly across the dark quay and stepped across to the junk's deck. In a shaft of light from a large building nearby three native policemen in their green jackets watched as the ropes were thrown clear and the vessel's sail was winched up; this filled and she moved out into the bay. A cool breeze swept the deck but every roll of the boat as it sailed into the darkness brought moans and whimpers from the injured.

CHAPTER EIGHT

The Escape Route

Pulau Moro 6th–17th February

On Friday, 6th February, the SS *Krian* was anchored off Pulau Moro, a small, jungle-covered island close to the Durian Straits on the main shipping route from Singapore. The *Krian* had left Singapore the previous day, 5th February, with the three men Colonel Warren had selected to run what became the escape route from Singapore. The three were on deck, two with their tommy guns and small packs, waiting for the ship's boat to return from the tree-lined cove.

Only two were going ashore. The third, Major Jock Campbell, was bound for Rengat in Sumatra to run the next part of the route. Captain Ivan Lyon, who was going ashore, leant on the ship's rail smoking his pipe as he studied the island. Although he was not familiar with this one he knew the area well. Before the war he often sailed his 3-ton yacht *Vinette* through these waters to escape the boredom of a peacetime army. On one trip he attempted to sail across the South China Sea to Indo-China but ran into a fierce storm. This badly battered and damaged the boat which stayed afloat long enough for Lyon to get her into the small harbour on the French island of Condore.

Although this was a penal settlement the French Governor made Lyon welcome and gave him every help to repair his boat. With the help of the prisoners and the moral support of the Governor's attractive daughter Gabrielle, the yacht was eventually ready for sea. But not before they had fallen in love with one another. They were married in Saigon on 27th July 1939.

The other person to go ashore was Corporal Morris RAMC, who was personally selected for the mission by Lyon, both for his calm, reliable manner and his medical knowledge. A Welshman from South Wales, Taffy Morris was keen to see action and lost no time in drawing a tommy gun from the armoury for firing range practice. After crating medical supplies and equipment he borrowed a lorry and took the supplies to the docks to be loaded on the *Krian*.

Morris had spent his last night in Singapore at the Union Jack Club, a hotel for other ranks, and joined the *Krian* the following morning. He found her tied up alongside Clifford pier, being hastily loaded by staff from the SOE School. All the dockers had long since disappeared. Despite the many daily air-raids she was mainly undamaged but peppered with shrapnel holes from too many near misses.

These raids also caused many injuries amongst the school's staff who refused to go to hospital and were looked after by Taffy Morris. After the ship sailed on Friday afternoon, 6th February, he spent most of the night patching up the casualties. Later he ferreted around the ship for food until he had enough to make a large pot of stew, sufficient for everyone.

Ashore on Pulau Moro, he and Captain Lyon settled in the small attap hut near the cliff top where all the supplies were stacked around the walls inside the hut. Lyon now decided to advertise their presence and spent most daylight hours amongst the islands in a small 17 foot sailing dinghy, calling on local headmen in nearby fishing villages. He wanted them to know that the island was occupied by the army and any vessels from Singapore should be directed to Pulau Moro.

Back in camp he and Morris shared the camp chores and every evening after supper, they would sit outside their hut with a bottle of whisky and absorb the atmosphere of a warm tropical night. In the distance they could hear the dull boom of artillery duels and watch the flash of explosions reflected against the night sky. They noticed the haze over the island turn black, as a belt of oily smoke from the ruptured fuel tanks stretched out from Singapore, over the island and beyond, to Lingga.

As there was every likelihood that the Japanese would attempt to seize the Durian Straits, Lyon and Morris took turns to stand guard and watch for any attempted infiltration; alone in the darkness while the other slept, every nocturnal sound gave flight to the imagination but the noises were often identified as some wild animal crashing through the jungle or birds and bats weaving their way through the trees above the camp. This tranquil life style lasted only a short 36 hours.

Most of the ships that sailed before the 10th reached Java, but those who risked the voyage by daylight were caught and bombed by early rising Japanese pilots. From their clifftop hideout they often watched the steady stream of ships run the gauntlet along

bomb alley. The larger vessels, which escaped with the *Durban*
convoy, raced through the Durian Strait on the 12th, fighting off
attack after attack from enemy bombers who seemed to be concen-
trating their attentions on the *Kedah* and the *Empire Star*. The smaller
vessels, delayed by that misplaced marker buoy at the mouth of the
swept channel, fled independently during daylight and were left to
fight their individual battles alone. The only firepower many had
was a small deck mounted gun and the support of the passengers'
bren and rifle fire.

Apart from the local steamers fleeing through the wide, cliff-
lined Straits they saw little boats of all shapes and sizes risking the
run down the channel. It was the crews of these small boats and
groups of deserters in stolen boats who were amongst the first to be
directed to Lyon's camp by the local fishermen.

About the same time local Malay fishing boats began to arrive
from the nearby islands with shipwrecked survivors whose boats
had torn their bottoms out on hidden reefs or run ashore on rocky
islands. They were found and rescued by the fishermen who ferried
them to Lyon's camp. But as each day went by fishermen brought
in more and more survivors, many suffering from wounds, sun-
burn, exhaustion and shock. Corporal Morris worked almost
single-handed for 72 hours as he cleaned wounds and probed for
shrapnel. The bombs and bullets had torn large pieces off the little
wooden boats, leaving Morris to carry out minor operations. He
extracted large chunks of jagged wood from open wounds before
carefully picking out the splinters left behind. He tried to comfort
children who had lost their parents in the sinkings and dealt with
patients who screamed with pain and shock. In what time he had
left, he helped bury the dead in a small clearing in the jungle.

Following the surrender of Singapore on the 15th a wave of
escapers reached Lyon's camp. After being supplied with rations
they were directed to the next staging post run by Major Campbell
at Priggi Raja, a fishing village at the mouth of the Indragiri River.
This was about 70 miles away and a two-day sea journey.

Any vessel that called at the island, whether it was a rowing boat
or steamer, Lyon made certain that it left with additional passengers. A large number were evacuated on the HMM/L *Hung Jao*
which was already crowded with survivors and escapers when she
arrived. She was followed by HMS *Malacca* and the launch *Joan*.
They arrived on Tuesday the 17th with news of the surrender.

The *Malacca* was a 211-ton Straits Steamship Company vessel, converted to a RNVR minesweeper, under the command of Lieutenant W.B. Bervis. Some of her passengers had been plucked out of the water and one group, marooned on an uninhabited island, were rescued when they attracted the crew's attention with rifle shots in the air. Amongst those rescued were twenty officers from the *Yin Ping*. Although the *Malacca* was overcrowded, Bervis agreed to evacuate some of the escapers and survivors at Lyon's camp.

The *Joan*, he discovered, was manned by a group of Welsh gunners who escaped on Sunday with the rest of their battery from Kallang. The launch was under the command of a young Argyll officer, Major Kennard. He and their battery commander, Captain Rowley-Conwy, had been at Marlborough together. His friend had remained with the rest of the battery on a beached junk, aground on a sandbank close to St John's Island. Kennard had left as they tried to refloat the heavy vessel with the help of some Malay fishermen from the island. Rowley-Conwy had ordered him to take men with him from the junk and try to reach Sumatra. Although the launch was crowded when Kennard reached Pulau Moro he also agreed to take off boatless escapers from Lyon's camp.

Their arrival coincided with news from shipwrecked survivors that their ships had been sunk by enemy surface vessels not bombers. This was confirmed by the Malay fisherman who rescued the survivors. Apart from people brought in by the fishing boats the number of escapers from Singapore had dropped to a trickle so after discussing the position with Morris, Lyon decided to close the camp down. After making arrangements for the fishermen to take any further survivors to the Indragiri River, Captain Lyon's last task was to write out, for escapers, detailed written instructions on how to reach Priggi Raja. This he pinned to the wall with a map. After a final look around the empty camp site with the lonely jungle graves, he and Morris picked up their weapons and scrambled down the well worn, steep path through the trees, to the beach and boarded the little dinghy. As they poled away the breeze filled the sail and, with a slight correction on the tiller by Lyon, the little boat slipped across the water towards Sumatra.

All went well until they reached the Brothers lighthouse, near the mouth of the Indragiri River. With a breeze behind them and the boat in full sail, the moon broke through the clouds to reveal a large enemy destroyer at anchor across their path. Somehow they managed to steer clear without being seen. Some distance away another was sweeping the shoreline with stabs of light from its searchlights. They passed this one in the darkness, off its seaward side and eventually reached the sanctuary of the river mouth.

Rengat 7th–27th February

The escape route ran from Priggi Raja, up the Indragiri River to Rengat, then across the mountains to Sumatra's west coast port of Padang. The man responsible for this part of the route was Major Jock Campbell. He disembarked at Rengat, from the *Krian*, about 7th February and made his headquarters in a small hotel near the quay. There he discussed his plans for the escape route with the local Dutch Controlleour. The Dutchman agreed to help and liaised with his colleagues at Taluk, Peranap and Sawahlunto, the districts through which military personnel would have to pass on their way to Padang. Stocks of food would be needed, petrol for the vehicles and if necessary the local Controlleours might need to arrange overnight accommodation for small groups of servicemen. The plan was to move well-disciplined bodies of men across to Padang where they would be evacuated by the Royal Navy. In practice the opposite occurred.

Campbell's next job was to set off down stream in a borrowed launch to check out two more suitable staging posts. The first choice was Tambilahan, a small riverside town some 40 miles downstream, used by coastal traffic and fishermen. It boasted of a wooden jetty and godowns along the waterfront which he anticipated could be used to house the troops. The town had been built around a large open market well supplied with fresh fruit and fish. Close to the market was the Assistant Controlleour's office. On the edge of the small town was the dispensary, with one small ward and a dresser. But no doctor.

As Campbell continued his journey downriver, the countryside, compared with Malaya, appeared to be completely untouched by the war but as he later found out, the local inhabitants were generally anti-Dutch. Apart from a curious glance his launch was largely ignored by the river folk as it chugged along. The river was flanked by thick forest inhabited by tribes of monkeys which screamed abuse as they followed his journey downstream, and high above his head colourful birds glided from bank to bank. Eventually, having sailed past gardens of floating flowers, the muddy river banks gave way to mangrove swamps. Near the sea the river became tidal, lost amongst small islands and narrow channels.

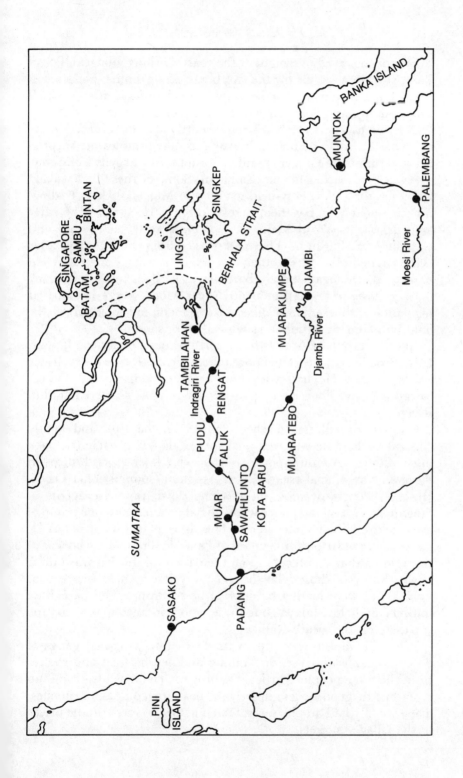

Campbell stayed overnight at the coastal fishing village of Priggi Raja, sited in a bay below the two breast-shaped hills. For a small reward the headman had been persuaded to look after a small supply dump and help anyone trying to reach Rengat.

The first escapers reached Rengat shortly after he returned to the town on the 9th. The first military to use the route came, surprisingly, from north Malaya, mainly Gordons and Argylls from units overwhelmed earlier in the campaign. Some of these had walked 200 miles through enemy-held territory in Malaya, before 'finding' a native boat to carry them across to Sumatra. One of the early arrivals was Sergeant-Major F. Colvin, a keen yachtsman, and Captain M.E. Bardwell. They had trekked from north Malaya after being cut off in the retreat, then escaped by boat to Sumatra. When he arrived at Rengat Captain Bardwell insisted on being flown back to Singapore, in a small unarmed Tiger Moth, where he married his fiancée, a nurse. He rejoined his regiment and took part in the final battle for Singapore and was taken prisoner.

Another group of Argylls from north Malaya included Captain D.K. Broadhurst, a Straits Police officer seconded to the Argylls for liaison duties. He had with him Sergeant Gibson and Lance-Corporal Gray. Their company was over-run and scattered at Slim River.

Captain Broadhurst reached Padang on the 15th and finally Australia where he was recruited into SOE and parachuted back into Malaya. Another police officer who later passed through Rengat as an official escaper, was Assistant Commissioner Davis. He had been responsible for tracking down Japanese agents in Singapore. Not all the police were official escapers and one group of six made off in a police boat. This type of action upset A.H. Dickinson, the Inspector General of Police in Singapore who was of the opinion that his officers should remain until the flag was pulled down. Many of those who did get away later joined the Special Forces and were landed by submarine or dropped by parachute into enemy-held Malaya, but those who remained slaved for the Japanese on the Death Railway.

While Singapore was still in its death throes, armed gangs of deserters came up river, demanding and getting food and shelter from the river people. Parties of European civilians also came up river but in good order, in private boats or company launches. They usually had ample funds, which helped to force up the prices in the village markets.

Throughout Monday the 16th, rumours in Rengat were rife that the British Army had surrendered. All day boatloads of escapers had arrived with what seemed to be wild stories about conditions in Singapore. Most of the new arrivals were official escapers, who were fed by the Dutch who also supplied lorries and buses to pass them along the escape route to Padang.

That evening in a small hotel near the quay, Campbell and a group of British officers in torn and dirty uniforms sat with Dutch friends around a Philco radio, trying to finely tune the set to reduce the crackle. Then came the unmistakable chimes of Big Ben and Churchill's strong dogmatic tones confirming their worst fears. 100,000 British and Colonial troops had surrendered to the Japanese.

As the week went by the Controlleour brought him more news. The first shock was that Wavell had abandoned Sumatra. At a stroke this put Campbell and the escapers some four hundred miles behind enemy lines. The island, the size of California, was given up without a fight following the seizure of the Banka Strait by the Japanese and the capture of the Palembang oilfields. The remaining British aircraft had flown from Palembang to Java, which left more than a thousand British airmen to be evacuated across south Sumatra to the Sunda Strait where they were ferried across to Java.

All the Dutch Civil Service, he told Campbell, had been ordered to remain at their posts to arrange for an orderly hand-over to the Japanese. The Dutch would stay while the British escaped.

The *Sir Hugh Frazer*, with Captain Ernest Gordon aboard, reached Rengat about Wednesday 18th February where Gordon found Campbell and the Dutch Controlleour at the quayside to meet his 75-ton barge. This vessel was often mistaken by some for a landing craft. As she nosed her way around the river bend and steered towards the quay Major Campbell could see she was packed with troops, some in uniform with their weapons while others were shirtless or wore scraps of native clothing. She carried more than 200 escapers to add to the hundreds already in the town.

Ernest Gordon's news of Singapore's last hours added meat to the bones of Churchill's announcement. But he also brought news of the situation down river which he described as a 'bonnie fine mess'. He told Campbell that Tambilahan was crowded with survivors and escapers. Food was running short in the market place and the increased demand from such a large influx of Europeans, simply forced prices up, certainly beyond the means of the almost destitute soldiers. A large number of injured were in the town's tiny hospital and many were lying around on the dispensary floor with only aspirins to ease their pain.

After listening to his story Campbell persuaded him to join his makeshift organisation and go back down river to take over the Tambilahan staging post. He also spiced the request with a suggestion that when it was all over there was a possibility of forming a jungle-based guerrilla unit. Gordon agreed to both suggestions and left armed with a note, signed by Campbell, authorizing him to act on behalf of the British Government. It also stated that 'any assistance given to him in the form of money, arms or equipment will be paid for at a later date. Any bills incurred as a military representative in Sumatra will be honoured'. Before he set off back down river he got Campbell's agreement to pass his passengers, and those on the *Joan*, through to Padang as soon as possible.

One of his passengers was a Londoner, Lieutenant Rigden RNVR. who had been in command of the *Trang*'s third lifeboat. When he heard from Gordon, that volunteers were needed to rescue people from the islands he opted to remain behind and help the search and rescue boats operating out of Rengat.

Another ship which docked that day was HMS *Malacca*. Like the *Sir Hugh Frazer* she too had rescued many survivors and had also embarked others at Pulau Moro and Tambilahan. She arrived with 300 soldiers on board including Indian and Australian escapers, who began to file off the ship and mill around the quay and riverside buildings. In the space of a few hours at least 500 penniless and hungry soldiers arrived, swelling the number of escapers to over 1,000.

Less than an hour later, more arrived on the *Tenggaroh*, including the Australian, Colonel Broadbent. He had with him 55 Australians who had made their own way to Sumatra and found by him along the route. Campbell was pleased to give him another 100 who had been roaming around Rengat making a nuisance of themselves.

One of the earlier parties of Australians that passed through the town had been befriended by a Javanese police inspector who opened his home to them. When he returned from work he found the twelve soldiers gone, his home ransacked and food, bedding and items from his dress uniform stolen. Initially the Dutch had been generous and sympathetic but incidents like this changed their views. An official report after the war refers to many cases of barbaric ingratitude and that the deserters, including Australians, blackened the reputation of their fellow countrymen that followed.

While Campbell coped with all the newly arrived troops the Controlleour faced the problem of what to do with some thousand civilian evacuees from Singapore and the shipwrecked survivors who also packed the town. Some of the early arrivals had been sent on by bus and lorry to Padang but they now arrived in such large numbers that they overwhelmed all the available transport. Most civilians stayed in the crowded Rest House or small hotels but amongst them were Asians, wives and families of Volunteers left behind in Singapore as well as civilian nurses from the General Hospital. Some Europeans found it hard to adjust to sharing the facilities with the Asian evacuees and occasionally quarrels broke out when the European women tried to maintain their social position.

To relieve the pressure in the town it was decided to move all servicemen up river to Ayer Molak, where the Controlleour had requisitioned an abandoned Dutch rubber plantation. This was to be used as an assembly area for escapers. They could remain there while transport was found to move them, and others stranded down river, to Padang. Colonel Broadbent remained with Campbell for a few days to help establish the new staging post.

Soon after this, Brigadier Paris arrived with more Argylls, including Major Angus McDonald from Argyllshire, red-haired 23-year-old Captain Michael Blackwood and Private Hardy, formerly batman to Brigadier I.MacA. Stewart, the Argylls' CO.

In the last hours before the surrender Captain Blackwood, with two of his men, used an anti-tank rifle to destroy the leading tank in the enemy column which had smashed its way through the last road block between it and the waterfront. This caused confusion amongst the following tanks in the enemy column and their supporting infantry, who eventually fell back.

When the officers learnt that General Percival was considering the possibility of surrender they made plans to save as many of their men as possible. They are believed to have finally escaped in Captain Blackwood's yacht, probably the *Cecilia*, seen by the *Hong Fatt* as the latter was on her way to Banka with 53 passengers on board.

The Argylls' party eventually reached Rengat where they found others including Sergeant Willie McDonald, a carrier platoon sergeant, and Gray. Sergeant McDonald had been hit in the neck in the last battle for Singapore and was in hospital when news of the surrender became known. Still heavily bandaged, he found his uniform and discharged himself. On the waterfront he persuaded a group of escapers to take him with them and he too eventually reached Rengat. He was later to die with Paris and other Argylls on the ill-fated *Roosenboom*.

Another launch to arrive on Wednesday the 18th and tie up alongside the quay was a 70-foot-long, diesel-driven, rather ancient launch, *Ko Fuku Maru*. This was Bill Reynolds's 90-ton old Japanese supply boat. It was used prewar to supply their fishing boats which operated off Malaya. As it pulled alongside the quay Campbell saw its deck crowded with a motley collection of soldiers and women interspersed with Chinese, some of whom helped to crew the boat.

Leaning out of the aft steering cabin was Bill Reynolds, a tall 60-year-old Australian, with large horn-rimmed glasses. A veteran of World War One, Reynolds didn't suffer fools gladly and he usually classed the military in this catergory. Since leaving Singapore he had already had one brush with a RN party when their whaler bumped his vessel at Priggi Raja. Without repeating himself once he gave the crew a dressing down in colourful Australian abuse.

Long after the surrender Reynolds remained behind in Singapore harbour collecting escapers and those marooned on nearby islands. Amongst these were twenty Chinese, some of whom had served in the ARP or acted as flash spotters for British artillery units. While he was collecting survivors off the islands he found a disabled Dutch vessel with 250 women and children aboard. With the help of the Chinese crew members he got a line on board and towed her to the Indragiri River.

All he wanted from the Dutch was sufficient food and fuel to go back down river to rescue more survivors marooned on the islands. He found them only too pleased to help and that evening the refuelled launch chugged back down river crewed by his Chinese which included a girl.

The news that three ships had been sunk off Pom Pom with heavy loss of life, leaving hundreds stranded on desert islands, reached Major Campbell about Friday 20th February. He persuaded the volunteers running search and rescue launches to risk the hundred mile trip through enemy-held sea lanes to rescue the survivors. The first to leave was Bill Reynolds in the *Ko Fuku Maru*, closely followed by the *Hung Jao*, which had only just arrived from Dabo. Unfortunately her engines broke down on the return trip up river. After her 100 survivors had been landed and Tambilahan, she was scuttled.

Two more vessels took her place. One was the 66-ton coastal launch *Numbing* under the command of Captain Rowley-Conwy. He and his battery escaped in a commandeered junk which ran aground near St John's Lighthouse. After many attempts to refloat her he arranged for Captain Kennard to take some of his battery on board the *Joan*. Others were ferried across to Sumatra by local fishermen and he finally left to get help to rescue the remainder of his men. At Rengat the Dutch gave him a launch which he took back to the islands to rescue the men he had left behind.

The other vessel was the *Plover*, a 30-foot-long, log-burning steam launch. Over the next eight days both vessels rescued 600 survivors from Pom Pom.

Many of the survivors who were either injured or in a bad physical condition were transferred to hospital. The others were found accommodation in the town except for the soldiers who were transhipped to the camp at Ayer Molak rubber plantation. While Campbell and the Controlleour were dealing with this latest influx of survivors a message reached them to expect a large vessel to arrive crowded with escapers. On Wednesday morning the 25th, six Australians walked into town after following the river path for about six miles. They reported that a large junk was stranded on a mudbank down river. From them Campbell learnt that on her journey from Singapore she collected escapers from Lyon's old camp at Pulau Moro, others were rescued from islands and 120 more joined at Tambilahan.

The *Plover*, which was sent down river to tow her in, found her well aground. Aided by a fast flowing current and a tow on her stern she was pulled off and brought up river. This vessel, Campbell discovered, was under the command of a young Artillery officer, Captain Norman Crawley. Like Rowley-Conwy, Crawley was determined to get his men away and when the rumours of surrender were confirmed he too commandeered a junk, out in Singapore Roads, and with his men sailed her to Sumatra. On one island they found seventy Australians whom they took along with them. At Lyon's camp they found more escapers, food and the map to the river.

The next stage took about three days. When they sighted the

mainland they followed it south until they identified the breast-shaped hills. One of the channels brought them to Priggi Raja where Crawley found Campbell's instructions and map pinned to the wall of a hut.

One of the passengers on board was Lieutenant Geoffrey Brooke who had joined her at Tambilahan. He remembers they were met by a bustling, bullet-headed officer with blue eyes and a sandy moustache. This was Jock Campbell. Because of all the trouble he had with previous escapers he made sure this batch didn't stay too long in town. As quickly as possible they were fed then separated into groups for the journey up stream on the wooden barges to Ayer Molak camp.

Their departure wasn't the end of his trouble with that party. On the following day one of the Australians, who had swum ashore and reported the vessel stranded, was admitted to hospital with gunshot wounds. About the same time Captain Crawley reported to Campbell that two sacks of rice had been stolen overnight from the junk. Linking the two events Campbell discovered that the Australians had stolen the rice and sold it to a local shopkeeper for the price of a taxi fare to Padang. After falling out amongst themselves their wounded friend was left at the hospital while they fled to Padang in the taxi.

The Dutch Controlleour was concerned about the Japanese and was anxious that the camps down river were cleared up before they arrived. So with Campbell's help Priggi Raja and Tambilahan were evacuated.

Captain Ernest Gordon had taken charge of the British troops when he returned to Tambilahan with food and medical supplies on the 20th. In just three days he found the conditions there had been rapidly deteriorated. Each day native boats brought more groups of shipwrecked people to join some 500 survivors and escapers already in the town. Having reached that point everyone was impatient to move on, particularly the escapers, who were determined not to be trapped in some unknown river town by the Japanese. It was every man for himself.

The Assistant Controlleour had requistioned an empty godown for the servicemen which provided shelter and a place to sleep on the hard but dry earth floor. The sheds stank of old rubber, fish and rotten fruit, their walls impregnated with a thousand smells of long forgotten stored cargoes. During the day the soldiers wandered aimlessly around the small town and just squatted along the river bank and watched for any boat heading up river.

Since his last visit Gordon found that doctors and nurses amongst the survivors had remained in the town to help the casualties. Not all the medical officers stayed behind to deal with the wounded but one who did was Lt-Colonel Hennessey, later Brigadier DGMS, FELF. He drew around him a small team which included a Major Kilgour and a Lieutenant E. Snood from the Queen Alexandra Hospital, Singapore (QMG Australian Division). Although they could provide the skills they lacked medical supplies and carried out operations without drugs or medicine. The overcrowded casualty-filled room, full of dead and dying became a charnel-house.

Into this mess walked a character who was to become a legend in his own lifetime, another Australian and a surgeon, Lt-Colonel Coates, from the 2/10 Australian General Hospital. He and other medical staff had been given a place on one of the escape launches which had been bombed and disabled. But before the boat sank they were found and rescued by fellow Australian Colonel Broadbent's launch. Having lost everything in the shipwreck, all Coates had was what he stood up in, his shirt and shorts, and was shoeless.

In less than two days Coates had carried out 15 operations, occasionally using an axe for some amputations. He and other volunteers worked non-stop for thirty-six hours dealing with the increasing flow of patients. By doing so they forfeited their own chance to escape.

Many of the servicemen who remained behind to assist the doctors and nurse the wounded had no nursing or medical training. They had been so sickened by the terrible conditions they found in the overcrowded ward that they remained to help. This lack of skilled help was overcome on Thursday the 20th, when they were joined by the matron and nurses from the 12 Australian General Hospital (AGH), rescued from the islands.

About this time another survivor, a young naval officer, volunteered to remain behind and take over the administration of the ward. Apart from scrounging food, since some of the medical staff had not eaten for five days, he also recorded patients' details and acquired adjoining premises to take the overflow of patients. The food problem was gradually overcome with the help of the resident Assistant Controlleour and the generosity of the local people.

The evacuees from Dabo began to reach Tambilahan about Tuesday 23rd February. Amongst the last to arrive was Geoffrey Brooke who wrote later that as they cruised up river, under tow from a steam launch, the thick jungle ran down to the river banks where wild pig could be occasionally seen. Along the water large water birds flapped ponderously off at the sight of the two boats.

They docked alongside a small landing stage where he was greeted by a well built Scot, Ernest Gordon. In Captain Gordon's opinion the Dutch were splendid, providing meals, and somewhere for the men to sleep. Shortly after daybreak Captain Gordon was at the riverside to watch a large junk creep in and moor alongside the landing stage. Its deck was crowded with soldiers from all regiments, Indian, Australian, the Norfolks, Gunners, Sappers and LDV. While Gordon watched the deck he picked out a young Artillery officer who seemed to be in charge with a bren gun cradled in his arm. When the officer came ashore he identified himself as Captain Crawley. He had seen Major Campbell's map and hoped to go upstream to Rengat.

Two days later Campbell sent a succession of boats down river to collect the escapers from Tambilahan. Captain Gordon left on the last launch with the stretcher cases. The Assistant Controlleour must have been relieved to see the British go, but his relief was short-lived when junks from Dabo arrived packed with wounded hardly fit to be moved. Each boat brought people in a worse condition than the one before. They were looked after by nurses from amongst the survivors, Mrs Stringer, wife of the director of Singapore's medical services and a lady doctor, Dr Thompson. She was badly injured in the leg and hopped around the ward from patient to patient.

Recalling that journey the badly injured Chinese nurse Janet Lim recalled that the boat's deck was so crowded that it was impossible to sleep. Children cried, patients screamed from either nightmares or from each jolt as the waves struck the vessel. When they reached the town the stretcher cases were taken to the hospital where they were examined by Dr Cuttwood. Gradually as other boats arrived the little room filled with casualties until Campbell sent the launches to embark them.

At Rengat Major Campbell had the Dutch Red Cross with vehicles waiting at the quayside to rush the wounded off to hospital. The medical staff who went with them found the fully equipped hospital manned by locally trained nurses and a German doctor. This doctor was technically an interned alien but the Dutch allowed him parole to carry out his duties. Although some people found him less than friendly his staff more than made up for his aloofness.

On the last boat from Tambilahan was Commander Alexander who went to the hospital to make sure his party were well cared for before he looked after himself.

*

The camp at Ayer Molak was probably set up about 20th February when Campbell transferred military personnel, in groups, up-river in open barges towed by a steam launch. A senior officer in one such group was Lieutenant-Colonel F.J. Dillon an old Indian Army officer. Known as Andy Dillon to many or as simply Dillo to his friends, he was a veteran of the North-West Frontier where he won his Military Cross. He had left his wife behind in India when he was ordered to join 18th Division which stopped at India on its way to Singapore and became the East Anglian Division's AA and QMG.

When his escape party reached Rengat, the highest navigable point of the river for sea going vessels, Campbell arranged for them to be fed before forming them up into groups to be marched down to the river where they boarded the barges. Dillon found himself amongst a large group of officers and men on one of the open barges. With its heavy tow the wood-burning steam launch barely made five miles an hour against the strong current and periodically made stops along the river bank to take on more wood.

The barge had some 150 soldiers on board, some mere boys of hardly nineteen who had probably never left their home towns before being conscripted into the Army. There were the older, regular soldiers who appeared to be self-sufficient and respectfully confident. Mixed in amongst them were the part-time soldiers, the Malay-speaking Local Defence Volunteers drawn from the civilian community in Malaya. With less than four months service behind them, they were more independent and still civilians at heart.

Most of the men on the barge were asleep, lying out on the deck or hunched against the side of the barge with their heads on the knees. The bow area had been taken over by an armed gang. The gang appeared sullen and threatening but made no overt moves. They kept to themselves, chatting and occasionally standing up to watch the tree-lined river banks drift slowly by.

Towards evening the thick forest thinned out and was replaced by long lines of rubber trees. Then in the gathering dusk the barge drew near the river bank and bumped alongside a wooden quay made of rough hewn logs. Close by were sheds for the rubber stocks. The camp already held a large number of escapers who were housed in the empty coolie lines or in the warehouses where the rubber had been stored. His contingent had been expected and the cooks had large containers of rice cooking, to be washed down with either tea or coffee.

Soon after Dillon arrived Brigadier Paris moved off with his Argylls and others, in two lorries provided by the Dutch. As senior British officer Dillon was now in charge of the makeshift camp housing some 500 escapers. Many grumbled that they had been deliberately kept there because the Dutch were under orders to remain themselves. Two lorries were found hidden in the trees but these lacked petrol and Dillon couldn't get any from the Dutch. It was only his strong personality that kept everyone under control.

One problem was the attitude of the Dutch authorities. When Dillon's repeated requests for transport seemed to be ignored by the Dutch authorities, the servicemen cooped up in the camp grew resentful and accused the Dutch of holding back the vehicles for their escape. There were also plenty of rumours which added to the discontent. One which caused the men to get most restless was that the Japanese had cut the road between them and Padang, which was untrue. But another, which was correct, was that the Dutch military were withdrawing all their forces to Fort de Kock, some 60 miles north of Padang. This would have the· effect of leaving the camp in a no-man's land.

In spite of all the problems, Colonel Dillon had the reputation of running the most disciplined and best organised camp on the river. To help him in this he had a Major Nicholson, who dealt with reception and administration, and Lieutenant Geoffrey Brooke, who, with a small band of helpers, looked after the feeding arrangements.

Dillon's plan for the evacuation of the camp when the Dutch transport arrived was based simply on the first in first out principle. But many were not prepared to wait that long and as individuals or in groups many slipped away in the night.

One of these was led by Captain Rowley-Conwy, who had stayed behind to help Campbell. When the search and rescue operation closed down he moved on up-river to Ayer Molak where he was told by Colonel Dillon that he would have to 'wait his turn'. This didn't suit his plans so he decided to leave and took with him a party of like-minded sailors.

They left that night, about 27th February, along the dirt track through the rubber estate. It was one of those black eerie nights with a slight breeze which rustled through the tree tops while the fast-moving clouds sometimes blocked out the light of the moon leaving them in complete darkness. Keeping bunched together they eventually found themselves at the entrance to the estate, on a metalled road. They marched on through the night at a steady pace and soon left the plantation behind. Along the roadside, in the thick forest, fireflies danced amongst the trees and they could hear the rustle of unseen animals in the undergrowth which seemed to keep them company. Shortly after daybreak their luck changed and they hitched a lift on a passing lorry, driven by a Chinese, which took them some 50 miles, half way to Sawahlunto.

In the camp next day Petty Officer Pickford reported to Lieutenant Brooke that about half the men were planning to abscond that night, en masse. This would not only cause trouble for the Dutch but such a large party, about 300 men, some armed, moving across the countryside without transport and living off the land could spark off the uprising and massacre the Dutch dreaded.

Colonel Dillon paraded the men as soon as he was told. He knew that he faced a serious situation as a large number of men refused to answer to discipline. They were armed and some were hostile. Nevertheless his impassioned speech calling for patience and the need to stick together and trust the Dutch worked.

This narrowly averted emergency must have had its impact on the Dutch who arrived next day and evacuated 100 men in four lorries. In spite of Dillon's initial plan to evacuate the men on a first come first out basis the growing indiscipline amongst the troops caused him to ask the RN personnel to remain to help run down the camp. The sailors were the most disciplined group and, as they still answered to their officers, they could not be relied upon if there was any trouble. The request wasn't well received and only after long talks from their officers did they grudginly agree to remain.

The hope that the evacuation had started was ill-founded and lorries failed to arrive the next day. Meanwhile Colonel Dillon kept up his pressure on the Dutch and eventually persuaded them to move a large number of sailors up river in *Faith, Hope* and *Charity*, the nicknames for the two wooden barges and the old steam-driven, wood-fired launch.

By the time the boats arrived from Rengat, heavy rains in the mountains turned the river into a fast flowing torrent and the little steam launch, battled against the current, to travel at about one knot. 'If you looked hard enough you could see the river bank moving past,' one escaper later commented.

Shortly after the naval river party left, the Dutch unexpectedly provided several buses and evacuated the remaining servicemen. Dillon soon closed down the empty camp and moved out with his helpers in two lorries.

While the camp was being emptied another group of sailors were making their way to Ayer Molak. The group was made up of survivors from the *Jarak, Scorpion, Dragonfly* and *Grasshopper* who were amongst the last to leave Dabo. At Rengat they found that Campbell had left and all the boats were upriver. The only alternative the Dutch offered was for them to follow the river path to Ayer Molak.

They left town the following morning and soon found themselves leaving the well-ordered plantations behind. The trek took them through the gloomy rain forest with thick foliage above their heads which allowed shafts of light to break through occasionally to lighten the forest gloom. In temperatures of 100 degrees Fahrenheit they trudged through the trees, clambered over fallen trunks and up and down banks – with the river often out of sight but audible. Flies and mosquitoes continually circled their sweating bodies and leeches dropped from branches as they brushed by.

Some four days later the forest path became a track which led past the empty coolie lines and plantation buildings to a large bungalow. It too was empty. A room had the appearance of being an office, in another room was a bed. Near the warehouse a large empty cauldron lay on its side blackened by countless fires. Their search for food produced nothing but a jar of Marmite and a little rice, which they collected in the small porcelain cups used by the rubber tappers to collect the latex from the rubber trees.

The Dutch had evacuated the camp on about St David's Day, 1st March. The buses took about 300 escapers to Basrha, a small town on the river, where the naval party coming upriver unexpectedly joined them. The Dutch then moved more than 600 British servicemen, in lorries and buses, 150 miles over rough terrain and dirt tracks until they reached Taluk where the military contingent met parties of civilian refugees and survivors. Both the military and civilians were now held up in the town because of the floods caused by torrential monsoon rains. The peaceful rivers had become raging torrents which blocked roads and swept away bridges.

The Dutch supplied the organisers with food, and accommodation was found for them in schools and empty sheds. Individual groups of servicemen making their own way along the route tried to beg food from the military field kitchens but Major Nicholson and his organisers refused to allow this unless they were prepared to join the official party and accept its discipline. Not everyone would do this and they travelled ahead of the official party hungry and resentful.

A lorry full of civilians arrived in town and were billeted in an empty house by the Dutch. Apart from that, unlike the servicemen, they had to fend for themselves and although some had Malayan dollars to spend on food in the market, others were left to barter away their jewellery and watches.

The flood waters began to recede on 7th March and the party was on the move again by the 8th. Major Nicholson, who was in charge of the movement of personnel, was told by the local Dutch military commander that his men were withdrawing to Fort de Kock and were back loading stores and ammunition. As they needed more lorries they were taking the two being used by the Royal Navy contingent. This was a blow made more difficult by having to tell the sailors, who had remained to help Dillon, that they were going to be stuck in this mountain town until more transport could be found for them.

The two lorries were parked near a growing pile of packing cases outside a large house which the Dutch Army had used as an ammunition store. Major Nicholson, Lieutenant Brooke, the Controlleour and the Dutch Commander stood nearby watching the Dutch soldiers loading the cases into their own trucks. Close by were a group of British sailors and local people – all watched silently. Eventually Brooke and Nicholson commented to the Controlleour that all the few remaining cases could, with a pinch, be squeezed onto the Dutch army lorries. The Controlleour got the Dutch Commander's nod and within minutes all the sailors were aboard the lorries and away down the road before anyone changed their minds.

The Controlleour and the Dutch Commander watched the lorries disappear around a bend in the road and out of sight. The officer gave a silent shrug and ordered his NCO to build a road

block outside the town. The Controlleour walked back to his office
to face his next set of problems and found a message waiting for
him. It said briefly that a small convoy full of casualties had left
Rengat by road for Taluk. The convoy was under the command of
a British naval officer, Commander Alexander.

Meanwhile the convoy of ancient buses and old lorries that had
just left Taluk, drove at breakneck speed along reasonably good
roads. These gradually dropped down to cross the flooded plains,
then climbed again, in a series of hairpin bends. All around were
towering peaks and cliffs, while hundreds of feet below the road, the
river torrents raged through tree-covered valleys. By nightfall most
vehicles had arrived at Sawahlunto, the main town in the heart of
the tobacco-growing region, and driven through its narrow streets
to the railway station. Along the main street the open-fronted shops
and pavements cafés were well lit and customers watched impas-
sively as the crowded lorries drove by.

The convoy drew up near the railway sidings and as the motley
dressed escapers emptied out of the vehicles they were met by
uniformed boy scouts who were to act as their guides. The Dutch
had mobilized the local community organisations and the chatty
scouts, eager to practise their school English took them along to a
large empty tobacco warehouse. Here they lined up and were
provided with blankets and ground-sheets. In the corner of the
building they found a buffet with plates of sandwiches and tea,
handed out by well dressed, pretty Dutch women. The Dutch had
also converted the shed at the rear of the building into a shower
room.

After checking out the possible accommodation those officers
who still had funds booked into the two small and overcrowded
hotels or found a room in the Rest House.

Some two hundred miles away, Commander Alexander's party
from Dabo left Rengat for Taluk. When they arrived earlier at
Rengat's hospital they were examined by the German doctor
accompanied by an Indian assistant taking notes. They moved
from bed to bed before going out along the verandah where the
stretchers were laid, side by side. The injured were separated into
two groups. Those considered too serious to be moved would
remain at the hospital. The others were loaded into the waiting
vehicles for the journey to Peranap. This was the group the
Controlleour at Taluk was told to expect.

*

When Colonel Coates arrived in Sawahlunto he found the hospital already crowded with about 130 patients, some of whom he had dealt with at Tambilahan. With them was an army officer, Major Jock Davis, a dermatologist, who forfeited his chance to escape to stay behind to act as liaison officer with the Dutch.

The flow of human wreckage which had passed along the escape route had finished up here and had overwhelmed the town's medical resources. The only answer, it seemed to Coates, was to move them out, and on to Padang by rail. Davis explained that the military in Padang would only allow the able-bodied escapers to use the Padang train. The logic seemed to be that should a vessel arrive to evacuate the escapers it wouldn't have room nor facilities to cope with the wounded. Secondly if the Dutch decided to resist the Japanese columns moving down from Medan in the north, the patients would be safer in Sawahlunto.

In a telephone call from Padang, the Deputy Director of Medical Services, Brigadier Sievers, 3 Corps and an official escaper, pointed out that the policy was basically to evacuate all able-bodied servicemen from Padang first. If there was room later then the wounded could be taken off – if not they were to remain behind and surrendered to the Japanese.

This news didn't meet with Coates's approval. Later, after checking on the patients, he discussed with Davis ways of getting them to Padang. The situation was resolved next day 1st March, when Sievers telephoned to say that three British naval ships had docked and between them were taking off escapers, including the walking wounded in Padang. He was leaving with them. Good luck and goodbye.

Putting the phone down Coates sat back in the chair in the hospital doctor's office. The hospital was on a small hill on the edge of town overlooking the valley. The rain had stopped and through the open shuttered window he could see the mist hanging over the tree-tops. The train's whistle shrieked its departure, taking another trainload of escapers to Padang. With Sievers gone, he Coates, was the senior medical officer. Any policy would be his policy and that policy was to move some fifty stretcher cases from Sawahlunto to Padang on the 11 am train the following day.

CHAPTER NINE

Padang

'Padang was a pleasant little town of about 60.000 inhabitants on the west coast of Sumatra,' remembered Warren. It was well laid out, for the most part, in Dutch colonial style with wide, tree-lined, main streets. The bungalows had wide verandahs, which overlooked well kept lawns and gardens, where the families sat during the evenings. The local people lived mainly in the crowded old town with its narrow streets and back to back houses.

About two miles away was the town's port of Emma Haven, with its warehouses packed with tobacco, rice and tin. Beyond the docks were long sandy, palm fringed, beaches which ran along the coast. This sparsely populated coastline was the resting place for huge waves which rolled unimpeded from the Antarctic Ocean.

Boris Hembry's SOE party arrived in the town on about 21st February. In contrast to the misery of the Indragiri River route, escapers who came through Djambi, as Hembry did, arrived in good order. He recalled that the SOE party arrived at Djambi about a week after leaving Singapore on Wednesday the 11th. They had spent the week amongst the islands laying supply dumps to aid troops trying to escape Singapore.

On about Tuesday the 17th they reached the mouth of the Djambi River and cruised inland along its course. Its muddy banks were fringed with mangrove swamps and later thick forest. On the mudflats basking crocodiles, disturbed by the chugging launch slid into the river with hardly a ripple. The town of Djambi was the furthest navigable point on the river and beyond the town one needed a shallow river craft to go any further.

They were met at the quay by the Dutch Controlleour who broke the news to Basil Goodfellow that Singapore had surrendered. While Goodfellow discussed their position with the Dutchman, Hembry and Sergeant Lamb unloaded the launch. Hardly had they finished than the air-raid siren moaned and an enemy bomber circled the town, the first they had seen since leaving

Warren's Men: From left to right: Captains Richard Broome and John Davis, who set up Warren's Sumatra guerrilla base. On the right Major 'Jock' Campbell and Captain Ivan Lyon. Between them they ran the escape route across Sumatra to Padang.

Head of SOE in Singapore, Basil Goodfellow with a Naval Officer, possibly Lt. Brian Passmore RNVR.

(Left) Lieutenant B.L. Jenkins, RNVR

(Below) Sergeant Walter Hughes, RAF. One of the ship-wrecked survivors on Pom Pom Island.

Singapore. Crammed into a narrow shallow trench they watched the plane's leisurely flight around the town before it began its bombing run over the riverside buildings. As they ducked down into the trench the earth shuddered with explosions as the bombs burst along the quay and amongst the warehouses. When the plane flew off Hembry scrambled out of the trench in time to see the launch, which had received a direct hit, break in half and sink. Boris Hembry had hoped to leave with Sergeant Lamb, in the launch, and to make contact with Colonel Warren further north but that was now impossible.

They gathered from the Controlleour that in the last 48 hours about 100 escapers and survivors had passed through the town on their way to Sawahlunto, a mountain town and the rail head for Padang. Apart from themselves a further twenty had arrived that day, including a few women. The Dutchman suggested that if someone could drive he would supply a lorry for the journey to Padang. Basil Goodfellow thought this was a good idea and nominated Boris Hembry as the driver. As Goodfellow was keen to travel fast and light he went off to search the town for a hire car for two RNVR officers, Morgan and himself. Although he had ample SOE funds he soon discovered that cars could be neither bought nor hired which left him no option but to join Hembry's group.

It was late afternoon by the time they drove out of town and dark when the lorry began its climb along narrow dirt roads through the Barisan mountains. The road twisted and climbed and occasionally on the bends its passengers has a moonlit view of the tree-covered valleys, hundreds of feet below. Hembry remembers stopping sometime during the night, at the side of the road, to allow everyone to stretch their legs and deal with the call of nature. As they wandered away they were warned not to roam too far and keep the headlights in view.

The following morning they reached Sawahlunto where the SOE party booked into the Rest House. They found the place crowded with evacuees from Singapore and Dutch families trying to reach Padang before the Japanese arrived and closed the harbour to shipping. All the SOE party could have, remembered Boris Hembry, was one bedroom for all six to share. As Hembry still had the airbed he slept on the floor leaving the others to squabble over the double bed and armchairs.

The party left early next morning with Hembry still behind the driving wheel. This time the journey was mainly a descent towards the coast. On the hillside above the road, rushing streams cascaded into long white waterfalls until eventually the forest became orderly lines of banana groves and palm oil plantations separated by stretches of terraced paddyfields. Then the twisting road began to straighten out as it met the railway track and followed it into Padang.

They found the British Consul's office near the seafront with a large Union Jack hanging limply from a pole above the door. Leaving the civilians in his care, Goodfellow, Morgan and the two RNVR officers went off to find a room in the Orangji Hotel near the seafront, leaving Hembry to mess at the Enderaach Club which the Dutch had turned into the British Officers' quarters. The other ranks were initially billeted in one of the town's two native schools but later the second school was also brought into use and used mainly by the Australians.

Another party on the road to Sawahlunto were survivors from Pom Pom. Amongst these were LAC Walter Hughes, from the RAF 250 AMES radar detachment. He had been on the *Tien Kwang* and was amongst the last to leave Pom Pom. He remembered that, 'At Djambi we were transferred to lorries and driven over the mountains to Sawahlunto. The following day we entrained onto a mountain railway. There was an old steam train on a chain and ratchet system with special gears to engage sprockets along the railway track. This helped to pull it up the steep hills. It crossed over some deep ravines on narrow, wooden arch bridges. These were constructed in a lattice work of tree trunks and looked very insecure but it got us to Padang.'

When his party arrived they were taken to a large single-storeyed school with playing fields nearby. Close by was the harbour. 'There was no sleeping accommodation,' Walter Hughes recalled, 'and the Dutch fed us mainly on cabbage and plenty of cold tea. There was never enough to eat. There was little organisation and no one asked us who we were or any other details.'

Boris Hembry remembered that Padang seemed full of evacuees from Singapore waiting for a passage to India or Australia. There seemed to be the same false sense of security he encountered in Malaya as both civilians and officers often let ships leave empty while they waited for a destination more acceptable.

Towards the end of February Colonel Broadbent and a substantial group of Australians arrived in town. These were quickly found passage to Tjilatjap on Java's east coast. There they transhipped to a fast cargo vessel, the *Van Dam*, which reached Fremantle on 6th March.

The Royal Navy diverted a destroyer to Padang but not everyone seemed interested in leaving on her. Boris Hembry remembers a notice appearing on the board in the Club announcing that 'a British naval vessel would be arriving, ETA 6 pm and leave later for a destination unknown. Anyone wishing to avail themselves of this passage out should report to the embarkation officer.'

Hembry and Sergeant Lamb chose to leave and joined about 100 others waiting outside for transport to the docks. The naval vessel was HMS *Encounter* and the sight of her tied up at the quay raised a cheer from the sailors in the party when the lorries drew alongside.

Shortly after 6 pm as darkness fell, the destroyer raced across the bar, through the minefield and past the islands. Hembry and Lamb found themselves a space on the crowded deck next to a young sailor from the *Repulse*. Soon it began to rain and the wind cut across the open deck. In the darkness they could see the white-topped waves covering the sea and the ship began to roll and pitch which sent the sea crashing over the bows.

Colonel Warren and three of his men, Broome, Passmore and Lind, arrived in Padang on 27th February. When Warren arrived at Bagan Siapiapi to set up the base for his operations against the Malayan peninsula, he was dismayed to learn that Singapore had already fallen. He needed to reassess his plans.

He had already put 30 armed Chinese guerrillas into Johore and a second party, Vanrenan and Graham, the explanters, were ashore further north trying to make contact with Spencer Chapman or any other stay-behind party. While he was waiting for their return he signalled his arrival to GHQ Java. A reply came from an Intelligence Officer, Colonel Field, requesting him to travel across to the west coast and assess the problem in Padang.

He knew Colonel Field from Singapore where Field had an office in Cathay Building and had been responsible for the operation of the strict news censorship. This led to the majority of the population in Singapore being unaware of the rapid Japanese advance down the peninsula. Possibly many civilians would have made more effort to leave if they had realised the extent of the crisis. Before Field left for Java in January he stopped an American CBS journalist, Cecil Brown, from broadcasting news programmes to America in case the news censorship in Singapore was broken by his broadcast being relayed from America.

When Warren set out for Padang he considered the trip nothing more than a reconnaissance for GHQ Java. In his opinion it could only now be a matter of a few weeks, if not days, before the Japanese occupied the island, so the took the opportunity to look for suitable bases for any covert operations. In particular there was an urgent need to open a base on the west coast to bring supplies in from India. One of the fishing villages he and his team examined on the west coast, was the little group of fisherman's houses straddling the tree-lined beach at Sasak where he noticed two large native craft at anchor near the beach. Later they drove back across the hills to the main road near Fort de Kock, Dutch Military Head-quarters, then drove south along the good metalled coastal road to Padang.

Reflecting on his arrival, Warren recalled that he found the town almost deserted apart from the local residents going about their normal activities. When he made enquiries regarding the senior British officer in the town he was told it was Brigadier Paris, commander of 11 Indian Division. He had taken over the town when Colonel Broadbent and his Australians left for Java but he too was leaving and was on board a small Dutch steamer in the harbour, SS *Roosenboom*. She was about to leave for Colombo with Paris and 600 troops and civilians on board.

Two other senior officers who also arrived that day were the Australian General Bennett and the Dutch Admiral Helfrich. The latter had commanded the Allied fleet in the Java Sea battles and had flown in from Bandung GHQ. He left the same evening for Colombo.

Although the town was only bombed once, the harbour pre-sented a grim sight, Warren remembered. Half destroyed build-ings, stained black from the fires while in the dock, masts from sunken ships stuck-out of the water. They parked the car close to a fire damaged building and climbed the ship's gangway to meet Brigadier Paris.

He noticed that the Argylls had taken up firing points all over the ship, determined to fight off any air attacks with bren guns and rifles. Every bit of deck seemed to be crammed with nurses, servicemen and civilians. One of the passengers was Doris Lim, a survivor from the *Kung Wo*. After she reached Dabo she was found passage on a second boat which was probably a naval motor launch. This took her on to Batavia. From there she was then evacuated on the *Roosenboom* for Ceylon.

Even as Warren and Paris talked a lorry drew up on the dockside below packed with nurses, wives, children, soldiers and business-men – all in rags and dishevelled. They clustered in small groups on the quayside until an officious officer bustled them up the gangway. Amongst the group were Mr and Mrs Nunn. He seemed to be the leader of the civilian party.

Warren learnt that they had been rescued from Pom Pom island, some five days earlier and taken to Sawahlunto via Djambi. From there they travelled by train to Padang where the Dutch provided a lorry to take them to the docks to catch this ship before it sailed.

Colonel Warren, who was generally unaware of the catastrophe that had overtaken the evacuation fleet, listened with horror as Nunn related the story of his escape from the island.

Brigadier Paris had heard many similar rescue stories at Rengat but he became particularly agitated when he heard that a Lieuten-ant Canty, who had been in charge of the rescue boat *Heather*, had met General Bennett at Djambi. It seemed that a friend of Canty's had rescued the General and his party from a boat at the mouth of the river. While Canty left to carry out his search and rescue mission to Pom Pom, Bennett, his British ADC and some Dalforce officers had been moved on to Sawahlunto in lorries provided by the Dutch.

Bennett's independent forthright views had not always been appreciated by his fellow commanders in Singapore and because of this Paris made it quite plain that he would have nothing to do with him. When, later, Bennett's British ADC came across to see him for funds, Paris told him to 'Let Bennett collect the bloody money himself.' However the Australian General had already made his own arrangements and reported his escape to General Wavell at ABDA Headquarters in Java. Wavell ordered a plane to fly to Padang and bring him out.

The *Roosenboom* sailed that evening, the 27th. Four days later she was sunk off Ceylon (now Sri Lanka). Brigadier Paris, all her crew and passengers were lost apart from Sergeant Gibson and Argyll, Doris Lim, the one-time British secret agent in north China, and two Javanese seamen.

After the ship sailed Warren and his men drove back into town which appeared normal apart from the continuous beating of a large drum which warned the inhabitants that the Japanese planes were about. During this short journey he pondered on the comment Paris had made that a large number of escapers were still arriving with their weapons. He mused that they could probably be formed into armed columns operating from jungle hideouts if the Dutch were prepared to let him have money, equipment and supplies.

His first call was to the Dutch Military Commander in the town. When he left he was sadly disillusioned. 'Sumatra was out of the war' the Dutchman had told him and he had orders to hand over the town to the Japanese. He hoped that neither Warren nor his men would do anything to upset the delicate nature of any negotiations that might take place.

What neither knew was that on his arrival in Colombo, Admiral Helfrich was given the responsibility for undercover work in Sumatra. On 4th March he was urged to find Europeans and natives who could work as agents there.

Disappointed by the Dutchman's attitude Colonel Warren was even more taken aback when he was told that as senior British officer in the town he was expected to control his men and to make sure that they didn't attempt to steal native boats. The Commander then went on to relate a 'grim story' remembered Lieutenant Lind who accompanied Warren as an interpreter, a story of demoralized British servicemen, largely out of control and without leadership who had flooded into Padang.

Warren pointed out he was only looking into the problem for military GHQ in Bandung and that he and his men would soon leave town to carry on their undercover work elsewhere. In rising anger the Dutch Commander accused the British of running away and that every senior officer who had taken charge of the embarkation arrangements had left almost the next day. Banging his desk with his fist he shouted that 'the British troops were fucking the native women in the streets and selling their weapons for five rupees. The soldiers were a rampaging mob.' Lind who was interpreting for Warren remembered that he had difficulty in keeping pace with the Dutchman.

What the Military Commander didn't tell him was that the nationalist leader and future President, Sukarno, who had been under arrest, was now free and hiding in the town. While he was being transferred from prison in Palembang to Padang his native military escort discarded their uniforms and deserted outside Padang. Sukarno, who was now alone, walked into town unnoticed and was given shelter by a friend. The Commander also knew that estate labourers had revolted and killed the Europeans in Medan. The situation further south was so bad that the Dutch were considering disarming the native police. So it didn't help to have the dregs of a European army, beaten by Asians, streaming into town. That same day Sukarno was holding a mass meeting near the town and one false move by the Commander could spark off a revolt by nationalists armed with weapons bought from the British escapers.

The Commandant wanted a senior British Officer to remain and deal with the escapers and as Warren and his men were accredited to General Overaaker's Dutch Headquarters he should be that man. When Warren objected the Commander pointed out that as Warren's unit wasn't included in Wavell's 'surrender of Sumatra' and that they were drawing money, food and supplies from them (the Dutch), Warren should take on the role as Senior British Officer. Reluctantly under pressure Warren agreed but as he walked away he resolved to get clarification from GHQ Bandung as to what the future role of him and his men should be.

Lind remembers that they went around to the Orangji Hotel to look for accommodation. There they bumped into Basil Goodfellow, deputy head of SOE's Orient Mission. He brought them up to date with the events leading up to his escape and the fate of his men. In the conversation he mentioned that Boris Hembry had reached Batavia and had been met at the dockside by Val St Killery, head of SOE's Orient Mission. The latter was last heard of in Bandung.

At the Enderaach Club, used by previous senior officers as British Military Headquarters, Warren found an Australian soldier, sitting on the step with his head in his hands nursing a king-size hangover. Relieved to see a British officer, the soldier immediately began to complain that he had been left behind.

While Warren sat at a desk in his new office and contemplated the future an orderly knocked and told him that General Bennett's British ADC wished to see him. He had seen Brigadier Paris before he left and was told in no uncertain terms that if Bennett wanted money he could come and get it himself. However the situation was resolved, the ADC explained, because General Bennett and he were flying out that night.

On hearing this Warren asked him to take a letter to Colonel Field at GHQ. (See appendix). While the ADC waited Warren wrote that if he must remain (to carry out clandestine work), he 'would require a wireless set, arms and money.'

But Warren was out of touch with the fast moving events in

ABDA HQ. While he was planning to put more men into Malaya, Wavell had selected Captain Laurens van der Post, a South African, to form 43 Mission and bring out the European parties left behind there. By the time that Bennett's ADC arrived with his letter Wavell and his headquarters were packing up to leave for India and Warren's letter to Colonel Field was ignored.

Like General Percival, Warren and his men had been abandoned.

1st March

'Yesterday *Roosenboom* sailed with more than 500 people on board. Since then hundreds more have flooded into town,' Warren recorded in his diary for St David's Day, 1st March.

LAC Walter Hughes also remembered St David's Day in Padang for a different reason. He recalled: 'One of the lads came into the school that day and said he had seen two British destroyers entering the harbour. So with a few friends we made off to the docks where we found two British destroyers, the *Scout* and *Dragon*, had put in for refuelling. Standing in our tattered uniforms on the dockside alongside the *Scout*, we shouted to an officer we could see on the deck whether we could come aboard. He gave permission and we lost no time in climbing up the gangway. We sailed that night for Colombo. At sea we transferred to the *Dragon* and later to the Australian cruiser HMAS *Hobart*.'

In the Enderaach Club an NCO rushed into Warren's office – not bothering to salute, but Warren promptly reminded him – announcing that the two British destroyers were in the harbour. His office emptied in minutes and with everyone else Warren made for the docks and joined the Dutch Commander standing on the dockside. The ships took off 700 and the *Hobart*, which also came in to refuel, took another 512.

The ships had hardly left when another train arrived with 500 more escapers and survivors. By the following day the figure had risen to over a thousand. The few stragglers that arrived first had travelled across Sumatra by their wits. They brought news of the grim scenes along the escape route run by his men and stories had also begun to trickle through of the behaviour of some troops during their passage across Sumatra. There was also the growing hostility of the native population which the escapers had to contend with.

Apart from those arriving via Djambi, some of the first to arrive were those escapers who had sufficient funds to hire their own transport. They were generally in better condition than those trapped at Taluk by the monsoon floods.

Warren recalled that the cooperation and forbearance of the Dutch deserved tribute. 'They had up until then seen nothing of the war or the demoralisation that inevitably follows defeat and disaster. There was a lot that they could not understand and much we could not explain. Certainly there was nothing in the situation for us to be proud of. But they did everything they could, and in the main refrained from insult and recrimination.'

When Warren heard that the local school had been turned into a billet for escaped Allied soldiers he walked across to make himself known and look at the accommodation. He recalled that he found every toilet in the overcrowded school blocked with paper and out of action. Unaccustomed to the Dutch habit of using a bottle of water for sanitary purposes, the troops used large quantities of paper which completely clogged the system. When he complained to the Dutch, he found that their sanitation authorities could offer no solution so in the end Warren scrounged dozens of buckets which offered some relief.

Lieutenant Lind who accompanied Warren on his round of inspection remembered that after seeing the general state of the men Warren decided to impose his will on the mob and restore some semblance of discipline. He ordered all the NCOs, from whatever unit, to get the men on parade for inspection. After this he addressed them to the effect that: 'You have come through desperate times. However that time is now over and if any man has got what it takes he will pick himself up.' He continued in this vein and closed by saying: 'You will again accept military discipline and I will try and get you away on ships by night. So it is essential that you are in your barracks every night and it is to this end that there will be a curfew at 6 pm each night.'

There was a hum of murmuring and shuffling footwear followed by calls for silence by the NCOs. Then it was all over and Warren marched away, with Lind following, leaving the NCOs to dismiss the men.

They had hardly got back to the office than they were told another train was approaching the town with 500 more escapers. Colonel Warren decided to walk across town, to the station, and meet this train. When it arrived he found that a large number of the passengers were in a bad way. 'Most of the troops had lost everything they had,' commented Warren.

2nd March

Warren wrote that: 'A few small parties under the command of young officers were arriving, still retaining their arms but, for the most part, it was a pretty sorry picture. Most of the troops had lost everything they had and many were practically naked or had no footwear.'

Referring to his own men running the escape route, the Dutch told him, 'They were somewhere along the trail and there was a pretty good mess in some places.'

More grim news from the Dutch which confirmed the rumour that the Allied East Coast Fleet had been sunk including the British cruiser *Exeter*. She had taken part in the hunting of the German pocket battleship *Graf Spee*.

Another item of news he gleaned was that an enemy fleet with transports was reported to be in the Sunda Strait, between Java and Sumatra. They had in fact seized an RAF airfield near the coast and the Dutch had stopped all flights to Sumatra.

More bad news followed. Enemy planes had attacked Australia and the Japanese fleet had broken into the Indian Ocean and intercepted and sunk many ships packed with military personnel and civilian refugees. Any vessels which had survived were being hunted down by enemy aircraft and submarines.

Later that day he was joined by Campbell, Lyons and Morris who arrived in Campbell's open tourer. About this time he also sent Broome back to Bagan Siapiapi for Davis, Vanrenan and Graham anticipating that the two ex-planters had returned.

Having their own transport helped Major Campbell and his team clear Taluk before the rivers flooded their banks. They told Warren that some 2,000 escapers, with about 100 in terrible physical conditions, were making their way across the mountains. They also brought an item of cheerful news. His stint as senior British officer in the town might soon be over. A possible successor was Colonel Dillon, an Indian Army officer in charge of a large party somewhere on the route. He could take over Warren's role in the town which would leave him free to carry on the clandestine work.

3rd March

The next day Coates' party arrived from Sawahlunto. He had previously discussed this move with Warren on the telephone. As a result he arranged with the Dutch for ambulances and lorries to meet the train. The local Red Cross had been mobilized and stood waiting alongside the track. They were joined by escaped medical staff who had reached Padang and by Major Meopham who ran the Salvation Army Hospital.

On the train the mood began to change as the track, surrounded by mountain peaks and deep gorges, began to run through gentle rolling hills, covered with terraced paddy fields. Somewhere a group started a sing-song and the strains of 'Tipperary' and 'Land of Hope and Glory' drifted along the carriages. Most of the children lay asleep in the arms of a parent or someone who had looked after them since their parents were lost in the shipwrecks. Gradually the train lost speed and drew up at the little railway station at the edge of the town.

As the military climbed down they were ordered to form three ranks and were marched away into town. Warren noted that many still carried their weapons. Coates had cleared almost a hundred from the hospital at Sawahlunto and these were dealt with efficiently and kindly by the medical staff and their helpers. The civilian wounded were placed in ambulances and lorries to be driven off to the Salvation Army hospital.

The badly wounded military personnel were lifted carefully out of the train on stretchers and loaded into the remaining vehicles. Colonel Coates watched the scene and when all the casualties were detrained he walked across to the waiting lorry and climbed in next to the driver.

The civilians were met by a representative from the British Consul and taken into town in a mixture of buses, lorries and horse-drawn carriages, called gharries. Warren and the local British Consul, a Mr Levison, worked closely with the Dutch to feed and accommodate the continual stream of new arrivals, pending a ship to evacuate them.

'The women survivors,' recalled Warren, 'were quite magnificent, particularly the nurses, and I was told that this was the case during the whole of their tragic journey from Singapore. A bath, a hair do, a clean frock and they reported in fine spirit for duty next day, looking after the sick and wounded who were starting to come in.'

All survivors had lost everything they had when their ships were sunk. Some were without footwear while many were practically naked. A clothes collection was organised from amongst the local population and the Dutch opened a second-hand clothes centre in the Town Hall. Women and children were allowed to select a dress, blouse, skirt, underwear, stockings and shoes. Some soldiers were lucky enough to be issued with new Dutch uniforms or civilian trousers and shirts. The unlucky ones received nothing at all or wore Chinese, pyjama like, black trousers or sarongs with their own torn or bloodstained shirts.

There was also the problem of pay for the troops. In the early days men were selling their weapons for food but now with the help of the Military commander and local community organisations this was overcome and everyone was at least fed. Some officers still had money or had managed to draw money at the local bank to cover their needs. But the other ranks were penniless. There were exceptions among the deserters who had acquired funds during their break for freedom. To overcome this fresh problem Warren drew thousands of guilders each day to pay newly arrived officers and military nurses ten guilders a day and other ranks five guilders.

Warren understood from the Dutch that they were expecting an evacuation ship, SS *Nizam*, which had left Colombo on the 20th and was due any day. In fact she was overdue. Lieutenant Lind recalled: 'We were also advised by cable from India that the British India vessel SS *Chilka* was being sent from Calcutta to evacuate the troops and refugees.' If she arrived Colonel Warren decided that he didn't want a repeat of the scramble that occurred when the *Hobart*'s flotilla came in. He wanted everyone to leave on her and her turn around time in the harbour to be mininal. As the Dutch didn't have sufficient vehicles just to stand by unused, he hired a fleet of horse-drawn gharries to be stationed at convenient locations around the town. These and the drivers remained on station day and night. The responsibility for this transport was given to Lieutenant Jennings, LDV.

Eventually Warren was told that the SS *Nizam*, for reasons not specified, had been recalled and had returned to Trincomalee on 22nd February.

CHAPTER TEN

The Last Goodbye

Extract from Warren's diary.

'5th March 1942. 1200 ton cargo boat from Batavia left Padang yesterday with 36 officers and 66 men on board. Amongst them were a crowd of Gunners who had sailed a Chinese junk from Singapore, hours after its surrender. Not a seaman amongst them, they managed to get as far as St John's lighthouse (beyond the Singapore Roads) before they ran aground. They were later rescued by native fisherman and passed on to Major Campbell's rescue boats operating out of Rengat.'

The cargo ship still had on board bombs for the RAF at Java. When she arrived at Batavia she was ordered to leave immediately without unloading her cargo.

Shortly after she left Padang a small coaster arrived and Warren persuaded her captain to take fifty passengers but he refused to allow women on board his ship. By this time all Warren's men, six seaman, an Argyll and Corporal Morris RAMC – from Bagan Siapiapi and Rengat – had arrived in town so he took the opportunity to include his NCOs and other ranks on the passenger list.

Two days after the ship sailed a look-out spotted a life-raft with two Javanese seamen clinging to it. At the time it was assumed they were the only survivors from the *Roosenboom* but somewhere in the vast Indian Ocean, drifting in the current, was a lifeboat with 150 survivors standing shoulder to shoulder in the small boat or clinging seven deep to each other's shoulders around her.

When the ship was torpedoed at night, by a Japanese I Class submarine, she sank in a few minutes and took with her a large number of escapers and refugees. Trapped in their cabin Mr Nunn managed to push his wife through a port hole before the ship slipped away beneath the waves taking him with it. Amongst those who reached the lifeboat were Brigadier Paris, who died shortly afterwards; Mrs Nunn and Doris Lim, the Chinese girl from the *Kung Wo*. This was the second shipwreck for both women. Another who reached the boat was Sergeant Gibson, an Argyll who had escaped from north Malaya.

In the next forty horrific days, some survivors just drifted away and drowned. Some were murdered and thrown overboard while others were killed and eaten. In the final days, Sergeant Gibson and Doris Lim, with a dwindling number of supporters, fought off and threw overboard the killing gang of soldiers. Eventually the lifeboat was washed ashore on the small island with Sergeant Gibson, Doris Lim and two crazed Javanese seamen on board.

In the week following the ship's departure so many sick and wounded arrived from Coates' overcrowded hospital at Sawahlunto, that they swamped Padang's medical resources. Both he and Warren realised something more substantial would be needed to cope, not only with those still to be moved but also with the cases held-up along the escape route. When Coates discovered that the local Dutch army barracks had a hospital he requested permission to transfer his remaining patients there from Sawahlunto hospital. This must have put the Dutch in a dilemma.

Sumatra had been abandoned by Wavell and the local Dutch military commanders were instructed to carry out a peaceful hand-over to the Japanese. The large numbers of wounded British servicemen at the hospital could be misunderstood by the enemy and might endanger the lives of both the medical staff and others. The British soldiers in the town were armed and patently had not surrendered. The rape and murder of military nurses and medical staff in Hong Kong and the killing of the military wounded and doctors at Queen Alexandra Hospital, Singapore, by the Japanese was fresh in everyone's mind. Whatever the reason the young Dutch doctor had orders not to admit them.

As far as Warren was concerned, apart from the humanitarian side of the argument he wanted everyone on hand to mount a swift evacuation should the SS *Chilka* arrive or any ship's captain be foolish enough to stop at the port. This couldn't be done with casualties some fifty miles away in the mountains. Unless they could use the Garrison hospital, Coates would have to bring his patients down to Padang and set up an improvised temporary hospital, possibly at the school. This alternative was unacceptable to both of them. The only option was the Garrison hospital.

6th March

The floods in the mountains brought a welcome lull in the flow of patients into Sawahlunto which left Colonel Coates free to look again at the possibility of a move to Padang for his remaining patients. On 6th March the hill town's little station was crowded with survivors and escapers. One was Captain Rowley-Conwy and a group of sailors. Around them, armed soldiers intermingled with the women and children while young Sumatrans in boy scout uniforms, helped mothers or led children by the hand to the waiting train. The Dutch Red Cross and members of the Red Crescent were also much in evidence and had set-up trestle tables nearby.

In his cabin the driver looked back at the length of the train with the extra carriage for the wounded. As he watched, an ambulance and a small convoy of lorries came down the road and eased its way through the crowd. They stopped alongside the last carriage with a freshly painted, large red cross on its side. The stretcher patients were carefully lifted out by willing hands and carried into the specially prepared coach.

This train arrived in Padang late afternoon and was met by Warren's reception committee made up of shipwrecked nurses and volunteer helpers from amongst the escapers. After the patients were transferred to the waiting vehicles, Coates climbed up alongside one of the drivers and directed the convoy to the Dutch Army barracks.

It was another hot day and the early morning rain had stopped, leaving pools of water glistening in the sun. The convoy of refugees and ambulances had become a familiar sight and no longer commanded attention as they drove through the crowded streets to the old barracks. At the gate the sentry watched the lorries, borrowed from the Dutch, drive in and follow the road alongside the square to park outside the hospital buildings. Off-duty native troops lounging outside their billets watched as the convoy stopped. The drivers and helpers climbed down, dropped the tailboards and helped the mobile casualties to the ground. Ambulance doors opened and stretcher after stretcher was carefully drawn out and laid on the gravel path.

At first the hospital staff, who came out to meet the ambulances, refused to take this batch of human wreckage, men and women with mangled limbs, blood-stained bandages wrapped around head wounds while others sweated with some obscure tropical fever.

From a distance the Dutch troops gathered in small groups as Coates threatened, cajoled and persuaded until eventually the medical staff, whose every movement and facial expression was followed by more than fifty pairs of pain-racked eyes, agreed to allow the stretchers into the hospital building to be out of the sun but not in the wards. Coates, with his battle half won, supervised the move to the verandahs and corridors.

The hospital doctor wasn't in but he soon arrived when the message reached him that the British were moving patients into his hospital. His car raced through the gates, across the square and braked hard at the tail of the convoy. He slammed the door and strode past the line of parked vehicles into the hospital and glared down the stretcher-filled corridor. Coates – a small slim man and a well known Australian surgeon – stood near the door in his faded army tunic and shorts and quietly waited. He didn't have long to wait as the doctor turned on him, looking down and almost shouting, demanded to know why his orders had been disobeyed. It was his hospital and he had specifically given instructions that these wounded soldiers should not be admitted.

The patients watched a second time as the wiry Coates stood his ground and argued his case. He had no alternative. If he couldn't use the Garrison Hospital where else could he take them? The Dutchman's anger gradually eased as he studied the stretcher cases and the sea of faces. 'Come' he said moving away to walk along the verandah, stopping to look at each patient's tag. Finally he stopped and looked at Coates who had followed him along the line. 'Let's get these into the wards.' Coates had won another battle for his patients and now the next step was to get them fit enough to embark on the next vessel into Emma Haven.

Recalling the incident Warren remembered Coates, by great effort, got most of the fifty limbless patients and others with minor wounds concentrated in the hospital.

The news Broome and Davis brought with them when they arrived, wasn't good. Captain Broome returned to Bagan Siapiapi with orders that John Davis, Vanrenan and Graham, together with the NCOs and men they had with them, should abandon the base and join Colonel Warren in Padang. However John Davis reported that the two ex-planters were missing.

The Chinese owner of the junk which ferried them to Malaya, was ordered to wait for them off shore. Some days later, when he and his crew were fishing, a Japanese patrol launch came alongside and they were questioned by its officer. The Japanese were suspicious so the owner left as he feared arrest if he stayed.

Reluctantly they complied with Warren's orders and closed the base down, destroying the last hope for any early contact with the men they had left behind in the Malayan jungle.

When they reached Padang they found Warren in his office. He listened to their report. It seemed like one blow after another but hiding his feelings he asked them to meet the train and look after a badly injured officer who had won the VC at Kuantan.

In the week since he arrived in the town Warren began to handpick individuals to help him run the evacuation organisation. One was Sergeant Major Road-night, Royal Artillery who looked after all the NCOs and men billeted in one of the schools. He was a regular soldier who had served with the Scots Guards and spent most of his service either in China or India. He learnt to box in the army and at one time became a professional fighter in America. For the disorderly and independent mix of troops at the school he was certainly the man for the job. In the last few days before Singapore fell he was ordered to take command of a large group of stragglers and mould them into a fighting unit. They fought until the end and, determined not to let them surrender, he brought his men out in a native craft across to Sumatra then across to Padang. With him at the school was Sergeant MacLaren who sailed the *Sir Hugh Frazer* to Rengat with Ernest Gordon.

He also brought officers into his staff. Three of the team were Lieutenant Geoffrey Brooke, ex-*Repulse*; Lieutenant Rigden, from the *Trang* and Major Rowley-Conwy. When Lieutenant Rigden arrived and reported to Warren, he was made dockmaster with orders to control the evacuation should a ship arrive. He had served his apprenticeship with P&O Steamship Company and stayed with them until he got his Master's Certificate. Later he worked for the Malayan Government and joined the RNVR. He co-ordinated the plans for the evacuation with Captain Jennings, Local Defence Volunteers who was responsible for the evacuation gharries.

These were located around the town; outside the Town Hall, which was a hostel for the women and children; at the two schools for the NCOs and men, outside the Enderaach Club and the two hospitals for the wounded. 'Just like lifeboat stations,' commented one sergeant drawn in to help.

Geoffrey Brooke and Rowley-Conwy were each made officer i/c of the two, Malay and Chinese, schools used as the men's billets. A large number of Australians were accommodated in the Malay School. 'Not all the officers were prepared to stay and help,' commented Warren after the war. It was not uncommon for an NCO at one of the schools to report to him in the morning that the officer 'had done a bunk, sir.' The men noticed this too and they were losing what little respect they had left for officers. When he chose both men he already knew them as 'leaders' who had a good track record for looking after their men.

Lieutenant Brooke had worked with Warren two months earlier when the Colonel and Commander Alexander organised the controversial evacuation of the Garrison and European civilians from Penang Island. Lieutenant Brooke was drafted to Penang with other survivors from the *Repulse* and the *Prince of Wales* to man the ferries.

Colonel Warren had first gone to 'Fortress' Penang, an island off the coast of north Malaya, to assist in its defence. Churchill had been looking for another Tobruk. When the rapid enemy advance down the peninsula was about to over-run the nearby mainland, GHQ in Singapore ordered Warren and Alexander to evacuate the island. Which they did despite opposition from the European community. While the Rt Hon Duff Cooper, Churchill's representative in Singapore, praised the operation, the Governor Shenton Thomas publicly apologised to the Asian leaders in Singapore that the local Asian community were not included in the evacuation. When both officers reported their escape to Admiral Layton C-in-C China Station, they were 'told off' for leaving behind undamaged boats which could be used by the Japanese. Their explanations that he was mistaken were brushed aside.

Captain Rowley-Conwy had only met him once before, when he and his party arrived on the train from Sawahlunto the previous day. Like everyone else his uniform was in rags but he sported a new green felt hat. When he learnt that Colonel Warren was running the town as SBO, he made his way the Enderaach Club and 'reported in'. When he was called into the office he gave a smart salute followed by name and rank. After studying this new arrival for a moment Warren quizzed him about the escape before he finally paid him ten guilders. Before he left the office he was warned to forget any ideas he might have of stealing another boat. The Dutch didn't like it. Although Rowley-Conwy had some 200 Malayan dollars on him the demand for any type of boat pushed the purchase price well out of his range.

Some 1,500 escapers and refugees were now trapped in Padang including New Zealanders, Australians, British, Asians and Indians from all three Services, Army Navy and Air Force. Hundreds more were still coming along the escape route. Having reached Padang they were restless because of the lack of ships and soon began to look for opportunities to get away on their own. Some, who walked to coastal villages looking for boats, were not well received, often abused and spat at. If a fisherman was seen by his neighbours to be considering selling a boat, they would threaten to report him to the Japanese when they arrived.

One group of sailors searched the docks and noticed that steamers were tied up without cargo or crew. When the local shipping offices refused to help them they tried to seize an empty vessel themselves. This led to another visit by Warren to the Dutch Commander who complained that the soldiers were drinking heavily, they harassed the local fishermen and they molested the women. Even the European women were afraid. Something must be done about it he insisted. As far as he was concerned this latest episode was the limit. All Allied military personnel in the town were to be disarmed and the weapons kept by the Dutch in their armoury. He was also strengthening the guard around the harbour and lowering a boom, trapping vessels in Emma Haven.

Warren had already thwarted one attempt to commandeer a vessel. He learnt that some escapers were planning to seize a barge and sail it away with the wounded on board. He discussed the possibility with Colonel Coates who had looked at the vessel and in his opinion it lacked shelter for the wounded and was quite unsuitable for the voyage. So they managed to kill the idea.

8th March

Throughout the day Colonel Warren received a succession of reports. Each one worse than the other. Commenting on that day 35 years later he reflected 'Some days are just bad days and 8th March was to be one of them.'

It was one of those humid days when the shirt stuck to his back with sweat, remembered Warren. He was in his office when someone brought the news that the Dutch were building sandbagged machine gun emplacements around the dock entrance facing the approach road. Although some men presumed it was perimeter defences against the Japanese Warren realised it was obviously an attempt to discourage any attempt by the British to seize one of the vessels.

Then the Dutch Commander sent a message that enemy troops were landing at Labuhanbilik, near the scene of some of his men's recent east coast activities.

'Here was crisis,' wrote Warren.

He already felt it was going to be a bad day. There was a noisy overhead fan which creaked away and got on his nerves. He found that he became irritated about trivial matters. Through the open door he could see into the large hall just outside the room he used as an office. This had become a dormitory for some of the junior officers whom he could see dozing on blankets on the floor. One or two just lay there, their hands behind their heads staring at the ceiling. As the morning went by he decided to go back to the hotel for a shower. The prospect of a long cold lager appealed to him more, so when he reached the Orangji Hotel he strode into the crowded bar. He had not been there long before a smartly dressed young Dutch officer pushed his way towards him through the throng.

'Sir, I have some bad news for you.'

As he studied the young officer's face, he allowed himself the luxury of silent comment. 'How much bloody worse can it get?'

'The liner you were expecting, it's been sunk.'

The Dutchman then went on to explain that the *Chilka*'s lifeboat under the command of its First Officer, had sailed into Emma Haven. He reported that the liner had been torpedoed off Nais, one of the islands off Padang. After the war Colonel Warren discovered that the *Chilka*'s skipper, in another ship's boat, had reached one of the islands where he took on fresh water and fruit. Then he sailed his crowded lifeboat 1,000 miles back across the Indian Ocean.

The young officer seemed hesitant. When Warren gave him a dismissive acknowledgement he spoke up. There was more. Java was surrendered yesterday he told Warren, and the Governor-General was negotiating the surrender of all forces in the Netherlands East Indies.

This meant that Warren and his men were the only active British unit operating in the whole length of the Malayan Barrier. After the officer left he drank his beer and surveyed the crowded dining room. At one of the tables sat the Gunner Officer Major Rowley-Conwy with two friends. At another was the Commandant's wife, waiting for her husband to join her for lunch. While he watched, the Commandant arrived, nodded to friends, went across to his table and bent over to speak to his wife. She burst into tears and as the dining room went silent her husband put his arms around her and they left the room.

Colonel Warren and Lieutenant Lind spent the next few hours in the Commandant's office, with both him and the Chief of Police trying to establish how the surrender of Java would affect their relations. More important as far as Warren was concerned, what was the military intention of the Free Dutch troops. 'Free,' the Commandant pointed out 'was a relative term.'

He explained that a strong enemy force was moving down from the north and although they may be held up by some, ill-equipped, road blocks it could only be a matter of days before they came racing down the road into Padang. A shrug of his shoulders said everything. Warren reflected that he could smell defeat in the air. It was Singapore all over again. Widening his review of the situation the Dutchman reported that the Japanese now occupied most of Sumatra. They had captured Palembang, occupied Djambi and Labuhanbilik on the east coast and were pouring battle-experienced troops, fresh from their Malayan victories into Medan in the north-east.

The Commandant looked tired. The Royal Navy had fled, he went on: Wavell had abandoned Java and the Japanese were sinking almost every ship that left the islands. All that he wanted was a smooth hand-over to the Japanese when they arrived.

After listening to the long list of reasons for not fighting, Warren again tried to persuade the Dutch to allow him to take his men into the jungle and organise a base for resistance. All his suggestions were brushed aside. 'Their deaths would not honourable,' the Commandant told him. 'If they are not killed by wild animals then the natives will get them.'

Their meeting closed with a comment that British sailors, survivors from the *Repulse* and the *Prince of Wales*, had again been warned off when they tried to board a steamer tied up alongside the quay. Some of those vessels in the harbour were needed to supply the islands. The others – the Commandant shrugged and pulled a face – 'Maybe the owners are worried about the submarine menace and the news of heavy losses amongst the ships fleeing from Java.' He wasn't prepared to take any more chances with the British servicemen, he told Warren, so he had placed sentries on all the ships and he was going to close the harbour mouth with a boom.

The humid weather had brought a storm and torrential rain beat across the roads and pavements as Warren and Lind walked back to the club. It had grown dark and in his dimly lit office the shutters rattled and bounced on their hinges. Above his head the slow moving fan creaked its way around sending a slight draught of cold air across his face.

Shortly after he and his men arrived in Padang they 'acquired a native sailing prahau' remembered Warren. If the *Chilka* had arrived and evacuated everyone he would have left the native prahau for any late arrivals in the town. But now with the Dutch about to close the harbour with a boom it was essential to get the boat out of harm's way before she too was trapped.

Recalling the occasion, Lieutenant Lind wrote that since their arrival in the town he and Warren developed a contingency plan to evacuate their own party if no further ships arrived to take them off. 'With Warren's permission and with the help of the Dutch Control-leour I purchased a good boat for 2000 Dutch Fls:. The next day it was gone and so was our money. We then took another one by 'force of arms' but without bloodshed. After putting a guard on it we set about storing it with food and water and any means of navigation.' On one of his scrounging missions Lind met a fellow RNVR officer, Lieutenant Gorham whom he had served with on the old HMS *Li Wo*. (See appendix.) He too now joined the team and helped provision the boat.

Discussing the boat one evening with Colonel Coates, Warren offered him the opportunity to get away but Coates replied that he would not leave the wounded, even if that entailed surrendering them to the Japanese. Warren also decided to stay, at least until Dillon's party arrived. Even though he intended to remain he realised that 'if the prahau was to get away she would have to sail immediately'. Lind recalled that when they initially discussed the idea of getting the prahau away Warren had insisted that 'only officers should attempt the trip to India. They should all be volunteers and he would select them.' He was referring to escapers reaching Padang and not his men who were still an operational unit.

'The task of selecting the personnel to leave was not easy,' wrote Warren, 'and the only qualification was their value to the war effort. This sounds pompous but it was true.' His own officers came first. Jotting the names down a paper he selected Richard Broome to lead the party with Jock Campbell as quartermaster. The self reliant Ivan Lyon could navigate. He had vast sailing experience and was an old hand at ocean voyages. Another was the ever reliable John Davis, the Chinese-speaking police officer and a member of his team in Malaya. He had many contacts amongst the Chinese Communist guerrillas placed behind the enemy lines.

Five naval officers provided additional seamanship, apart from

Lind and the old man of the team Lieutenant Brian Passmore. There was Lind's friend, Garth Gorham RNVR, a merchant navy officer who had spent many years trading around the China coast. Warren added Lieutenant Geoffrey Brooke to the list, who had been with him during the Penang evacuation.

Then there were Alexander's men, two RNVR officers from the *Trang*, Richard Cox and Holly Hollywell. They had given up their chance to get away when they stayed behind to help Alexander in Dabo. They told Warren that his old friend the Commander was on the escape route somewhere.

Looking at the list of possible passengers he had pencilled down, he ticked Dr 'Doc' Davis who had stayed behind to help Coates at Sawahlunto and the Japanese-speaking Lieutenant Clark, Intelligence Corps. He was half Japanese and oriental looking and wouldn't last long in enemy hands. He survived the sinking of the *Scorpion* and brought ashore with him his nine Japanese prisoners. He then marshalled these across the escape route hoping to get them to India. They were now in the Dutch jail.

Two of the remaining six places went to Major Spanton, Manchester Regiment and Major Waller, Royal Artillery who together 'found' a rowing boat near the Raffles Hotel and rowed away until picked up by Ernest Gordon. In Padang they became part of Warren's team of co-ordinators. It was Waller who was given the task of rounding everyone up.

Finally he had four places left. Two would obviously go to Broome's servant Loo Ngiop Soon, from the days when he was a District Officer in Christmas Island and a Malay policeman who accompanied Davis, Jamal Bin Daim. He later trained as a parachutist and dropped back into Malaya as an agent.

This left two places, including one he had reserved for himself. Decision time. He wrote in his diary that he sent a message 'telling a young Artillery Officer to join me. He had evacuated his battery from Singapore.'

When Rowley-Conwy arrived Warren broke the news that there was a place on the boat for him – and added –'There's also room for one of your officers.' Since his escape from Singapore Rowley-Conwy had worked closely with two others, Douglas Fraser and Davies. They had shared many adventures together and were close. Rowley-Conwy briefly described the qualities of each to Warren, who listened and finally asked which one was he going to choose.

He chose Fraser. Douglas Fraser was a product of the war in Malaya. A prewar planter with a pilot's licence. In the months before the war he joined Malayan Air Force Volunteers. When war broke out he flew unarmed Tiger Moths on reconnaissance missions from Penang and took part in the evacuation of that island. When he reached the mainland at Prai, he returned to his home to collect his motor bike then drove his Triumph Tiger to Kallang airfield, Singapore where his unit was stationed. Rowley-Conwy's battery was also positioned there as part of the airfield's ack-ack defences. When the RAF flew out to Sumatra he found himself out of a job so he sauntered across to Rowley-Conwy, the battery commander and asked to join his outfit. He remained with the battery during the escape as its only Malay-speaking member. He worked with Rowley-Conwy on the search and rescue missions and finally they set out for Padang together.

Warren assembled his team and the escapers in a large bungalow near the edge of town. It was dark by the time everyone finally arrived and he was anxious that they should leave before the Dutch carried out their threat to block the harbour entrance.

Apart from his own men the reason for the meeting had remained a secret from the others who waited around in a large room with a drink in their hand wondering if he was going to announce a mass evacuation. Lieutenant Brooke wrote later that 'the air was electric.'* In another room Warren spoke to his team and gave overall command to Captain Broome. The departure he insisted must be carried out in absolute secrecy, especially from the Dutch as nothing was known of the surrender terms agreed in Java. Lind then recalled receiving written orders from Colonel Warren which said, 'You are to raise anchor, set sail and proceed to Ceylon.' He then sent Campbell out to bring in the others.

Describing the scene Geoffrey Brooke remembered Warren standing in the middle of the room and everyone stood in a semi-circle around him. After studying each in turn as if to imprint the faces to memory Warren commented that he didn't expect any more ships to arrive. The Japanese however could arrive at any time and unless those who wished to escape left that night it would be too late. He expected everyone still in town tomorrow to become prisoners of war.

He then went on to say that he had authorised one of his men to

---

* *Alarm Starboard* Geoffrey Brooke, Patrick Stephens

Colonel Warren talking to Lieutenant Lind RNVR aboard the *Hin Leong* before the aborted first attempt to leave Singapore.

This photograph was taken by an officer in the Royal Engineers when he and his men were returning to Singapore after they had destroyed oil tanks on nearby islands. This scene, once described as 'Hell's Port', shows a launch, probably packed with escapers, and Singapore burning in the background. Keppel Harbour is on the left covered in smoke while the high-domed Supreme Court can be seen to the right with St. Andrew's Cathedral barely visible above the smoke.

The Navy returns. Collyers Quay, August 1945.

Both photographs on this page were taken by Frank O'Shanohun who as a major with SOE was parachuted on to Singapore racecourse to negotiate the Japanese surrender.

Japanese military personnel descending the steps of the Municipal Offices after signing the surrender.

purchase a prahau which had been provisioned and was anchored five miles up the coast. He had selected them to leave Padang onboard that vessel. He had intended going himself after handing over command to Colonel Dillon. But he had not arrived and Warren thought he and his party had already been captured. So he had no option but to remain.

'You sail tonight,' he said. 'Any questions?'

For a brief moment there was complete silence until finally Lieutenant Clarke spoke up saying that he couldn't possibly go as he had been ordered to stay with his prisoners. Warren dismissed the excuse with a sweep of his hand. 'Leave them, I order you to go.'

When Captain Rowley-Conwy learnt he was to leave he dreaded breaking the news to his friend Lewis Davies who had been with him since Singapore. He never forgot the look on Davies's face when he realised he was being left behind. Nor did he ever find out what eventually became of him.*

The crisis point had also arrived for Lieutenant Brooke who walked out of the room onto the verandah. Everything was so quiet apart from the whirring of the crickets and the call of a night bird in the trees. Across the lawn fireflies flickered amongst the shrubs. The night sky was black and he could see the stars. Here was a chance to escape, he reflected, but a fellow survivor Lieutenant Fairfax who assisted him at the school, was waiting for a telephone call from him to muster the men for an evacuation. Then there were the men at the school who would wake up the following morning and find him gone. In the middle of this mental turmoil Lind joined him on the verandah and told him not to do anything foolish. He was followed by the commanding presence of Colonel Warren. He was standing no nonsense, 'I order you to go,' he told him.*

The prahau was hidden some miles away so Warren had arranged for the party to move off in a convoy of gharries which waited in the road outside. He made a point of speaking to everyone as they waited on the verandah, especially Rowley-Conwy. He remembered Warren's last farewell that night. As the party moved off towards the gharries Warren laid a hand on his arm.

'You're a lucky man. I intended to make you Commandant of the British troops in Padang. Lucky for you you're too young so you get this trip and I stay.'*

* *Marines don't hold their horses* Ian Skidmore, W.H. Allen

Warren watched their dark shapes move along the drive and small groups form as they mounted the high wheeled pony traps. Then with a great deal of cluck clucking from the drivers and the rattle of wheels on the metalled road the gharries moved off and the road was empty.

CHAPTER ELEVEN

A 'Busted Flush'

The next day Dillon, with some five hundred servicemen, arrived in town from Sawahlunto. Morale was high as the train climbed down from the hills on the chain and ratchet track. Each coach had its own sing song party. Having walked through the train to see if everything was all right he relaxed in his seat and dozed with the motion of the carriage.

The train followed the metalled road which ran alongside the track. Either side were paddifields, and banana groves which tried to hide the tidy decorative native houses. The landscape had changed from mountains to flatlands. Bullock carts moved leisurely along the road with the drivers raising an arm in reply to shouts from the train. War could be a thousand miles away.

The train drew up at the side of a small brick station building, and the passengers were met by a well organised reception committee. Nearby were ambulances and lorries. The Dutch Red Cross were very much in evidence and a small number of British and Dutch officers waited near the track. The few civilians and children on board were taken away in a lorry to the Town Hall. The servicemen, after climbing down from the train, were lined up alongside the track and ordered to place any weapons on the ground. Then they formed-up into three ranks and marched off to the school. The weapons were later collected by the Dutch and Warren suspected that they were dumped into the harbour. The officers had the choice of going to the Enderaach Club or to try and find accommodation in the overcrowded Orangji Hotel.

After seeing that all the casualties were looked after, the nurses climbed aboard a waiting lorry and were driven to Warren's house at the edge of town. There they were greeted by a tall Englishman with a beard, remembered one nurse. He recorded their names and Service details then allocated them accommodation around the town.

The Asian nurses were billeted in the Roman Catholic Convent where the nuns ran a private girls' school in the town. The girls had been sent home because of the war. Civilian women amongst the late arrivals were also billeted there.

Dillon's party was soon followed by Alexander's group. He had with him about fifty limbless patients whom he had shepherded from Dabo. Some were stretcher cases and a few hobbled along on home-made crutches. The group had been held up by the flood at the small town of Peranap and billeted in an empty house. When the walking wounded went to the market place they found the local population were appalled at their condition. Many shopkeepers refused to take money for the purchases and a collection around the town brought in clothes to replace the rags they wore.

When the floods receded the party had moved off in two trucks. The journey to Sawahlunto took almost twenty hours. Everyone was exhausted by the time they arrived. Sleep had been impossible as the lorries chugged their way across the mountains. They only stopped when they had engine trouble or when they ran into floods. Each time that happened the passengers dismounted, apart from the casualties and children, and everyone waded across. The cold mountain flood waters were often waist deep. The lorries followed slowly behind and if the water rose too high on the waders the vehicles reversed and the drivers waited until the water level dropped.

Finally the party was stopped at a Dutch road-block in the mountains outside Sawahlunto. At first the soldiers were reluctant to let them through but an officer intervened and the obstacles were removed. The lorries drove on through the darkness into the brightly lit streets of the town recently evacuated by Dillon.

In Padang Dillon and Alexander joined Warren at the Orangji Hotel. Coates arrived later after dealing with the latest influx of casualties. The dining room was full but they found a place in the bar in high-backed plush seats. Over drinks Warren briefed them on the events so far and finally commented that the whole mess was a 'busted flush'.

After all the efforts and trouble all three had gone through to get their parties to Padang they expected and hoped to find a ship waiting for them. Warren's report was like a blow below the belt. The discussion turned to opportunities to get escape parties away. The Dutch had ships in the harbour remarked Warren but they wouldn't release them. They all belonged to local shipping firms and the crews didn't want to risk meeting enemy warships. Furthermore it seemed that the Dutch and Japanese would need them to reach the islands. The harbour was, in any case, now a 'no go' area and the Dutch had placed machine gun posts around it.

They all agreed it was useless for all four to remain but Coates emphasised that he intended to remain with the wounded. Alexander adopted the same attitude and wouldn't leave those he had shepherded from Dabo. The conversation was interrupted by a recently arrived officer, an Australian, who cradled a bren gun in his arms and pushed his way through the crowded bar. Like each new arrival his clothes were torn and dirty, he was unshaven and he smelt. Warren watched his progress and mused that the 'Dutch will soon have that off you m'lad.' He caught Warren watching him and sat down next to Coates. Looking at the four senior officers he smiled and announced that he'd just arrived from Singapore. This fell on rather deaf ears so he continued in a louder tone, trying to impress, 'I found this bloody Chinese in bed with his wife so I kicked him out and made him row me all the way to Sumatra.' He smiled again. 'Everytime the bastard tried to stop I waved my gun under his nose.'

March 10th

No news of any evacuation ship. The Dutch announced that Darwin had suffered a heavy raid and in a big sea battle before Java surrendered, the Allies had lost five cruisers and five destroyers. Only four old American destroyers escaped and fled to Australia. In the north on the mainland, Rangoon had been captured by the Japanese.

Warren decided to walk along to the British Consul to send a message to the Royal Navy. In the park close to the Town Hall, groups of soldiers hung around idly chatting and watching the girls or playing cards on the grass. The Town Hall was a hostel for civilian women and the Dutch ran a second hand clothes stall in the building.

As he passed, a group of Asian civilian nurses from Singapore General Hospital came down the steps crying. He recognised them as a group who had remained behind to help on the islands. They had arrived the previous day with Alexander's party from Dabo. Most of the civilians knew Warren and told him, when he asked, that the Chinese nurses were upset at the weight they had lost. This meant that none of the fine clothes would fit them and they would have to still wear their torn clothes. One of the European women, who had herself escaped from Singapore, was overheard by them to scornfully remark that, 'They should be thankful they're here. If they were in Singapore they would have had their heads chopped off by now.'

Levison, the British Consul listened to Warren's request for his security codes, so that a message could be sent to Colombo. The Colonel wanted to find out what was happening. No reply had been received from British Military HQ in Bandung before it evacuated to India and he had hoped to bypass the Dutch and get permission to take his men into the jungle. If not, he wanted news of any plans to evacuate everyone.

He was too late, Levison told him, acting on instructions he had destroyed all his codes.

Every evening Warren called all the officers together to give them updated information on what was happening. As everyone wanted to hear news of the evacuation ship, each night was an anti-climax. He also heard that individuals were slipping away to make their own escape. He didn't blame them but he hoped they didn't run up against any anti-Dutch elements who wouldn't know the difference between being British or Dutch.

13th March
The Dutch in Java signed the formal instrument of surrender the previous day and Padang was declared an open city.

'It was evident that the Japanese were closing in on the town,' wrote Warren 'and in a talk with the Governor I offered (again) to form a unit to co-operate with the Dutch troops and carry on guerrilla warfare.' The Dutch commander refused his offer and warned him against letting his men 'go on the run', repeating that 'their end will not be honourable.' In Warren's view the Dutch were fearful of the reaction of the natives who were restless and impatient for independence and had already given signs of Japanese sympathies and influence. He commented after the war that followed the surrender of Java he never discovered what the Dutch policy towards Sumatra was, but he realised that the Japanese would soon have complete control of that island.

The discipline amongst the troops had improved and there were less complaints about their behaviour from the Dutch. This was partly due to a meeting held at the school where Warren read out the 'riot act' to the assembled servicemen. But his NCO's at the school still reported that some officers, put in charge of troops at the school, had gone.

Near the gates of the convent a Chinaman was doing a good trade buying jewellery from the women. Watches, diamond rings and brooches were traded away for money or food. To try and take their minds off their desperate position the nuns helped the women set up sewing and language classes to keep them occupied. Like the military their main thought was when would the evacuation ship arrive.

That evening, Friday the 13th, Warren held his daily meeting. As British Commandant in the town he had decided that he must stay with the men. That left Dillon free to lead an escape party. Warren promised to let him have whatever money he needed to buy a boat and gave him the two cars his team had driven to Padang.

As he sat at the green baize-covered table Warren watched the last few seats being taken in the crowded room. The murmuring died down when he stood up. It was hot and someone opened the shutters which also helped clear the air of cigarette smoke. He had decided to give everyone a complete picture of the situation. There was no ship. The Dutch had surrendered and at this very moment a Japanese column was racing across from Medan on the east coast to put them all in the bag. With the other ranks' feelings in mind he told the assembled officers that he intended to remain. Although this last comment was an attempt to reassure his men, some officers were angry that he gave his word not to escape. It was an officer's duty to escape, was their opinion. This news had a sobering effect on his audience and as they crowded around the doors to leave a number decided it was time to take individual action to escape.

Warren slept that night in the Enderaach club. At about 2 am he awoke to the sound of what he thought was a heavy bombing raid on the town. The building shook with explosions, cracks raced up the wall near his bed and plaster tumbled down from the ceiling above his head. Throwing his sheet aside and clawing his way from the mosquito net, he ran outside with his pistol in his hand and dressed only in his trousers and steel helmet. Behind him in the club 300 officers were stumbling out of their beds demanding to know what was happening. He recalled that it seemed to him that 'the enemy had arrived and were opening up on the town'.

In the nearby convent terrified women ran screaming from the building, some dressed in bra and knickers others naked, to hide in monsoon ditches and slit trenches. Running behind them came the nuns, fully dressed, trying to calm them.

Outside the club everything seemed relatively calm. The gharries were still parked at the kerb although the horses seemed to be a little troublesome. Their drivers just sat there half asleep mumbling in Malay to reassure the animals. They just stared at the tall shirtless officer who was waving a pistol about. In answer to his question they replied that the mountains were volcanic and the noise was only an earthquake.

By the time he finally finished walking through the club calmly announcing that it was only an earthquake dawn was near. At about 4.30 am Dillon appeared fully dressed carrying a small pack with money and food for the trip. He had decided to take Warren's advice and go north to Sasak where two ocean going junks had been seen. The two walked along the narrow streets to the school where Dillon had arranged to meet the rest of the party. After saying his last goodbye and wishing him luck Warren watched Dillon and his party drive off as the sun's rays broke across the grey skies. He looked at his watch, it was five o'clock.

One officer who felt a little put out when he heard that Dillon's escape party had gone was Captain Jennings, LDV. He had escaped from Singapore and later joined Dillon's group when they were stranded by floods in central Sumatra. The previous evening a naval officer who acted as the troops' paymaster asked him to pay-out the following day. Apart from thinking it a bit odd he agreed but then discovered that he was landed with the job as his fellow officer had left with Dillon. Within a few days he made his own escape bid in a small open outrigger canoe which he tried to sail down the coast in an unsuccessful attempt to reach Australia.

Throughout the next two days escape parties were formed and groups set out to search the beaches and villages around the town for boats. Although the Dutch had warned them they didn't appreciate the depth of nationalist feelings. They found themselves threatened and mocked and even spat at. Some soldiers clubbed what little money they had but found they could only buy boats far too small for the journey. Nevertheless Warren was prepared to fund any well considered escape plan. As far as he was concerned the latter proviso was just a matter of form, as there was nowhere to go except to the jungle or to the string of islands about one hundred miles to the west. 'There were hardly any boats left in Padang,' he recollected. 'The real criterion was the character of the leader. Provided he had the will to make a break and show some appreciation of what he was up against we did what we could for him.'

About eight parties eventually left. The favourite destination was
Burma via the Andaman Islands to the north, but some chose to
make for Australia.

A message from the Dutch told Warren that the Japanese had
reached Fort de Kock, some sixty miles away. They were expected
next day and when they arrived in Padang the Governor would
surrender Sumatra. Warren realised that Dillon's party was
directly in their path and wondered how they had fared.

Having sent a soldier to warn Major Meopham and Colonel
Coates of the latest position he walked through the narrow empty
streets, avoiding heaps of cow dung which seemed everywhere.
News of the enemy's approach had already reached the residents,
and shopkeepers were hastily putting up their shutters. Above in
the streets windows opened briefly then banged shut and bolted
noisily, leaving white sheets dangling underneath. Little Japanese
flags were pinned to doors and near the Convent a small crowd of
Chinamen gathered at the gates.

Inside the women could be seen doing their chores in the yard. A
rumour had circulated that the Japanese would sell the Asian
nurses so the men were doing a little window shopping. Warren
sent a message to the nuns to close the high, wooden double doors
and that all nurses should wear a red cross armband. The news of
the approaching Japanese came as something of a shock to many in
the convent who were confident that the Royal Navy or the British
Government would get them out. One nurse remembered that
dinner that evening was a silent affair.

There was trouble outside in the streets as looters began to break
into businesses and homes. The Dutch were very much at risk. As
for the other-ranks Warren ordered Road-night to confine them to
the school billets. Levison, the British Consul instructed the
civilians to concentrate at the Salvation Army hostel or at the
Town Hall. No one should go out of doors.

Later that evening when Warren was told that the Japanese were
expected at any time he, with a Japanese speaking escaper
named Waite, left the club at 7 pm to walk to the Governor's office.
He remembered that there was a strange hush over the town and
the streets were deserted except for a half-crazed European civilian
who walked past clutching a spaniel. He was trying to retrace his
steps across Sumatra to try and find his wife.

What follows is Warren's recollections of that evening:

'As we walked through the narrow streets to join the Dutch

authorities for the last act of this debacle I thought of all those
anxious men and women who were awaiting the result of the
night's work; of the prahaus at sea, of the men hiding in the jungle;
of the defeat and ruin of Singapore and the mainland beyond.

'What was the why of it all?

'We were about to see the end of three hundred years of history.

'It was 1 am on the morning of 17th March. There was a
spattering of gravel outside the main entrance of the Governor's
office and a certain tenseness was felt around the large table at
which we were sitting. The Governor and his staff were sitting
opposite me, immaculate in full-dress white with gold embroidered
collars and cuffs, stiff, dignified and obviously concealing consider-
able emotion. A Dutch army captain and warrant officer in jungle
green sat awkwardly on my left, seemingly conscious of their
inferior rank and work-a-day clothes. The small, worried-looking
man in a white tropical suit, who sat at the end of the table was the
British Consul. He had insisted on attending the ceremony in his
official capacity and had assumed responsibility for my civilians.
His Dutch wife was very ill and he really needed to be with her.

'My own khaki shirt and shorts were dirty and smelt, for the few
other belongings I had were on board the prahau now somewhere in
the Indian Ocean.

'The main door of the outer hall was rudely burst open and we
turned to watch a young Jap officer stride through the room, his
new yellow riding boots squeaking and thumping on the polished
wooden floor. He was followed by a Dutch police officer and a
bearded bespectacled Jap soldier, armed with rifle and bayonet.

'A bearded Jap? Not a good beard but nevertheless a beard.

'The Jap strode up to the table, arrogant and truculent, and
stood with his legs apart turning his head to glare suspiciously at
each of us. Slowly we all came to our feet and returned his stare.
Whatever effect it had been intended to produced was interrupted
by the bearded sentry dropping the butt of his rifle heavily on the
floor, which he followed immediately by emitting a loud belch.
Instinctively we turned our heads towards him, a ridiculous and
owlish self-conscious figure.

'The officer slumped quickly into a chair between myself and my
interpreter, with a characteristic hissing intake of breath through
his teeth. He seemed suddenly tired of acting his charade and
removed his cap to mop his shaven head with a dirty neck cloth he
was wearing. He ostentatiously selected a cigarette from a shining
new silver cigarette case, lit it and started to talk. He had the

appearance of being slightly drunk or doped but was nevertheless in full possession of his senses. The interpreter told us he was asking for a drink and when a glass of water was brought he turned up his nose. Laboriously he started to scribble on a sheet of paper and giggled childishly to himself. He thought the girls in Singapore were lovely and this seemed to be his only topic, so the interpreter informed us and he was trying to draw one of the lovely girls.

'This was opera bouffe. Our tension relaxed and we talked more easily among ourselves. The Dutch police officer said that he had met the Jap by arrangement at Fort de Kock and had been driven into Padang with a gun in his ribs, for the Japs suspected some treachery. A general was to be expected in an hour or so to receive our formal surrender. He told me that my friend General Over-aakers, military commander in the Bagan Siapiapi area, had been compelled to surrender and his troops considered it was useless for them to carry on the struggle after Singapore and Java had fallen.

'While the Dutch exchanged news and talked among themselves and the interpreter kept the Jap officer in conversation, the purpose of the gathering around me struck me with some force. Were we really so impotent that we had to surrender ourselves and our men to trash like the fool on my right or the belching sentry behind me? The war had not so far killed my morale even though my experience had to date been all scuttle and run. Norway and France in 1940? We had come out of that with our tails high even though we knew out country had its back to the wall and was hanging on by a shoe-string. But this Malaya business had been different somehow, even allowing for the same lack of aircraft, tanks and other necessities of modern war. The country, the jungle, had been so unknown to our men; most of them couldn't tell a Chinese from a Jap, Malay from an Indian. The *Prince of Wales* and the *Repulse* had somehow started the rot, though God forbid that I blame the Royal Navy for our position.

'I had been in the War Room at the Naval base in Singapore when Admiral Phillips had made his decision to put to sea and I remember thinking as I watched him that here, indeed, was history in the making. An historic moment! But that effort had also gone wrong somehow. We still had so many fine fighting types. If I had seen the demoralisation and lack of manhood in some, I had also seen the other side of the penny – men taking their bombing and machine-gunning and coming up with the age-old grins of defiance and contempt.

'Was it our leader? Was it me, even now sitting here waiting to cash in my cheque while my men lay in darkened billets awaiting the results of my night's work? What did they think about it all?'

'An hour passed and there were sounds of movement outside. The Jap officer dropped his childish behaviour and shouted something at us as he jumped to his feet and made for the door.

'"They're here, sir" — from my interpreter.

'This was it!

'They entered noisily and we stood up as the sentry banged his butt. This too was a play, but a grim one. They strode purposefully in with the air of conquerors, kicking their legs in front of them, their muddy boots striking heavily on the floor, their curved swords jangling as they walked. The general went to the table opposite me with a few of them, the remainder, ranging themselves behind me. A few words were snapped out.

'"Chairs," said my interpreter and the Dutch moved to get them.

'Treating us all as if we did not exist the general sat and talked with two of his staff while the others were being seated. All this to the accompaniment of noisy throat clearings and hissing intakes of breath as though the coming proceedings were going to be something of great relish.

'I glanced about me. It was as if the pages of history had been rolled back. Vague memories stirred in my mind. Here were Genghis Khan and Tamerlane and the Mongol hordes of centuries past. These were good fighting men, crude, fierce, proud and confident. There was little of the undersized myopic Jap in this bunch with the broad, flat, yellow faces with cruel eyes and long wispy moustaches under beehive-shaped sun helmets, bleached and dirty and long past their best. Their clothing was stained and made of some cheap cotton material with the sleeves half-covering their short gorilla-like arms. A jangle and scraping of chairs as swords were placed between their bow legs and they settled down, filling the room with the sour smell of sweat.

'The jabbering and hubbub gradually died down and we turned our eyes towards the general. He was wearing a British soldier's tropical helmet and shirt with no trimmings or badges of rank that I could see. Helmets were removed and an officer on the right of the general opened the play by suddenly pointing a pencil at me and asking something in Japanese.

'"Do you command the British troops?" My interpreter took up his role without further invitation.

'"Yes," he replied.

'"How many troops are here? Where are they now? Where did they come from? Where have you come from?"

'So it went on, the interpreter putting the questions to me and passing the answers back. The questions were simple and there was no point in concealing from the Japs what they would learn in a few hours time. We handed over our written surrender and a statement of the dispositions of all British nationals in the town. These were read with interest and carefully filed away. They appeared to understand what was set down. The story I told was that I had been sent over from Java just before it fell to look after the British in Padang. I was silent as to the real purpose the port had served or the thousands who had passed through.

'Now the Dutch captain had his turn. He was vague and confused in his answers and the irritation of the Jap was plain. A map was demanded. A thing the size of a postcard was brought in which showed nothing even to the Dutchman. The Jap became suspicious and he started to shout. A map on a large wooden frame was brought, so enormous that some difficulty was found in getting it through the door. The situation was getting slightly ridiculous and I had time to study the officers grouped behind the general. One had a fine head and an aesthetic face and carried himself with aloofness and dignity. The proceedings had little interest for him and he seemed to take pains to show his contempt for them. I put him down as the artillery commander and tried to sort out the remainder of the staff. I was somewhat distracted by the snorting, honking and hissing of a fat, uncouth ruffian immediately behind my chair whose path I was later to cross when he filled the role of Town Major.

'So the affair dragged on. The Governor was questioned closely. Coffee was demanded but none was forthcoming from the back premises; glasses of water were produced instead.

'It was about seven o'clock when the party broke up and the bulk of the Japs departed leaving half a dozen or so behind. I was instructed to keep all my men in their billets and was given a pass to return to my headquarters. This was fastidiously written out in Japanese, with my name in both Japanese and English, by the staff officer who had questioned us. He spoke good English and could not resist telling me he had been to a military academy in France. He was certainly no fool and I felt some satisfaction that here at least was someone with, apparently some civilisation in him.

'I left the building with a sense of unreality strong upon me and walked down the middle of the road with my interpreter. The latter

– Waite by name – had done well, though there was little in the miserable proceedings which could be regarded as cause for satisfaction. I felt, however, that our request for decent treatment for the sick and civilians had been fairly received, though I could not understand the farewell remark of the Governor's assistant "Your people will have a bad time," spoken kindly with tears in his eyes.

'The native population stared curiously at us as we passed. All roads were jammed with Jap lorries but the drivers took little notice of us. They were busy on their engines or crawled like monkeys over their vehicles doing odd jobs.

'I decided that it would be safe to make a detour and call at one of the schools where several hundred troops were housed. On the way we passed several natives with baskets of live hens. We told them to follow us for we were doubtful of the food situation. They did so with some caution.

'We gave the commanding officer our news, the chickens and some money and then went on our way to my headquarters.'

The troops at the school were vocal in their opinions especially of Churchill and Wavell and those officers who had taken the opportunity to run away while they were forced to remain, remembered Warren.

At the Club 'Three members of the Kempei Tai — the Jap secret police – were waiting to interview me. They were undersized little rats in shoddy civilian clothes. The questions were a repetition of what I had answered previously, and I told them the same sort of story. They wanted to search the building for arms but I assured them that all arms had been collected into the Dutch armoury. In actual fact we had hidden, around the building, about six revolvers, a few compasses and other escape items. At the school Japanese guards took over.'

Later, with Warren's permission, Sergeant Major Road-night decided it was now or never and slipped away under cover of darkness.

The following is an extract from Colonel Alan Warren's diary hastily scribbled when he arrived back from Government House:

'8.30 a.m. March 17th. 1942. Padang, Sumatra. A Japanese motorised column arrived last night from Fort de Kock at 1.30 a.m. Awaited the arrival of the Jap Commander in Government House in company with the Dutch Governor, his staff and the Dutch Military Commander. Made my formal surrender. St Patrick's Day and my first day as a prisoner. And now what?'

CHAPTER TWELVE

An Outpost Too Far

The arrival of the Japanese signalled the outbreak of civil disorder that the Dutch had dreaded. With the Commissioner of Police arrested and the local police disarmed, looters and nationalists swept through the town. Japanese sympathisers came out into the open and acted as guides informing on those who worked for or were friendly with the Dutch. Looters, men, women and children, roamed the streets with large baskets plundering the homes and businesses of those arrested or under suspicion. Many Dutch families fell victims to the gangs and were murdered. The nuns rescued two young Dutch girls, victims of the mobs, and hid them in the convent. The situation calmed down when the Commissioner of Police was set free and his men rearmed.

All the European women and children evacuees, and Dutch who were interned, were transferred to the convent which became a temporary prison camp. The military personnel and the Dutch men were moved into the barracks.

Sergeant Major Road-night escaped into the mountains, later found a boat, set out for Ceylon. Somewhere in the Indian Ocean he was seen and rescued by a British naval vessel enroute for Australia. When he arrived there no one believed his story and he was arrested as a suspected deserter but later his story was confirmed and he was awarded the Distinguished Conduct Medal.

On transfer to India he joined the Chindits and took part in long range penetration operations behind enemy lines. After the war he volunteered for the recently formed Malayan Scouts. The relatively unknown unit, led by the ex-Chindit Colonel Michael Calvert, operated in the jungle against the communist guerrillas. Their role was taken over by 22nd SAS and under Road-night's guidance the men soon developed the knowledge and feeling required for this type of warfare. Many of his training methods are still in use today at the Hereford SAS base.

Some hundred servicemen set out from Padang in small groups to reach Burma, Ceylon and Australia but nothing is known of their fate. Warren's men, in the *Sederhana Johannes*, reached India on 19th April. Allen Lind recalled that after leaving Warren they rode in the gharries to a creek five miles up the coast beyond the boom the Dutch had lowered to stop the ships leaving. The forty feet long boat which had been built for coastal trading, had a freeboard of only 18 inches. Her sails were so thin that the stars could be seen through them. From the beach the three masted vessel didn't look too inspiring. From out of the darkness Malay fishermen appeared with four dug-out canoes and the party were paddled out to the prahau anchored half-mile off shore.

Warren's men were familiar with the vessel and had previously taken trips around the bay under the watchful eyes of the Malay crew. So after some hours of sailing around to get the feel of her again the crew were disembarked and, with Lyon as navigator set out for Ceylon. The first few days had its problems. One day the anchor snarled up on a coral reef. Then the wind blew in the wrong direction. Meanwhile they discovered that the boat was over-ridden with cockroaches which swarmed over them as they slept at night.

While Warren pondered on their fate, as he sat waiting to surrender the servicemen in Padang, they were almost 100 miles out into the Indian Ocean. In the next thirty days they alternated between being becalmed or the victims of strong winds which tore their sail, already showing signs of wear and tear. On a number of occasions they were sighted by Japanese planes. Although this caused a mild panic aboard, and everyone fled below to hide leaving the coolie-like helmsmen on deck, the planes just flew by and assumed them to be just another fishing boat.

By 28th March they had travelled 784 miles but being blown before the wind they were sailing in the wrong direction and running short of water and food. Then the wind dropped and they wallowed around. When they found the wind again Brian Passmore fell overboard and by the time they managed to bring the vessel about they were more than a half a mile away with everyone on deck trying to keep him in view. Eventually Lyon brought her around and eager hands leaned over the side and hauled him in – only feet away from a fast moving shark's fin.

One morning in April a Japanese fighter suddenly appeared and instead of just ignoring them, as others had done previously, it circled so that the pilot and gunner could take a good look at them. Rowley-Conwy, who watched the attack from beneath an attap covered shelter on deck, remembered that the plane seemed to fall from the sky. With all guns firing the plane roared overhead and above the noise of its guns came the thuds of bullets hitting the hull and the whine of ricochets. Everyone clung to the deck or tried to squirm into gaps much too small for them for protection. Then it was gone. As they were some 1,000 miles from Sumatra the plane probably came from a Japanese aircraft carrier, part of Admiral Nagumo's fleet heading for the British Naval Base at Trincomalee, Ceylon.

The water supply was down to half a mug a day. No one knew their precise position but the wireless set they brought with them, although unable to transmit did, occasionally pick up the Greenwich time signal which helped Lyon plot their position. This set was issued by SOE and brought out of Singapore by Basil Goodfellow remembered Warren. Before he left on the Australian cruiser for Colomba, Goodfellow gave it to Warren who in desperation tried unsuccessfully to contact Ceylon on it. All the wireless sets issued to the Orient Mission were quite inadequate for the job.

Then on 12th April, after being at sea for 32 days, they sighted low cloud on the horizon. This became mountains. It must be Ceylon but where?

The next day the prahau followed a long line of golden sands and palm tree lined beaches but could not find a suitable spot for Lyon to bring the boat ashore. They dare not try to beach her in case the hull collapsed and everyone was far too weak to swim ashore. On the following day they sighted a British freighter, the *Anglo Indian*, and tacked towards her. She changed course away from them but when Ivan Lyon brought her around on the new bearing the vessel turned away.

When the ship's master eventually decided to pick them up they discovered that he was suspicious when he first saw them and thought they were a Japanese ruse to lure his vessel into a trap for a submarine attack. The ship was on its way to India and, as the Japanese task force was heading towards the island, he wasn't prepared to go back and land them in Ceylon. They found no difficulty in agreeing to sail with him to India and transferred across to his ship, leaving the prahau to be sunk by gunfire.

Broome and Davis joined Goodfellow in India and between them set up the Malayan section of Force 136, which took over Warren's role. Both went back into Malaya on a number of occasions, remaining in the jungle with the communist guerrillas. After the war John Davis played a prominent role in that country with the security forces during the Emergency.

The Australian Bill Reynolds, who remained at Rengat after Campbell's team withdrew to Padang, eventually left about 13th March after being told by the Dutch Controlleour that the Japanese were about to come up river. With a crew of Chinese, including a girl crew member, he went back down river for the last time. In the enemy-held Malacca Straits the launch was attacked by a Japanese fighter; it eventually flew off without causing casualties but leaving the boat peppered with bullet holes.

Their first landfall was the Nicobar Isalnds, between Sumatra and Burma. Suspecting that it may be in enemy hands he didn't attempt to land. The Deutz diesel engine, with a mind of its own, decided it would stop, causing Bill Reynolds to spend the next five hours with his head down inside the engine casing. Eventually it fired and the boat pitched and rolled her way 1000 miles across the Indian Ocean to Bombay.

In India he again met Ivan Lyon, who talked him into joining SOE. The old Japanese fishing supply boat was renamed the *Krait* and shipped to Australia. Lyon also tracked down Corporal Morris to a military hospital and rescued him from a life of bedpans. The three formed the nucleus of a team which carried out a successful raid on Singapore. This entailed sailing the *Krait* from Australia to Singapore and sinking enemy shipping there with limpet mines.

Lyon was killed in a copy cat raid on Singapore in 1944. The Japanese were more alert and intercepted the raiders as they approached Singapore in follboats. The chase back down through the islands lasted two months with the final boat captured only 400 miles from Australia. All his men had been killed or captured during the raid. Those who were caught were imprisoned in Changi and beheaded five weeks before Japan surrendered.

Unknown to Ivan Lyon, his attractive wife and his son were in a prison camp near Palembang, possibly some 100 miles from where he was killed. Their ship had been intercepted by an armed German raider who took the crew and passengers prisoners to be handed over later to the Japanese.

Not selected for the second raid on Singapore, Captain Reynolds was recruited by the Australian and American special services. He was last heard of as a prisoner in Borneo where he disappeared. Corporal Morris remained with SOE until the end of the war and retired from the RAMC in 1965.

The *Mary Rose* went south and the 'elderly naval officer in charge' refused to land the DALCO officers in Sumatra, remembered Frank Brewer. As the launch approached the Banka Strait she was intercepted by a Japanese vessel. After some debate on whether to surrender, they agreed to do so and the only white flag they could find was someone's underpants which was hoisted from the mast.

After they went ashore they were searched. Frank Brewer had lost all his kit during the fighting so Mr Bowden, the Australian Government representative gave him a small pack he had spare. When this was opened the Japanese found a rifle butt and cleaning rags in it. When they began to angrily question Brewer, Bowden intervened and tried to explain both who he was and also how Frank Brewer came to have the pack.

This annoyed the Japanese even more and they took Bowden away. He was made to dig his own grave before they bayoneted him to death. Survivors from the *Vyner Brooke* who managed to reach Banka shared the same death.

The group of escapers, including sailors from the *Jarak*, who remained behind at Dabo, were eventually given a native boat by a Chinese schoolmaster. They followed Reynolds' course up through the Malacca Straits, avoiding the Japanese transport ferrying men into Medan. They too reached India but nothing is known of the fate of a second group, all Australians, who proposed to capture a Japanese patrol launch and sail it to Australia.

Doris Lim, who survived the sinking of the *Roosenboom* and the *Kung Wo*, was murdered in a village outside Padang in 1944. Another Chinese girl, a nurse from the temporary hospital in Outram Road who was on the *Kuala*, was Janet Lim (no relation to Doris Lim). She reached Padang and she was interned at the convent. After the war she became a matron in a Singapore Hospital.

Patsy Li, the six-year-old girl whose mother thrust her on to wreckage when the ship was bombed and sank near Pom Pom, was found six months later in Guadalcanal, wandering around the battle zone by American Marines. She was taken care of by the RC Army Chaplain and sent to a convent school on a nearby French island. With the help of the Chaplain and the nuns she went to America to be educated and was reunited with her mother after the war. As Guadalcanal is in the Solomons Group in the Pacific it remains a mystery how she reached there. The obvious theory is that a group of escapers or survivors rescued her and eventually reached the island where they may have been killed by the Japanese.

The NCO from 101 Special Training School, Gabby Gavin, and his party were captured still paddling through the islands by the Japanese. The drunken Argyll roaming around the quayside when the nurses were waiting to be ferried out to their escape ships, was captured and survived the Death Railway. He still had a drink problem in 1968 and was on social security. The 200 civilian nurses who refused to run the gauntlet at the dockside were interned. This included four Auxiliaries, three of whom were wives of senior army officers.

In those final two weeks before the surrender an estimated ten thousand servicemen, mainly officers and specialists – from a total of some 87,000 on the island were evacuated before 10th February. A further 3,000 officers and specialists, were evacuated on the night of the 13th. A large number were drowned, many were captured and some managed to reach Warren's escape route. These were joined by some three thousand escapers and deserters.

An estimated 7,000 civilians and servicemen used the route across Sumatra organised by Warren's three man team, the makeshift cadre of volunteers and the Dutch Controlleours. One can only guess at what might have been had GHQ and the Royal Navy prepared a plan which was supported with sufficient resources.

Colonel Coates survived the war. He went with a party to Rangoon then up-country to build the Burma end of the Death Railway. He became a legend amongst the prisoners, frequently exhorting them that the way home was through the bottom of their mess tin.

The Japanese separated the RN personnel and transferred them to Changi. Alexander and Warren went with this group. Both suffered badly at the hands of the Japanese guards. Warren was one of the first senior officers to go up country to build 'the railway'. Mainly because Japanese secret police were looking for him as head of the stay-behind parties and guerrillas, he decided the best place to hide was 'up country.' Colonel Warren tried to pass off his imprisonment lightly by saying there were bad times and some good times. In spite of the risk of drawing attention to himself he used a local Thai river trader to make contact for him with a lady friend in the French Embassy in Bangkok. While the Japanese searched for him, he smuggled drugs and medicines to prison camp hospitals on the river, all paid for and supplied by the attractive wife of someone working in their Embassy in Bangkok, and brought up river by traders.

When he heard the war was over, picked up on secret radios hidden in the camp, he marched up to the Japanese Commandant and demand transport. In this he and fellow officers, dressed in peaked hats and 'Jap Happies' (loinclothes) drove to Bangkok, marched into the Japanese Headquarters and demanded access to a wireless transmitter, clothes and money. Having obtained all three they then made contact with British HQ in Ceylon. When Whitehall learnt he had survived, they wrote asking for receipts and signatures for the money borrowed from the Dutch in Padang. He had used this to pay the escapers.

He met some of his men as he travelled home and commented that Broome and Davis, both now lieutenant-colonels like himself, had done an excellent job in Malaya. In Colombo he was surprised to find himself out-ranked by Jock Campbell, a colonel and OBE.

Within 24 hours of arriving home he found his marriage had broken up. Having nowhere else to go, he telephoned a friend who was Commanding Officer of a nearby Commando Unit, and stayed at the camp.

*

Dillon's Escape

Colonel Warren recalled that shortly after he arrived at Changi POW camp he saw Dillon's party arrive. From them he learnt that the journey to Fort de Kock had been uneventful but beyond the town they had met large numbers of retreating Dutch and Javanese native troops resting by the roadside. The Dutch were reluctant to let them through but after much persuasion they drove on until they met a road block at a bridge, manned by Dutch troops. Again they needed to persuade the military to let them across. Evidently the Japanese were expected at any moment and hardly had they crossed the bridge than the cars were shaken by a blast. Behind them the bridge disappeared in a growing cloud of dust and debris.

Dillon decided to get off the main road on the first suitable track to the left. In less than a mile they found a track which twisted and turned up into the hills. Again fate was on their side. Minutes after they took the side road they saw a tank led Japanese convoy of lorries racing along the road towards the Dutch lines.

In the afternoon they reached a large coastal village where the

Controlleour had his office. He was pleased to see them and produced a crate of beer to wash the dust of their travels away. He listened with interest to their news of Fort de Kock and the Japanese advance. Finally he went to his desk and wrote a letter to his assistant at Sasak for Dillon to give him.

It was late when they reached the village, built close to the mouth of a river. The two native boats were still there, at anchor in the river. They finally bought one, the *Setia Berganti*, for two thousand guilders. The Malays seemed delighted with their bargain and Ernest Gordon believed, from their smiles, the escapers didn't get the best of the bargain.

They had brought with them for supplies a ham, a case of milk, a case of fish and a case of beer, the last item bought from the District Controlleour. Seeing an opportunity to trade, the locals opened an instant market alongside the river. Baskets of limes appeared for sale to be joined by dried fish, yams and sweet potatoes, pineapples, eggs and chickens, all spread out on the ground for the escapers to choose from.

One member of the party discovered and bought six, fifty-five gallon oil drums for the water supply. Eventually these with two full sacks of rice, coconuts and green fruit were hauled aboard and stowed away.

They sailed the following day. She wasn't in such good condition as they first thought and her sails and running gear were rotten. Dillon did take the precaution of buying a bolt of sail cloth, twine, needles and rope before she finally sailed. This was to prove a wise move.

Her crew took her out across the bar and showed the escapers how she worked, then left them. They left Sumatra behind doing about seven knots with the wind behind them. All went well until dawn when a change of wind split the sail to tatters. Dillon's first thought that they may have to abandon the voyage but he then decided to put into Pulau Pini, one of the long islands lying about 100 miles west of Sumatra. He hoped to make repairs there and if possible buy a new sail. Although the mainsail had gone they still had the jib, stay and missen.

With this they reached Pulau Ayer, another small island in that group. A Roman Catholic missionary there told them that survivors from the SS *Chilka*, the torpedoed British India Liner, had reached this spot before sailing on to Nais, a larger island in the group. While ashore the local Dutch Controlleour sought their help. A riot had broken out on the island between two tribes. It had all started because one young lad of the neighbouring tribe made some remark about a girl from the other tribe, who then set out to settle matters with their neighbours. There were many dead and more with terrible injuries. Would they join him in a show of force, the Controlleour asked.

After talking the problem over with his fellow officers Dillon led them ashore armed with pistols. They found a very relieved Controlleour waiting for them on the beach and, led by him, they strode towards the scene of the skirmish. On they way they passed a long walled native hut which Crawley found to be full of wounded, groaning and crying with no one to give them any attention. When he enquired as to the number they were about to quell the Dutchman told him about 600. The path they were following began to open out into a large clearing bordered by two rows of Malays, armed with vicious looking parangs (native knives) glaring at each other. Without any hesitation the Dutchman led them between both columns. At this point Dillon wondered what on earth they had let themselves in for but felt that they had to give the Dutchman every support in his thankless task. To Gordon's surprise and relief both sides began to melt away in two's and three's until eventually they were alone on the battlefield. Dillon later negotiated a peaceful solution with the elders of both tribes and the party lost no time in getting away, leaving the Controlleour the thankless task of welcoming the Japanese.

A few days later all the shore party went down with a mysterious fever. Then on 31st March Lieutenant Hooper's hand became poisoned from a splinter and became swollen and painful. On April Fool's day, they were spotted by a Japanese patrol plane which circled the prahau several times then flew away. When the same thing happened the following day it was obvious to Dillon that their position was being reported. He told Warren later that he estimated that they were some three hundred miles into the 1300 mile journey when three large Japanese tankers, which had just completed refuelling the fleet, emerged from a thick rain squall.

Everyone fled below to hide leaving the steersman, a Sapper, on deck in a wide conical hat and long shirt, hoping that he could pass off as a native at that distance. The ships, about a mile away passed across the beam and sailed on. Down below everyone began to sigh with relief as he called out the enemy's course. Suddenly there was a distant bang and a round splashed just ahead of them. One of the tankers had stopped and there was nothing else he could do, Dillon told Warren, but to bring the boat up in the wind and eventually bring her alongside the Jap ship.

Above them the tanker's rail was crowded with enemy sailors looking down at them. A rope ladder was dropped down the side for them to climb and a Japanese naval officer on deck ordered them all to board his vessel.

They left their vessel with its missen sail still set, gently rising and falling in the swell. On board in the galley, breakfast was left half-cooked and, amongst the sand brought aboard as ballast, their coconuts were sprouting. Her only occupant on board, he recounted, 'was a lizard which had made a home directly over Hooper's sleeping place on the sand. The lizard had regularly woken him up by dropping his morning packet on him.'

The irony of the last comment wasn't lost on Warren. He remarked that the lizard was just one in a long line from Churchill, his Chiefs of Staff and the European businessmen, who by their misguided decisions copied the lizard. Initially the resident Europeans considered the soldiers to be socially inferior and looked down on the young soldiers sent to defend them. Eventually the army of some 85,000 was abandoned in Singapore, as some 2,000 escapers were in Padang. In its short life an estimated 7,000 survivors and escapers used the escape route. Almost one fifth of the European troops in Singapore. If GHQ had provided a coordinated escape plan and rotated a flotilla of small boats to Sumatra, far more could have been saved.

On St Patrick's Day 1942 the escapers trapped in Padang, under the command of Colonel Warren, faced three and a half years of starvation, fever, sadistic guards, torture and brutal treatment. Thousands died. Unlike prisoners of war in Europe these men disappeared from sight. No Swiss visitors, only a rare Red Cross parcel or, even more rare, a letter from home.

Their families suffered agonies for three and a half years not knowing whether they were dead or alive. Next of kin died, children were born and some wives found others to be with. Instead of taking the advice of his senior officers on the spot Winston Churchill influenced the battle from Whitehall. The loss of the army in Singapore was a disaster.

Reporting the debate on Singapore in the House of Commons Hansard devoted three columns to the successful escape of the *Scharnhorst* and the *Gneisenau* from Brest up the English Channel.

Singapore, which was the second item in Churchill's speech that day, merited only one column.

In the battle for Malaya and Singapore 130,000 British and Empire troops were captured and 8,000 killed or wounded. Ten thousand more died in captivity. Australia's share of the losses was 15,395 captured, 1,789 killed and 1,306 wounded. A heavy price to pay for an empty naval base.

For Churchill, the Japanese thrust south brought America into the war on the side of the British.

Singapore was a sideshow in the Japanese thrust towards the American oilfields in Dutch Sumatra. For successive British Governments it was an outpost too far.

The Known Fate of the Little Ships

Ampang, HMS: 231 ton. Sailed on the night of 11th/12th but was so badly damaged by bombs as she left harbour that she was scuttled on 14th February.

Andrew: An Auxiliary Patrol launch which sailed on the 10th with Asiatic Petroleum Company (APC) staff on board from Pulau Sambu. She was sighted on the 13th bound for Rengat.

Anking: The 3,472 ton vessel was built in 1925 and later used as a baseship in Singapore. When she reached Tandjong Priok (Batavia) she became a depot ship which provided accommodation for the RN drafts from Singapore. She was later sunk escaping from Java with some 400 RN personnel on board. See report in appendix II.

Appleleaf: This 12,370 ton RFA oiler escaped from Singapore. No details known.

Aquarius: The 6094-ton liner is believed to have been sunk following a heavy air attack in the Durian Straits. Of the 1,000 passengers on board, mainly women and children, three survivors may have been picked up by *ML310*.

Auby: 636 tons, was built in Genoa in 1908. Prior to the 1914/18 war she operated a service from Paris to London. Later she was bought by the Sarawak Steamship Company and crewed by Sarawak Malays. She formed part of the evacuation fleet from Singapore and reached Tandjong Priok, Batavia, where she was abandoned both from lack of fuel and in need of repairs.

Bagan: A 244 ton, coal burning ferry from Panang, left Singapore on 11th with 100 Harbour Board staff as passengers. She was later sunk and some survivors were rescued by the *Tenggaroh*. There is another report, however, that she reached Palembang and was scuttled in the Moesi River on the 16th to avoid capture by the Japanese coming up-river.

Ban Hong Liong: A 1,671 ton auxiliary patrol launch which escaped with servicemen and civilians on board and is believed to have reached Java.

Barline: This was probably the *Barlane* built in 1938. In reports from prisoners of war she is known to have escaped from the harbour but nothing further is known of her fate.

Barricade: Ex-*Ebgate*, built in 1938 as a 385 ton, small, coal fired boom defence vessel which worked the boom at Singapore. She had a complement of 15. One of her crew, CPO A.R. Taylor, remembered that they received orders to 'coal ship, provision and steam at all speed to Batavia.' She sailed in company with two other boom defence vessels, HMS *Barrier* and HMS *Fastnet*. *Barricade* and *Barrier* escaped but *Fastnet* was abandoned at Tandjong Priok.

Barrier: 385 ton coal fired boom defence vessel. See *Barricade*.

Blumut: Sailed on 13th with 29 passengers and captured at Muntok by surface vessels on the 17th.

Brunei: A Straits Steamship Company (SS Co) vessel which traded, prewar, to Labuan. During the battle for Singapore she was used as a tender to ferry evacuees from Clifford Pier to ships waiting in the Roads. She was probably the only SS Co vessel left in harbour on Saturday the 14th when the captain, Matt Bin Ali, collapsed from exhaustion. His place was taken by Captain Chamberlain. She was eventually scuttled to avoid being seized by the Japanese.

Bulan: Reached Tandjong Priok, Batavia, after leaving Singapore on the 10/11th.

Camiron: Described as a handsome 10 ton yacht built to its owners specifications. She was equipped with a five horse power auxiliary petrol engine with a tiny cabin aft and another larger one forward. Each with two berths. She was berthed at the Yacht Club where someone stole her compass and charts. On Wednesday the 11th, she was commandeered by the RAF who provided a crew and passengers, mainly RAF officers. She took part in the evacuation of small boats that day and despite problems with her petrol feed she reached an island near St John's Lighthouse where she was taken in tow by *Rompin*, a seaplane tender. When the flotilla reached Muntok, in the Banka Straits, the *Rompin*'s engines failed and she continued the journey with a second yacht, the *White Swan*. In the Banka Strait they rescued the crew of a Wellington bomber marooned on the islands. See entry for *White Swan* and *Rompin*.

C14: A yacht which sailed from Singapore crowded with passengers. She was seen by the *Mary Rose* but her fate is unknown.

C450: Harbour craft. Fate unknown.

C451: Harbour craft. Fate unknown.

Cecelia or *Corelia*: Described as a motor launch but may have been a yacht. She sailed on the 15th with 44 selected passengers on board, including Brigadier Paris, Major McDonald and a number of Argylls. She was sighted at 10.30 on the 16th by the *Hong Fatt*. Her passengers passed through Rengat and moved on to Padang. Most of her passengers embarked on the ill-fated *Roosenboom* and were drowned.

Changi: She sailed on 14th from Pulau Brani for Sumatra. On board were Royal Engineers and Royal Army Service Corps personnel who had carried out demolition work amongst the fuel tanks on the island. She sailed in company with five motor launches, the *Hastings Anderson, Rosemary, Swift* and *Swallow*. The fifth unknown launch which might have been the *Jane*, ran aground on Pulau Batam, near the western entrance to Singapore and all on board her were eventually taken prisoner. Apart from that wreck the others are believed to have reached Rengat in Sumatra.

Changteh: A 244 ton Straits Steamship Company tug converted by the RN to an auxiliary minesweeper. She sailed on Sunday the 7th with 70 passengers on board with three other company vessels, *Rahman, Klias* and *Hua Tong*. She was last seen by HMS *Dragonfly* in the Durian Straits, covered in smoke and ablaze after being heavily attacked by enemy aircraft. She finally sank on the 14th and about 30 survivors reached the Warren's escape route.

Chuting: A 207 ton tug built in 1921. Fate unknown.

Circe: A 778 ton trader built in 1912 at Taikoo. She was originally a Blue Funnel vessel. She and her sister ship *Medusa* were bought by the Straits Steamship Company for £15,000 in 1927. She traded around Borneo until she was taken over by the Royal Navy at the outbreak of war, in 1939, and converted to a trader/minesweeper. Her skipper, Captain A. Brown was commissioned in the Royal Navy Reserve as lieutenant.

Shortly after the causeway was blown Brown was ordered to bunker with coal and be ready to sail. He found the coal wharfs in a mess with coal and cargo intermixed. There were no dockers but his loyal Asian crew volunteered to haul the coal aboard. This continued throughout the night in rain and blustering winds. Occasionally when the wind changed they were engulfed in thick oily smoke from the burning fuel tanks.

Finally when she was fully loaded and trimmed HMS *Laburnum* informed him that he should dismiss his local crew and replace them with sailors from the *Prince of Wales* and *Repulse*. Despite his protestations that he didn't have either food or accommodation for them he was also ordered to embark military personnel including the Pay Corps clerks and pay records. She sailed on 2nd February and the last he saw of his crew they were huddled against a godown for shelter against the rain, covered in coal, soaking wet and hungry.

She left harbour at 4 am in company with her sister ship *Medusa*, *No 51* a motor minesweeper and HMAS *Maryborough* with orders to sweep the sea route from Berhala Island to Banka. When this was completed she continued her journey to Tandjong Priok. After Captain Brown objected to receiving contradictory orders from the RN shipping officer in Batavia, he was dismissed from his command by the RN STO which left him free to make his own escape to Australia. Later the company gave him the *Kepong* which he commanded throughout the war in almost every war zone.

Daisy: This 110 ton diesel-powered water boat, probably used to ferry passengers to the waiting evacuation ships, left Singapore on the 13th. She was described as being a barge with a tiny bridge aft which broke up her low profile. Under the command of Sergeant Walmsley, and lacking compass and charts, she eventually reached the Djambi River. On the voyage through the Berhala Strait they sighted the *Yin Ping*.

At the mouth of the river he found a white police patrol boat with General Bennett and his party on board. This group followed the barge up river to Djambi then on to Muar Atebo. Here the Dutch provided transport for the escapers to reach Sawahlunto and join the SOE escape route to Padang.

Darvil: Under the command of Captain W. Lutkin. She was taken over by the Royal Navy in 1939. When the Japanese invaded Malaya she carried gunners to bomb-blasted Rangoon. Later she embarked others for Palembang. In late January she formed part of the convoy of little ships sent up the coast to rescue British and Australian troops trapped behind enemy lines at Batu Pahat. Hardly had these been disembarked in Singapore, than she set off for Sultan Sands to rescue survivors from the old *Empress of Asia*, on fire and sinking after a heavy air attack. A week later she took on board men of the 2/3 Australian Reserve Motor Transport Company. Like other local vessels the RN had ordered the captain to dismiss his native crew. These were replaced by volunteers from amongst Australian Motor Company. She sailed on the 9th in company with SS *Kinta*.

Derrymore: A 4799 ton freighter loaded with ammunition being backloaded to Java. She cleared Singapore at about 7 am on 12th. At Banka she found the Straits packed with shipping of all sizes evacuating Palembang because of the threat of the Japanese invasion fleet. She joined four tankers escorted by HM Ships *Stronghold* and *Jupiter* but some fifty miles north of Batavia she was torpedoed and sunk.

Dowgate: A 290 ton boom defence vessel built in 1935 at the Hong Kong and Whampoa yards. In the evacuation she was used as a harbour boat and was scuttled to avoid her being seized following the surrender.

Dragonfly, HMS: This 585 ton paddleboat was designed and built for the Yangtse River Flotilla. The gunboat, described as looking like a Mississippi river boat, was 197 feet long and 33 feet wide and armed with 2 × 4 inch guns and a 3.7 howitzer. A flat-bottomed boat, with only a 5ft draught and all her decks above water.

Following the evacuation of Shanghai she was based briefly in Hong Kong but escaped when the Japanese invaded. Based in Singapore she took part in the rescue of troops from behind enemy lines in Johore. She returned to harbour unscathed but received a direct hit while tied-up alongside the HMS *Laburnum*, the RNVR depot ship.

On the 13th/14th, she cast off at 3.10 am and joined the evacuation fleet with 77 passengers aboard. She and her sister ship HMS *Grasshopper* escorted a slow convoy made up of two paddleboats and a tug. Early the following morning the convoy was sighted by an enemy plane which launched an attack on the *Grasshopper* causing bomb damage and casualties. Later, when the convoy was in the Berhala Straits, it was attacked again by three formations of bombers. This time the *Dragonfly* received three direct hits and some eleven near misses which caused her to capsize and sink in three minutes.

There were some 45 survivors who later joined up with others from the *Grasshopper* and made their way to Dabo and to Warren's escape route.

Durban, HMS: A cruiser which raced into Singapore on the 11th to rescue airmen and sailors. With her were HM ships *Kedah, Stronghold* and *Jupiter*. The *Durban* embarked 57, the *Stronghold* took 150 and the *Jupiter* a further 150. When they attempted to leave under cover of darkness they found many ships at anchor around the entrance to the minefield because the marker buoy was missing. At dawn the *Kedah* led the way along the swept channel leaving the *Durban* to cover the rear and give fire cover should the ships be attacked. Later the larger, faster vessels were formed into a convoy and, escorted by the *Durban* and destroyers, raced for Java.

Dymas: Captured in the Banka Strait on the 17th with 21 passengers.

Ebond: Scuttled to avoid capture.

Edang: Sailed on the 11/12th with eleven other vessels which formed the second, slower, part of the evacuation fleet which left that morning. Once clear of the harbour each ship made its independent way to Batavia via the Banka Strait.

Elizabeth: Although described as a tug she may have been a sizeable armoured motor launch. She left Singapore on the night of 13th/14th with a crew and 12 passengers. These included Lieutenant R.C. Beckwith RN, a survivor from the *Prince of Wales*, who was in command, three Royal Marines, six RAF servicemen and 2 soldiers.

She was intercepted on the 16th close to Banka Straits by enemy surface vessels and order alongside a Japanese destroyer. Beckwith was taken aboard for questioning. He was then told that his vessel was to be set adrift, with his crew and passengers, and sunk by gunfire but he could remain on board and become a prisoner of war. He refused this offer and was allowed to rejoin his launch. As the destroyer steamed away she opened fire and blew the launch out of the water. Only two survived including a seaman Stoker Farrow. Lieutenant Beckwith's body was never recovered.

Empire Star: A 10,800 ton Blue Star liner under the command of Captain Selwyn Capon, sailed on the 11th with some 2,000 passengers, including service families and special officers and technicians. She was also boarded by deserters who shot and murdered the Captain of the Dockyard, Captain T.K.W. Atkinson RN, who tried to stop them.

Excise: A motor launch which sailed from Singapore with seven passengers including one civilian and four army personnel as passengers. Captured off Muntok, Banka Island on 17th.

Eureka: She left on the 13th but was accidentally beached in the Durian Straits on the 14th.

Fanling: May have been named after a district in the Hong Kong New Territories, ten miles from the Chinese border. She was a motor launch which sailed on the 13th with 47 passengers. Both she and the *Elizabeth* were in sight of each other on 16th when they were intercepted by surface vessels as they approached the Banka Straits. The enemy vessels opened fire and sank her leaving only four known survivors, Lt-Colonel A.H. Long, two Rajputs, Seamen Andrews and Basham and Stoker D. Kerr. They were rescued by a junk, also escaping from Singapore, under the command of Lt-Colonel Scott, RAOC. This boat was also fired on by a second junk manned by Japanese who swept the boat with automatic fire. Everyone abandoned ship and leapt overboard and attempted to swim to the nearby island in the strong currents which swept through the Straits. The number of survivors is not known.

Fastnet: A Royal Navy boom defence vessel which operated the boom at Singapore. She left on or about 14th February for Batavia in company with HMS *Barrier* and *Barricade* and was later abandoned at Tandjong Priok.

Florence Nightingale: A RAMC launch, also referred to as a Red Cross launch, not only ferried casualties from Singkep to Rengat but also carried out search and rescue mission amongst the islands seeking marooned survivors. She went aground and lost her propeller at the mouth of the Indragiri River.

Fuh Wo: Owned by the China Navigation Shipping Company this 953 ton vessel was built in 1922. She was the senior ship in the company fleet. In 1940 she was taken over by the RN and converted to an Auxiliary Patrol vessel.

She sailed on the 13th/14th with two other company ships, the *Li Wo* and the *Ping Wo*, with some 46 passengers on board. As her charts had been stolen her skipper directed the *Li Wo* to lead the way through the minefield. A report by prisoner of war claimed that she reached Banka Strait where she was beached but in fact she reached Batavia and transferred to the Sunda Strait Patrol.

Gemas: An auxiliary minesweeper, sunk south of Java on 2nd March.

Giang Bee: This ancient 1,646 ton Chinese-owned coaster was armed with a 4-inch gun and depth charges. She was built in 1908 with accommodation for 25 passengers including her cargo. Like most local ships she too was taken over by the RN at the outbreak of war and converted to an Auxiliary Patrol vessel.

On 11th February she embarked Malayan Broadcasting employees being evacuated to Java but her skipper refused to take female members of the staff. He also limited the number of passengers to 25 claiming he was restricted to that by the Board of Trade regulations. While his disappointed would-be passengers searched for other escape ships to take them, the ship sailed and was well out into the Roads when she received a signal from the RN STO recalling her. Despite his protests the captain was ordered to take on board a further 200 passengers. Amongst these were Robert Scott, Head of Information at Cathay Buildings, his Chinese cook who now doubled as the ship's cook and an MBC engineer who became the wireless operator.

Two days later she was stopped by enemy destroyers. Unable to understand their signals the captain replied that she was unarmed. While awaiting their reply all the women and children lined the ship's rail to prove she was a merchantman carrying civilian passengers. All the while the RN white ensign flew from her mast. The enemy destroyers stood off about a mile from the vessel occasionally signalling incomprehensible messages. Finally the captain ordered everyone into the lifeboats but at least a hundred were left behind by the overcrowded lifeboats. As the ship was abandoned one lifeboat pulled towards one of the destroyers which waited until it was almost alongside and moved away.

Suddenly all the ships opened fire on the abandoned vessel setting her on fire from stem to stern with the final salvo crashing through her plates. She began to list and then slid beneath the waves in a quick rush, leaving 200 dead.

There were 70 survivors including 42 in a lifeboat under the command of Lt E. Morton RN. These landed in a small bay on the Sumatran coast. Those on board included two Royal Marines, Hayes and Williams, Miss Hicks a 38-year-old Australian from the YMCA, a 51-year-old New Zealand schoolteacher, Sona Grick an Eurasian and an Eurasian hairdresser from the Capitol cinema. Shortly after the lifeboat was beached they were seen by the *Tapah*, a Straits Steamship Co., which had been hugging the Sumatran coast. Although overcrowded, she took off 28 survivors leaving 15 to sail the lifeboat to Java which they reached on 8th March only to find it in enemy hands.

Gorgan: The *Gorgan* was one of three Blue Funnel ships in Singapore. Her sister ship, the *Phrontis*, had sailed the previous day and another company ship, SS *Talthybius* was on fire tied up alongside the quay. The *Gorgan* left on the 11th with 358 passengers, half her cargo still unloaded and with mail sacks brought on board by Sergeant Isaacs SSVF. He was offered the post of ship's clerk – and the opportunity to escape – but he declined and rejoined his regiment.

Like the other vessels that night her departure was delayed because of the misplaced marker buoy. Once through the swept channel she joined the fast larger vessels, escorted by the *Durban* and *Kedah*, and raced for the Banka Straits being continually attacked by enemy aircraft. When she reached Java all her military personnel were disembarked but the women and children were ordered to remain on board for passage to Australia.

Grasshopper, HMS: This 585 ton Yangtse riverboat was a flat-bottomed paddleboat built in 1939 specially for Yangtse Flotilla. She had an overall length of 197 feet and carried a complement of 74 men. She left Singapore on the 14th with nine Japanese prisoners of war on board, Royal Marines and civilians. Amongst the latter were three Dutch women, two in a very advanced state of pregnancy and the other blind.

She and the *Dragonfly* escorted two other paddle boats and a small tug, all crowded with escapers. This convoy was found by a lone bomber at about nine o'clock the following morning entering the Berhala Straits. Two hours later as they approached Pulau Posic they were again attacked, this time by 27 enemy aircraft. The *Dragonfly* sank almost immediately. A second wave sank the two overcrowded paddle boats; the tug received a direct hit and disappeared and the *Grasshopper*, pursued by the remaining aircraft, ran for the island where the skipper intended to beach her but she was sunk some 600 yards from the beach.

Hastings Anderson: A motor launch which left Pulau Brani at 200 hrs on 14th with REs and RASC personnel who had destroyed the fuel and supply dumps on that island.

Heather: a 110 ton diesel powered waterboat described as a barge with a tiny bridge aft to break up the barge-like line. She escaped on the 14th loaded with military personnel and under the command of Lieutenant Canty assisted by his sergeant. Without the aid of charts or compass he navigated her some 200 miles to the Djambi River. They moved up stream until they reached the Muar Atebo. Here the Dutch Controlleour provided transport to take his passenger north to Sawahlunto where they joined Warren's escape route to Padang. Canty and his sergeant remained behind tinkering with the engine probably intending to go further up river. Soon her sister ship arrived, the *Daisy* escorted by a white police patrol boat with soldiers on board.

After an initial alarm that the latter contained Japanese she tied up at the quay to disembark a group of officers, including General Bennett. He was impatient to move on and asked the Dutch Controlleour to arrange for transport to get him to Padang. Meanwhile the Controlleour had other worries. He had information that many hundreds of survivors were trapped on Pom Pom island in the Rhio Group and wanted volunteers from the escapers to carry out a rescue mission.

After some discussion amongst themselves Canty and his crew volunteered to go back down river, leaving the others to escape to Padang. The Dutch loaded the barge with blankets, bandages, medical supplies and fitted cots. From directions provided by the Controlleour, Canty eventually reached the island where he found the Head of Singapore's Public

Works Department, Nunn, in charge. The island was crowded with survivors, including many casualties. Canty took all the casualties and a further 100 survivors including David Miller, Director of the Chartered Bank and Nunn and his wife.

On their return trip they saw the last vessel to leave Dabo captured by a Japanese destroyer. She had on board all the medical staff, shipwrecked survivors themselves, and the remaining casualties. Preoccupied with their victim the Japanese failed to see the barge, low in the water, sneak by. She reached Djambi on 26th February and found the Dutch had vehicles ready to continue their escape. Those fit enough to travel reached Padang on the 28th, minutes before the Dutch KLM *Roosenboom* was due to sail.

Herald: A harbour boat scuttled to avoid capture.

Hiep Hien: A 130 ton native junk anchored in the Outer Roads and stolen by escapers. On her voyage across to Sumatra she rescued survivors in the water and embarked about 100 more from Lyon's camp on Pulau Moro. She was directed to Priggi Raja and then to Tambilahan where she embarked more passengers for Rengat.

Hong Chuan: A steam engined trading launch used by SOE to stock secret supply dumps to assist would be escapers. On 2nd February she stocked Pulau Moro and Priggi Raja at the mouth of the Indagiri River. On the 11th, back in Telok Ayer Basin she was loaded with more supplies by Lieutenant Boris Hembry LDV, who had just returned from a mission behind enemy lines in north Malaya. With Sergeant Lamb as coxswain they were joined by the head of SOE in Singapore, Basil Goodfellow and Captain F.L. (Careful) Morgan and two RNVR officers, one being a Commander Pretty. After leaving Singapore they spent the next few days stocking a dump on Pulo Salu, ten miles south west of Singapore and two more en route to Djambi. The headmen of the fishing communities on the islands were asked to help guide escapers to these dumps. The SOE group reached Djambi about 17th and travelled on to Padang.

Hong Fatt: She was captured at Muntok on the 17th with 53 passengers on board, including 20 British officers and 33 Australians. One escaper died and was buried at sea – Sergeant West, a Gunner, AIF.

Hong Kheng: 6,167 tons. Sailed on the night of the 11th/12th.

Hong Kwang: This vessel left Singapore on the 13th and reached Java where she was abandoned on 9th March.

Hua Tong: This 208 ton vessel had been owned by a small Muar based shipping company which collapsed during the shipping slump in the 1920s. She was built in 1927 and sold nearly new. Ten years later she was taken over by the Royal Navy and converted to an Auxiliary mine-sweeper. On Wednesday night the 11th she was ordered to embark passengers for Batavia. She eventually reached Palembang where she was sunk in the Moesi River by enemy bombers in a prelude to a two-pronged parachute landing and seaborne attack on the town. Amongst the crew were its Chief Engineer Mr D.R. Horn, Gunnery Officer Lieutenant J.C. Tongue and her commander, Lieutenant Brown.

Hung Jao: A HMM launch which sailed on the 13th. When she reached Dabo her crew agreed to ferry some of the shipwrecked survivors there, to Rengat. From there they volunteered to stay behind and join the search and rescue operation being carried out jointly by the SOE and the Dutch. It is believed that they rescued some hundred stranded survivors before the engines failed with 17 officers on board. She was scuttled in the Indragiri River and her passengers and crew made their way to Padang.

Imperial Airways tender: This left on the evening of the 15th following the news of the surrender, carrying eleven passengers. These were four young officers from the Volunteers, F. Gibson, R.F.W. Leonard, D. Richards and Noone together with seven civilian staff from Masefields/Straits Steamship Company staff: F.L. Lane, W.A. Kempster, W.M. Oak-Rind, A.T. Wedgewood, F.E.E. Hindley, E.D. Rushworth and P.A. Holt.

As the tender crossed the harbour it ran aground and was held fast on a reef. When everyone climbed overboard to lighten the load she drifted free, causing a panic as they scrambled to hold her and climb back on board. As the crowded boat chugged through the night past St John's Lighthouse they discussed where the next port of call should be. The civilians, whose launch it was, were intent on reaching Palembang but the officers opted for Rengat. As they couldn't resolve the situation, the officers agreed to be put ashore on a suitable island. They eventually made their way to Priggi Raja and escaped through Padang. The civilians sailed south and were captured off Banka Island.

Ipoh: The 1,279 ton SS built in 1908 was the oldest Straits Shipping Company vessel still afloat when the Japanese besieged Singapore. On 7th February she was badly damaged in an air-raid when two near misses burst alongside and punched more than forty holes above the water line. Some were as big as a man's fist and were all patched up with bolts, washers, and tarred paper.

On the 11th her skipper, F.W. Jennings, was told to bunker and prepare to embark 300 RAF personnel for Java. All his Malay and Chinese crew had been dismissed on RN orders leaving him with only the ship's engineer. HMS *Laburnum* found him Australians from the 3rd Australian Motor Company to crew and act as stokers. He was also joined by the company chairman, Mr. W.W. Jenkins, and two senior members of staff, Mr J. Crighton and Mr. F.S. Gibson.

When crowds of civilian evacuees on the quay saw her about to sail they rushed the gangway and clambered aboard. When the RAF eventually arrived the captain pleaded with civilians to leave but his pleas were ignored. A compromise was finally reached and the officer commanding the RAF detachment agreed to allow his men to travel in the hold providing they could come on deck for air and exercise.

Later that afternoon when the old steamship began to belch smoke and prepare to leave, no one could be found to go ashore and release the hawsers. At that moment three formations of enemy aircraft appeared and began to pattern bomb the waterfront. A member of staff from the shipping office, who had arrived to see his company chairman off, realised the problem and ran along the quayside pulling off the ropes and casting them into the sea. As the last one was flung over the side the bombers flew overhead and he leapt into a nearby trench as the bombs exploded in a line amongst the buildings. Then more explosions threw up curtains of sea water as bombs rained down. Finally when the sound of the planes began to recede he peered over the rim of the trench and the last he saw of the *Ipoh* was her stern, almost covered with spray, as she steamed belching thick black smoke, towards the outer harbour. What he couldn't see was the gaping hole in her side caused by a near miss which exploded only twenty feet from her. On board were 300 RAF servicemen and 200 women and children.

Jalavihar: This 5,330 ton steamship sailed on 11th February. After being heavily attacked by enemy bombers in the Durian Straits, she reached Tandjong Priok, Batavia and eventually Colombo.

Jalakrishna: Sailed at 5 pm on 11th February without passengers. She was attacked by enemy aircraft at the southern end of the Banka strait and was badly damaged, with a hole in her port bow. She reached Colombo via Tandjong Priok.

Jalibahar: Sailed at 5 pm on 11th February.

Jalratna: A 3,942 ton steamship, she sailed on the night of 11/12th February. She sailed from Java on 19th February for Tjilatjap.

Jane: A launch which sailed from Pulau Brani at 2 pm on the 14th with REs and RASC personnel. By 1200 hrs she was aground on Pulau Batam.

Jarak: The *Jarak*, a 209 ton Straits Steamship Company vessel, was built in 1927 and taken over by the RN in 1939 for minesweeping duties. She had a crew of about 40 under the command of Lieutenant E.A. Hooper, former Chief Officer on the *Kedah* and one time harbourmaster at Singapore. For the first twelve months she carried out daily sweeps for mines, returning to harbour each evening. Following the outbreak of war in December 1941 the crew noticed the changing scene each time they docked in Singapore. Towards the end the smell of the fires and clouds of smoke was apparent some fifty miles away.

As the war developed the period away grew longer. On one occasion on their way home they discovered another company ship, the *Tapah*, in the middle of wreckage, trying to rescue survivors from the SS *Tai Sang*, a Jardine vessel. The *Jarak*'s crew pulled nine survivors from the sea. When she landed the exhausted and shocked crew she was ordered to join the *Dragonfly* and *Scorpion* and a flotilla of small boats, about to set out to rescue some 1,000 Australians and other, trapped behind the lines at Batu

Pahat. The convoy left after dark with the *Jarak* towing six sampans to ferry the trapped soldiers back across the shallows.

When she returned to Singapore the following day, HMS *Laburnum* ordered her to sail to the now deserted naval base and rescue equipment left behind by the Royal Navy. The base was under enemy guns which shot-up anything moving on the far shore. In spite of the difficulties she crept forward under cover of the night, found the gear and towed it back; all the time raked by machine gun fire and straddled by enemy artillery.

She was then sent out on another sweep and everyone kept a sharp look out for enemy aircraft which by this time were almost continuously overhead. When ordered back to harbour Lieutenant Hooper was instructed to keep her topped-up with oil, to dismiss his Asian crew and replace them with RN ratings. That night, Friday 13th, he embarked 34 Service Specialists but instead of sailing with the evacuation fleet, he was ordered to station his vessel at the mouth of the swept channel to mark the entrance for shipping. Throughout the night Hooper found himself watching ship after ship emerge from the blackest of nights he'd every known. Some would go by with mysterious flashes from their Aldis lamp while the remainder treated her with suspicion and disappeared into the oily smoke which rolled across the sea leaving oil smuts over the ship.

Finally, early in the morning one passing vessel signalled that the *Jarak* should break station and leave for Batavia. Hiding by day and sailing at night she crept through the Lingga Group of islands, then across the open water of the Dempo Strait to make a dash for the Banka Strait. It was then she was spotted by a Japanese reconnaissance plane which brought three cruisers and a destroyer racing to the scene.

On board the *Jarak*, Hooper saw their guns sparkle in the distance, the next moment his ship was straddled with near misses. The plane acted as a spotter for the enemy guns and only once ventured close to the *Jarak* to check the damage. Once was enough and she was met with a burst of fire from rifles, bren guns, a grenade thrower and the ship's four inch gun. Badly damaged the plane banked and flew off in a trail of black smoke. This caused an enemy destroyer to hurtle forward like a demented animal firing her guns at close range reducing the ship to a shambles, filled with dead and wounded. Hooper had no alternative but to abandon ship. The enemy vessel stopped firing and began to circle the burning ship watching the survivors launching two seaworthy lifeboats.

It was late afternoon when the attack began and the sinking ship was abandoned somewhere near the island of Saya. By the time it was dark the two boats had reached the island but as they couldn't find anywhere to land they slept in their anchored boats. At first light they circled the island and discovered it was a crescent shaped volcanic island, walled in on three sides with an opening to the sea. It was through this gap that the two boats rowed and found themselves in a sheltered bay with a gently sloping beach. Hooper sent one party to find water and fruit while the others scrambled to the top of the hill for an all round view.

This last group soon returned from the hill to report that a steamer was approaching. This was soon recognised as the *Jarak*, now drifting in the current. Delighted by the news Hooper swiftly assembled a boarding party which he sent out to bring her in. From the top of the hill the survivors watched the lifeboat go alongside and she was boarded. Soon a signal was hoisted that she was under pilot and she began to move slowly towards the gap in the reef.

Once she was safely in the bay everyone boarded her and began to carry out repairs, clear the wreckage and bury the bodies. While they were busy with this someone spotted two people on the hill and everyone scrambled for their weapons.

The brief moment of panic receded when the strangers identified themselves as local Malay fishermen who had with them a large amount of fruit as a gift. They had been sea fishing the previous night and had witnessed the seabattle. They added that many more shipwrecked Europeans were at the town of Dabo and their Sheik had asked all his subjects to scour the neighbouring islands for more. They also reported that beyond the horizon were many more large warships.

The following day the crew and passengers patched-up the holes along the water line and repaired the engines. All her deck structure had been smashed during bombardment and the bridge was almost totally destroyed by fire. The engine room was also in a bad way but the Chief carried out repairs and restarted the machinery. Their previous melodious thump, thump however was replaced by clanking and a mysterious whine of tortured parts.

The engines despite their complaints were running and the ship did answer so after ordering everyone back on board Lieutenant Hooper steered her out of the lagoon back into the open sea and headed for Dabo. All day her engines almost shook themselves to pieces but they lasted out to Tanjong Buku, a headland on the island of Singkep. Hooper anchored close in-shore and had the stores unloaded and ferried to the beach. Then she was taken out to deep water and scuttled.

Soon after being marooned they were found by a Malay searching for flotsam. From him they learnt that they were only twelve miles from Dabo. On hearing this news the ship's boat was manned and set out for the town, later returning with two native boats to rescue the remaining passengers and crew.

They found the town packed with hundreds of shipwrecked survivors and the food situation was becoming critical. The survivors were being evacuated to Sumatra by Commander Alexander who was running a ferry service to Warren's escape route up the Indragiri River.

With hundreds of survivors waiting for passage on the occasional launch or native boat, Lt Hooper decided to take independent action. In the small harbour he persuaded the crews of two prahaus to take them to Priggi Raja. One party led by First Lieutenant A.H. Huntley finally reached Ceylon. Hooper's party which left later was less successful. When they reached Padang they found all the ships had left.

After some two weeks waiting for an escape boat, Hooper was selected to join Colonel Dillon's small escape party. This group bought a native prahau and left Sumatra on 16th March but two weeks later they were captured by tankers refuelling the enemy fleet attacking Colombo.

Jeruntut: A 217 ton Straits Steamship Company vessel purchased in 1927. Taken over by the Royal Navy she was converted to an Auxiliary mine-sweeper. She sailed on the 11th and was scuttled in the Moesi River, Palembang to avoid capture.

Jeram: A 210 ton RNVR vessel under the command of Lieutenant J.H. Evans. She took part in the evacuation and reached Tandjong Priok, Batavia on the 13th. She was later sunk on 27th February at Tjilatjap, a major seaport on the south coast of Java.

Joan: A launch under the command of an Argyll, Captain Robert Kennard, company commander of C Company and a product of Marlborough College. He had been badly wounded in the groin when trying to stop the enemy advance along the Grik Road in north Malaya. The company lost half its men and he was left for dead. After crawling for three days through the jungle, narrowly avoiding capture he reached the Perak River and launched himself afloat on a log. He clung to this for many miles as it swept down river until eventually he was seen by Indian troops covering the rear guard. These mistook him for a Japanese trying to infiltrate the front line and shot at him. When he was recognised as a European a soldier swam out and pulled him ashore.

He was in a Singapore hospital when the final battle for the city took place and he obtained Brigadier Paris's permission to try and escape if he could. He met up with a school friend from Marlborough College, Captain Rowley-Conwy who was in command of an ack-ack battery at Kallang airfield and was invited to join the battery's escape bid.

Rowley-Conwy had acquired a junk and 'found' a launch in the nearby boat yard. Captain Kennard took command of this launch, the *Joan*, and the two vessels set out on the 15th for Sumatra but both ran aground on the same sandbank near St John's Island. Although the *Joan* lifted off at morning tide the heavy junk, with 120 soldiers on board, remained firmly aground; in spite of attempts by the launch to pull it clear.

Eventually it was agreed that the two vessels should go their own ways and, after taking on board six more gunners, from the junk, Kennard and some 30 men set off again, without charts and with only a four inch compass to steer by. They were soon lost amongst the many islands but eventually sighted a small steamer going in the right direction. When they drew alongside to ask directions they found she was the *Sir Hugh Frazer* under the command of Captain Ernest Gordon, another Argyll officer.

The two vessels landed at Pulau Moro where they found Captain Ivan Lyon in charge of a supply dump for escapers. From him they received news, food and directions on how to reach Priggi Raja. After taking on board shipwrecked survivors sheltering at Lyon's camp the *Sir Hugh Frazer* and the launch set out that evening and eventually reached Rengat.

Junks: Amongst the many local boats used in the escape, four junks have been specifically mentioned. Three are listed below and the fourth was the *Hiep Hien*, listed under her name.

(a) One, under the command of Lt-Colonel Scott RAOC, rescued survivors from the *Fanling* as she approached Banka Strait on 17th. The Strait was already occupied by a large enemy naval force, which captured or sank all vessels entering the area. His boat was intercepted by a second junk, manned by enemy soldiers, which opened fire causing everyone on Scott's boat to leap overboard and try to swim ashore.

(b) Another was under the command of Captain Norman Crawley RA. This was crewed by his Gunners with little or no experience of sailing especially a native junk. Never the less they overcame all the initial problems and navigated her through the minefield.

On the voyage to Sumatra he rescued a detachment of 70 Australians marooned on an island and later took off more escapers from Pulau Moro camp. Without charts or compass, he crept through the islands and eventually reached Priggi Raja. Along the way they rescued more survivors from the water and found others shipwrecked on the islands. Apart from his own men, military discipline amongst the escapers had almost broken down and the young officer enforced his control with bren gun and the support of his own men.

At Priggi Raja the headman directed them up river to Tambilahan where he collected another 100 servicemen including Lieutenant Geoffrey Brooke RN from the *Kung Wo*. He had now been at sea for some ten days. About six miles downstream from Rengat the vessel ran aground on a mudbank and a group of six Australians volunteered to swim through the crocodile-infested river to the shore, and walk to the town to get help. The Dutch Controlleour, when he heard of their plight, sent a small launch, the *Plover*, downstream to pull them off and she later towed the junk to Rengat.

The Dutchman and Major Campbell organised everyone to be fed and sheltered while casualties were dealt with in the nearby hospital by a German doctor. The following morning Captain Crawley discovered that the Australians, who had previously swum ashore, had returned to the unattended vessel during the night while she was tied up alongside the quay and stolen two sacks of rice. They had been sold to a local trader for the price of a taxi to Padang. Meanwhile the group had fallen out amongst themselves and one was admitted to hospital with gunshot wounds. His friends left by taxi before the theft was discovered.

(c) The third junk carried a battery of gunners who had manned ack-ack guns near Kallang. When the commander, Captain Geoffrey Rowley-Conwy, later Lord Langford, realised the end was near he prepared plans to evacuate his men. After attending a meeting at Fort Canning on the

15th when news of the surrender negotiations were announced, he commandeered a large 70 ft, two masted, junk with battened sails, at anchor in the Roads. He had already acquired a launch, the *Joan*, from the nearby boat yard.

In these two vessels he embarked his 120 men and set sail for Sumatra. Some miles off shore a group of armed soldiers in a rowing boat attempted to intercept them but were warned off. Near St John's Island, beyond Blakang Mati they were caught in a strong current and the junk was driven ashore on a sandbank. The launch had also run aground but she was refloated by 6 am the following morning. Despite fruitless attempts to tow her off by the *Joan*, the junk remained fast. After a 'council of war' Rowley-Conwy decided that the *Joan* should take six more gunners from the junk, and make her own way to Sumatra.

Next day while they were still aground, they were approached by friendly Malays from a nearby fishing village. They had seen the Gunners in trouble and came out to offer their help to get the boat refloated. All attempts were doomed to failure, so eventually small groups separated from the main body of escapers and assisted by the fishermen, island-hopped to the escape route. When eventually the junk was refloated there was no one left behind capable of sailing her. So she was finally abandoned and those who still remained were ferried to Sumatra by fisherman.

Katong: She sailed on 1st February and following an attack by enemy aircraft on 5th in the Banka Strait, sank four miles from the bar light vessel, at Palembang.

Kedah: This 2,499 ton vessel, built in 1927, was the pride of the Company's fleet. She had a large lounge and comfortable saloons to accommodate 88 first class passengers. She was also designed to carry 960 deck passengers, normally native workers travelling to the tin mines and plantations being opened up in the jungles of north Malaya.

When taken over by the Royal Navy as an auxiliary destroyer she was armed with a 3-inch, high angle gun, two quick firing 4-inch guns and a pair of pom poms. In January 1942, when the Japanese broke the defence line in Johore she was in the Naval Base having an engine refit. She and other vessels still in the Base were swiftly made ready for sea. The *Kedah* sailed with 500 airmen to Tandjong Priok, Batavia. Hardly had she reached port than she was ordered to return to rescue more airmen and sailors from Keppel Harbour.

She sailed in company with the cruiser *Durban* and two destroyers, *Jupiter* and *Stronghold*. As they raced north and entered the Banka Strait they were attacked by nine planes and although they managed to avoid any serious damage, there were casualties. A brief report simply states that 'we buried our casualties at sea'. On the approach to Singapore on the 11th, they encountered the fog of oily smoke some 70 miles downwind of the burning city. By the time she reached the north end of the minefield close to the Durian Strait the haze had become the thickest oily black smoke her captain, Commander Sinclair, had ever experienced.

The Chief Engineer, Lieutenant R. Lowe, recalled being called to the bridge 'to look at what you will never see again'. The ship was heading for the western entrance at 18 knots and a force five NNE wind blew across the ship smothering everything and everybody in oily smuts. Nothing familiar was to be seen and fires were burning fiercely on Pulau Sebarok and Pulau Sambu. Small islands abeam were also alight.

Suddenly from the shore an ammunition dump exploded momentarily lighting up the scene and Sinclair saw the *Empress of Asia*'s three funnels above the water on Sultan Shoals which confirmed his position. Then the guns on Blakang Mati blasted off their shells and for one horrible moment he thought the convoy had been mistaken for the Japanese. This was followed by more explosions and the fuel tanks on Pulau Bukum erupted in a huge fireball of flame, roaring skywards to some 600 feet turning black darkness into daylight.

The waterfront was almost a continual line of fires and the fire fighting unit, now overwhelmed, left them to burn themselves out. As the ship closed in on her wharf Commander Sinclair remembered a large warehouse nearby was a furnace and when she berthed she seemed to be surrounded by flames. They found the servicemen sheltering amongst the burnt out godowns patiently waiting to be rescued. The quay was covered with luggage and personal items from previous evacuations. The wharf was coated with oil from spillage from the fuel feeder pipes simply thrown away after use, by previous crews in their haste to get away. As the 345 passengers trooped aboard they brought this oil with them and walked it throughout the ship.

Any attempt to leave before first light was out of the question when they found the marker buoy had been misplaced, forcing the naval units to anchor with other ships. As soon as possible that morning, with the *Kedah* leading the way, the ships fled through the minefield before the enemy bombers arrived.

The larger ships that followed her through the minefield, assembled into a convoy and raced through the Durian Straits. At about 9 am they were caught by a series of enemy bombers in an attack that lasted some three hours. Close behind the *Kedah*, the *Empire Star* was struck by three bombs and the *Kedah* slowed to give covering fire. She then became the enemy target and for the next three hours fought off wave after wave of attackers. She weaved and dodged and Sinclair would leave it until the last moment when he could almost see the bombs falling, before he ordered the change of direction. Below decks, her steam pipes burst, the oil pipes on the turbines cracked and the generator was wrecked. Once the convoy was through the Banka Strait the planes withdrew.

The *Durban* had already docked when the vessel reached Tandjong Priok, Batavia, and as she sailed past the crew of the cruiser lined the decks and cheered her in.

Kelana: A 300 ton auxiliary patrol vessel which was bombed and later scuttled. She was later salvaged by the Japanese and became *Sukei No22*.

Kinta: This 1,220 ton vessel sailed with the *Darvil* on the 9th with a total of 1,000 servicemen on board both ships, including 2/3rd Australian Motor company who helped crew both vessels.

Klias: She and her sister ship, *Jarak*, were built at Sungei Nyok yard in 1927. This 207 ton vessel left on 7th, in company with *Rahman*, *Changteh* and *Hua Tong*, with an estimated 400 passengers on board. All their crew had been dismissed and replaced by RN personnel, but the stokers knew nothing about coal burning engines and were soon belching thick, black smoke which marked her trail through the islands. Her speed eventually dropped to about three knots as the clinkers built up in the furnaces.

She headed first for the mouth of the Indragiri River, then south; hiding by day and steaming by night. Near Singkep they converged on a number of surface vessels including a destroyer. The initial alarm receded when they were recognised as HMAS *Bendigo* escorting the two Straits Steamship vessels, the *Jeram* and the *Sin Aik Lee* on passage to Palembang. The *Klias* reached that port some days later but was scuttled on the 14th.

Klang: Very little known apart from the fact that she may have taken part in the evacuation. Six years previously she was the scene of a macabre crime when a Malay passenger ran amok with á large sword killing nine passengers, wounding sixteen more and almost disembowelled its large, bearded Scots captain. She sailed from Tandjong Priok on 21 February 1942 for Fremantle, Australia.

Krian: A 845 ton, Straits Steamship Company ship built in 1914. Prewar she ran a fortnightly trading service between Singapore and Sabah. At the beginning of February 1942 the captain was ordered to dismiss his Asian crew and presumably wait for RN personnel to be allocated to her. About this time the SOE Orient Mission, which ran the secret training school at Tanjong Balai were ordered to move its Establishement to Rangoon but were unable to find a vessel. Its Chief Instructor, Trappes Lomax, saw this vessel tied up alongside the quay and introduced himself to the ship's master who agreed to give them passage on the assurance that SOE would provide the crew.

She sailed from Clifford Pier on about the 5th and called at Pulau Moro to dump more supplies for the escape route. She may have also called at Rengat to disembark Major Campbell who was to run that route. On the 17th she reached Tandjong Priok where the School's staff were reunited with the commander, Major Jim Gavin and his wife Barbara. He had earlier been transferred to Rangoon but had been held up in Java. All air flights had been reserved for VIPs leaving for Australia and the flights to Rangoon were suspended because of the uncertainty of the extent of the Japanese advance.

Gavin and his wife hitched a lift on the *Krian* which left Batavia for Rangoon on the 28th. This ship, almost out of fuel and food, eventually diverted to Ceylon.

Kuala: The *Kuala* was a 954 ton Auxiliary Patrol vessel built in Scotland in 1911 to cater for 1st Class passengers on the coastal run between Singapore, Port Swettenham and Penang. This was about the time when Malaya was opened up and young civil servants and their families moved up-country to take up posts in the Malay States. Tin mines and rubber estates were being developed which in turn created a demand for engineers, planters and workers. As the Malays preferred their own relaxed mode of living to the heavy work demanded by the developers, the gap in the market was exploited by contractors who brought in immigrant Chinese workers. So the *Kuala* was specially designed to carry as many as 600 such additional passengers.

She sailed from Britain on 13th February and her superstitious owner doubled her insurance. His forebodings were justified: she ran aground on an island in the Red Sea on her maiden voyage. Taking advantage of their windfall, she was picked clean by the local inhabitants who made off with bedding, furniture, equipment and even the brass fittings. Later the hulk was towed to India to be reconstructed and refurbished.

Thirty-one years later on 13th February 1942, her earlier owner's superstitions were again justified. On that Friday she was alongside Telok Ayer godowns when she was caught in an air-raid and received a direct hit. At the time she was embarking some 400 evacuees. Amongst the casualties was a nurse from the General Hospital and the husband of an Eurasian woman. They were buried at sea later. Other passengers included colleagues of the dead nurse from the General Hospital, Queen Alexandra nurses and specially selected officers and technicians.

One passenger was Tengku Haji Mohaiden, the second son of the Rajah of Patani. A prewar member of the Federal Legislative Council, he volunteered for the Malay Regiment and fought alongside his British counterparts during the long retreat down the peninsula. As the enemy thrust towards the city, he took part in hand to hand fighting on Kent Ridge until he was ordered to leave in the secret military evacuation. He later joined Force 136 and dropped into Siam to organise resistance against the Japanese.

After some two hours taking on passengers, the *Kuala* cast off at about 1900 hours and joined the queue through the swept channel where the *Jarak* acted as a lightship. The following morning she anchored off Pom Pom island where the captain intended to hide the ship for the day. She found the *Tien Kwang* already sheltering close inshore and another vessel, the *Kung Wo* – badly damaged and with a list – close to another nearby island Dankau.

While the ship's boat was sent ashore to collect fronds for camouflage the *Kuala* was attacked by enemy aircraft and hit by two bombs. One exploded on the bridge and the other crashed through the deck to explode in the engine room. On fire and sinking the *Kuala*'s undamaged lifeboat, which had been sent to the island, came alongside and began to take off the women and children. Life boats from *Tien Kwang* and a launch from the *Kung Wo* began to circle the burning ship and pick up the passengers who had jumped overboard.

A Chinese mother Mrs Li, with her two daughters aged two and six, was one of these. She managed to save her eldest girl by pushing her onto passing wreckage. After some time in the water the mother was rescued by a liferaft but her younger daughter, now unconscious, slipped away and was drowned. Her elder daughter was found 3,000 miles away, on the Japanese-held island of Guadalcanal in 1943 by American marines when they invaded the island. She had a gaping bayonet wound and was feverish. They handed her over to the RC padre who nursed her back to health. Eventually he arranged for her to be looked after by nuns at a catholic orphanage on the island of Estate and she continued her education in the USA. She was reunited with her mother after the war.

Hundreds of passengers were swept away in the strong currents, amongst a long slick of wreckage which now spread through the islands. Some were found by Japanese surface vessels and rescued, others were pulled from the sea by Malay fishermen while many more managed to reach the island and join the survivors from other vessels. About 800 were shipwrecked on the island and almost all of these were taken off by search and rescue boats, either from Dabo or from the Warren escape organisation based at Rengat.

Kung Wo: An Indo-China Steam Navigation Shipping Company vessel of 4636 tons built in 1921 with a speed of about 15 knots. She was built for the Yangtse River trade and her high-box like superstructure was once decribed as looking like a Mississippi Riverboat. She was a coal burning vessel with a very tall, thin funnel amidships. After fleeing from China during the Sino-Japanese war, she reached Hong Kong where she was later damaged by bombs when the Japanese seized the colony.

When she reached Singapore she was taken over by the Royal Navy and converted into an unarmed minelayer. Her captain and six officers were all RNVRs. She was again damaged during a raid on the naval base when she received a direct hit near the funnel which wrecked most of her cabins around the saloon.

On the 13th she took part in the secret evacuation and embarked about 120 RN personnel under the command of Lt-Commander Terry. Most of these were survivors from the *Prince of Wales* and the *Repulse*. There was also a group of 20 airmen including Flight Lieutenant Downer; a Mr Mackintosh, who was a fireman and two colleagues, and a group from the Government Information Services. Amongst these were Captain Steel, Public Relations; an American from Associated Press, Yates McDaniel; an Australian reporter, Athole Stewart; Mr Welby from the Censor's Office and Doris Lim, an attractive Chinese girl dressed in a blouse and blue trousers. She had been a British agent in north China but escaped through Shanghai and was now on the Japanese wanted list.

The ship embarked passengers from alongside HMS *Laburnum*, surrounded by small craft of every description each loading passengers and equipment. While at anchor she was approached by a number of launches looking for berths for their evacuees. But when they discovered how badly damaged her lifeboats were they hawked their passengers elsewhere. Apart from being damaged at the Naval base she also survived very near misses while taking on passengers that afternoon. Although the hull received only minor damage the lifeboats were peppered with shrapnel holes.

Having stood by under steam for some days her coal stocks were low so she steamed across to the coaling berth at Keppel Harbour to recoal. When she returned to HMS *Laburnum* the place was deserted and she couldn't get any reply to her signals requesting permission to leave. Finally a large armoured motor launch with only a Commander Pool aboard, came out to the ship. He called up to the bridge that he had seen their signal but everyone had left and he was only waiting to evacuate Admiral Spooner. All the other small craft had also gone.

It was now 7.30 pm and the captain decided not to wait any longer. Eventually she got under way and sailed past the burning fuel tanks dotting the islands surrounding Singapore, acknowledged signals from the *Jarak* at anchor then into the islands until she reached Pom Pom island at daylight.

Close to the nearby island of Dankau she was caught by enemy bombers in daylight. She received a direct hit in the second bombing run when a bomb crashed through two decks before exploding, blowing out part of the ship's side amidships. A large number of passengers were lost when they leapt overboard and swept away but many reached the island including Lieutenant Geoffrey Brooke, RN. From there the survivors witnessed the raid on Pom Pom which sank the *Kuala* and the *Tien Kwang*. Later they sent medical orderlies across to help with the casualties.

All the survivors were evacuated over a period of seven days to Dabo, either by passing launches or on junks sent from Lingga. Lieutenant Brooke was the last to leave. Most of the survivors from the *Kung Wo* were later drowned when the *Roosenboom* was torpedoed after evacuating survivors from Padang.

Kulit: A launch which sailed from Singapore on the 12th with civilian men and women on board. She was seen heading south but her fate is unknown.

Launches, motor

ML36: Sailed on 13/14th with six British and twelve Indian soldiers as passengers. She was captured at Muntok on the 16th.

ML53: A RAF launch which left on the 10th. All her passengers taken prisoner.

ML310: A Fairmiles B class motor launch built at the Singapore Harbour Board yards. A 73 ton vessel with a complement of 16. She had an overall length of 112 feet and was armed with one 3 pdr, two .303s (Lewis guns) and two 1 MGs.

This was the launch that answered the *Kung Wo*'s signal on Friday evening near HMS *Laburnum*. On the morning of 27th February, four Australian and two Dutch ships anchored at Merak, NW Java, sighted a prahau flying the White Ensign. On board were Lt-Commander H.J. Bull, captain of the 'lost' *ML 310*, two RN sailors and two natives, the Javanese Controlleour of Pulau Tjibea with his native assistant. The gunboat had been missing since it set out on the night of the 13/14th, from Singapore, with Rear Admiral Spooner and Air Vice Marshal Pulford amongst its thirty passengers.

Bull recounted that they reached the Jibbia Islands in the Pulau Tiyoh Group, some 30 miles from Banka, on the 15th. She was seen and chased by an enemy destroyer, and in an attempt to escape, ran aground on Pulau Kaibang. Her passengers and most of her crew dropped over the side and fled into the jungle to hide but Bull and a few sailors remained near the boat, hoping to persuade their pursuers that they were simply sailors trying to escape.

When the destroyer's landing party arrived, they lined up Bull and his men against the beached hull facing a row of armed guards. Behind them they could hear the vessel being searched and ransacked until finally they were joined by the landing party's young officer who calmly stated that they were not taking any prisoners. They watched as the Japanese sailors smashed holes in the *ML310* then ran back down to their whaler and returned to the destroyer. Hardly believing their unexpected reprieve they rejoined the others hiding in the trees close by.

The marooned party were eventually found by local villagers who reported the position to the Controlleour. He helped all he could and eventually found them a small native boat which they repaired and provisioned. Lieutenant John Bull RNVR, Leading Seaman Brough and Able Seaman Hill and the two Javanese sailed the boat some 350 miles through enemy occupied waters to Java where they were seen and rescued by HMAS *Maryborough*.

After the war Admiral Helfrich in his unpublished notes commented that at the time they didn't know anything about the story but 'if I had known, it would have been easy to rescue them by sending a submarine. The *K14* was near the place.' One reason why he wasn't informed may have been that he was ordered to Colombo the following day and the rest of Wavell's staff were already destroying records and papers and evacuating as quickly as possible to Australia or Colombo.

The report obviously reached the American HQ in Sourabaya Java, as an American submarine actually set out in March to find them. Throughout the journey north she was constantly attacked by enemy surface vessels and despite the danger of discovery in those shallow waters her crew made two night landings by rubber boat but failed to find any trace of the escapers.

Meanwhile the shipwrecked party were dying of malaria, dysentery, exposure and later malnutrition. Admiral Spooner died on 15th April and Pulford soon afterwards. Eventually the surviving members found an abandoned native boat which they managed to repair and make seaworthy. Under the command of Wing Commander Atkins this was launched and the survivors tried to reach Sumatra, however after a harrowing sea journey they were finally picked up by a Japanese surface vessel and transferred to prison camps.

ML311: A Fairmiles, RN motor launch under the command of Lieutenant Christmas, sailed on the 13th with 57 passengers and crew 55 of whom were RASC and RAOC personnel. By daybreak on Sunday she had reached the village of Pegu on Sugi Bawah, some thirty miles from Singapore where the small group of escapers said morning prayers in the shade of the palm trees flanking the beach. That night they set off again. Occasionally in the darkness they heard distant thunder and flashes over the horizon. Rain showers swept across the sea and the gunboat bounced across the heavy swell.

As dawn broke she left the cover of the islands and roared across the open sea to Banka Strait with her high bow wave and the White Ensign stretched out behind her. The Strait was flanked by the jungle covered Banka Island with the town of Muntok clearly visible on one side, with the mud flats of Sumatra mainland on the other.

The bay seemed full of ships and, as she swept around the point, her dash was watched by hundreds of passengers who lined their decks. Within minutes the gunboat was amongst a fleet of small boats and launches which fussed around the anchored fleet. Who recognised who first, may never be known, but the scene soon erupted into salvoes of shells, the bark of rifle fire and the stutter of bren guns. Amid the noise came the boom boom boom of the *311*'s pom poms as she dodged and turned, sometimes completely hidden by fountains of water. Within minutes the destroyers were under way pumping shell after shell at her, bringing down a curtain of gunfire from which she didn't emerge.

Picking through the wreckage later Japanese sailors rescued fourteen survivors, eight of whom were badly wounded and taken ashore at Muntok.

ML432:A Fairmiles armed motor launch which sailed on 13/14th with 75 passengers. She was captured at Muntok on the 17th without casualties.

ML433: A Fairmiles armed motor launch which sailed on the 13/14th. She was sunk by surface vessels at the north end of the Banka Strait. Of the 60 RAF and Army passengers she carried there were only six survivors.

ML1062: This was a 45 ton harbour defence motor launch built locally at Walker, Son and Company yards. She was armed with one 1 pounder and 4 Lewis guns. She sailed on the 13/14th with 35 passengers but was sunk by surface vessels at the south end of the Banka Strait. Ten survivors were rescued.

ML1063: This was also a 45 ton motor launch designed for harbour defence work and built at Walker, Son and Company yards. Armed with a 1-pounder gun and four Lewis guns she sailed on 13/14th and may have reached Java. If she did reach Batavia, this vessel may have been the one which rescued Doris Lim.

Larut: She was commissioned in 1927 together with another Straits Steamship Company vessel, the *Perak*. In February she was sunk at Sabang in N. Sumatra. The skipper joined Warren's escape route at Padang and was taken off by a destroyer, possibly HMS *Encounter*. As the ship drew into Tandjong Priok he recognised the *Perak* at anchor. After hitching a lift on a passing launch he boarded her only to find a ghost ship. Although all the cabins were prepared for passengers and the dining tables laid for dinner she appeared to have no officers or crew. Eventually he discovered two company employees on board, one a deck hand from the *Auby* and the other an engine room hand. Both crew members had lost their ships. When they reached the docks they also recognised the company's vessel and had come aboard hoping for help.

Leaving the two crew in charge he went ashore and eventually met two more company men from lost ships, Captain Durrant of the *Kinta* and Captain Bulbrook of the *Auby*. Together they mustered a crew from amongst the many stranded seamen and escapers in the port, scrounged stores then embarked a large number of passengers. These included two officers in SOE, Boris Hembry and Michael Lowe. The *Perak* sailed on 28th February in another last minute evacuation when the Japanese invasion fleet was sighted heading for Java. Other Singapore ships which cleared harbour that day were *Matang, Kepong, Kajang* and the *Krian* with more SOE Orient Mission staff on board.

Li Sang: Sailed at 17.30 on 11/12th and reached Java.

Lipis: She was a 845 tons auxiliary patrol vessel built in 1927 mainly for the east coast trade. She had a special refrigerated room to supply fresh meat, vegetables and stores from Singapore and would return loaded with tin. This trade was reduced when the Singapore Cold Store opened a branch in Kuantan. In the floods of 1926 the Pahang rose 78 feet and the *Lipis* sailed upstream to carry out rescue work.

Like other local vessels she was taken over by the RN in 1939 and converted to an armed trader. With Commander W.E. Steele in command she sailed on the 11/12th with 300 passengers. She must have been one of the last through the minefield as she was caught by early morning enemy bombers off Sultan Sands, close to the remains of the *Empress of Asia*. Three bombers came in low astern and despite her Captain's attempts to dodge the bombs she was hit many times, killing Steele and setting the ship on fire. The first officer took command and ordered everyone to abandon ship. Amongst the dead was the ship's Chief Engineer Beeton who served with the Scottish Light Horse in the Boar War and in submarines during the First World War.

Li Wo: A 707 tons, flat bottomed Auxiliary Patrol vessel owned by Indo-China Steam Navigation Company. She was taken over by the RN who overpainted her peacetime red funnel with a black top with camouflage and armed her with a four inch gun. Apart from that she already had

thin armour plating around her bridge to protect the ship's officers from
the random shots of river pirates in the Yangtse.

She was built in Hong Kong for the Yangtse river trade and has been
described as being ugly and the smallest ship in the company's fleet. She
had a draught of eight feet and was designed to negotiate the upper
reaches of the Yangtse. Above decks there were three tiers of boxlike
cabins which extended the whole length of the ship.

One of the few ships to escape from Hong Kong before its garrison was
overwhelmed by the Japanese, she took part in her second escape on the
11th. On the 14th, as she approached Banka Strait, she met the Japanese
invasion fleet on a converging course. She hoisted a second White Ensign
and engaged the enemy with small arms fire and the four inch gun before
ramming a destroyer. As she withdrew leaving a hole in the ship's side she
was blown out of the water and sank. Thirteen survivors were rescued by
the Japanese.

Loch Ranza: 4,958 tons, was bombed and later beached following a heavy
attack by aircraft on 3rd February at Abang Island at the north east end
of the Rhio Strait. She was backloading stores, important radar sets,
wireless transmitters and anti-aircraft guns for the defence of Palembang.
The wreck was found by HMAS *Toowooma* who rescued the crew from the
desert island. Unaware of this, as the *Toowooma*'s signal never got through,
Rear Admiral Spooner ordered the *Woolongong* with HMAS *Bendigo*, to
divert and rescue the stricken vessel's crew. These two vessels were the
last Australian ships to leave Singapore.

Lugate: A 290 ton Gate Vessel built in 1935 at Hong Kong and Whampoa
yards. Her overall length was 98 feet and she was armed with a 3-inch
anti-aircraft gun. She was captured by the Japanese.

Malacca: The 211 ton *Malacca* and her sister ship *Jeram*, 210 tons, were
bought from a local shipbuilder, Taikoo Dockyards in 1927.

She was under the command of Lieutenant W.B. Bervis when she
formed part of the evacuation fleet on the 13th. On the voyage to Sumatra
she rescued 20 officers from the *Yin Ping* and is believed to have called at
Pulau Moro where she evacuated more escapers. On the 14th she was
attacked by enemy aircraft causing sufficient damage for her master,
Lieutenant Bervis to scuttle the vessel at Chanako on the Tjemako River.
He and his passengers reached Padang where they embarked on a vessel
to Tjilatjap, on the south coast of Java.

Mary Rose: A 40 foot, diesel-engined launch, which was probably one of
the last official evacuation vessels to leave Singapore. She carried a cross
section of some 38 officers from Fort Canning. These included Colonel
Dalley, Commanding Officer of the disbanded Dalforce, a unit made up of
mainly Chinese volunteers; ex SOE Lieutenant Frank Brewer; Mr Bowden, the Australian Government's representative in Singapore and his two
assistants and an Intelligence Officer from GHQ.

The elderly Naval Officer in charge of the launch had been told to take passage through Banka Strait but the Intelligence Officer pointed out that he believed this could be occupied by an enemy task force. Frank Brewer and Dalley pressed for the launch to go to the Indragiri River where they knew Warren had an escape route. They were also anxious to move on from there to Bagan Siapiapi, further up the coast, to join Warren's under cover work behind the lines in occupied Malaya.

The commander refused to disregard his orders and continued to Banka. The voyage was uneventful, remembered Frank Brewer, although each day they saw enemy planes searching the islands for larger escape vessels. Wreckage and bodies were spotted and one day the yacht *C14* with military and civilians on board was seen.

When the launch reached Banka on the 17th they were intercepted by a heavily armed, enemy patrol boat. As she approached, and after some debate, it was decided that they should surrender. In the absence of a white shirt they hoisted someone's white underpants. The enemy launch closed in and signalled them to follow her to Muntok.

Medusa: Built in 1915, 793 tons. She was taken over by the Royal Navy and converted into a minelayer carrying 52 mines and 10kts. On 2nd February she left for Batavia with another Straits Steamship vessel and converted minesweeper, HMS *Circe*. With them went the motor minesweeper *No 51* and their escort HMAS *Maryborough*.

Mata Hari: This 1,020 ton vessel was built in 1915 and like other local vessels was taken over by the Royal Navy at the outbreak of war. On the 11th she embarked 483 civilian and military nurses and staff from Ministry of Information, Malayan Broadcasting Service, others from the Colonial and Foreign Offices together with a few Argylls and Royal Marines. After waiting at the entrance to the minefield for daylight, because of the missing marker buoy, she escaped and hid amongst the islands.

One night her lookouts spotted survivors in the water and rescued six from the ill-fated *Scorpion*. Two of these were a Lieutenant Arnold and Able Seaman Milne. When she reached the Banka Strait on Sunday the 15th she was approached by enemy destroyers, ordered to drop anchor and receive a boarding party.

All around her in the bay were other captured vessels and small boats were ferrying the prisoners to the long jetty at Muntok. This already held a long line of people and their possessions. On the beach were three abandoned steamers which had been run aground. As the day developed the passengers watched the *ML 311*'s dramatic arrival and brief engagement.

Norah Moller: This 4,433 ton merchantman was attacked by aircraft just after noon on the 3rd, in the northern leg of Banka Strait. She had on board 57 passengers including women and children. The enemy planes

were driven off by the arrival of cruiser HMAS *Hobart* and its destroyer
screen, HMAS *Tenedos*. The ship was ablaze after being hit amidships and
badly damaged. Amongst the survivors aboard *Tenedos*, 6 of the 28
wounded had died before they reached Tandjong Priok the next day.

Oriskany: 1,644 tons, sailed on 11/12th. No further information.

OK: A launch – possibly used by escapers. Fate unknown.

Pahlawan: A 60 ton RNVR launch with an overall length of 76 feet, and
built for the Straits Settlements RNVR by Thornycroft Yards, Singapore.
Her complement was 10 and she was armed with a 3pdr gun and one
Lewis gun.
   She escaped on the 13th with 26 servicemen and crew. Two passengers
were later reported missing following capture on 15th, 30 miles north of
Banka Strait.

Pangkor: A 1,250 ton Auxiliary Patrol vessel built in 1939 and named after
a low lying, steamy island in the Malacca Straits some ten miles from the
Kinta River. She left Singapore crowded with escapers and reached Java.
Her passengers were evacuated from there in late February. In 1943 she
was used as an accommodation vessel.

Panglima: A 60 ton Straits Settlements RNVR launch built at Thornycroft Yards, Singapore. It sailed on the 13th with military personnel and
later reached Tandjong Priok, Batavia.

Panji: A 60 ton Straits Settlements RNVR launch built at Thornycroft
Yards, Singapore. She escaped with military personnel on the 13th. Fate
unknown.

Pelandok: A Harbour Board boat. Fate unknown.

Pengail: A RNVR launch which escaped from Singapore on the 13th with
military personnel. Fate unknown.

Pengawal: A RNVR motor launch which may have been used as a tug
boat: sunk in the Durian Strait on the 14th by enemy aircraft. Fate of the
passengers and crew unknown but they may have reached the Lyon's
camp on nearby Pulau Moro.

Penghambat: A RNVR motor launch simply recorded as being lost.

Peningat: A RNVR motor launch simply recorded as being lost.

Perak: A Straits Steamship Company vessel. See *Larut*.

Ping Wo: This 3,105 ton ship sailed on the night of the 11th and anchored
in the Outer Roads until daylight because of the missing marker buoy.
She plucked some 200 survivors from the sea from previous shipwrecks
and finally sailed with some 400 passengers. Being one of the larger vessels
she was amongst the first through the swept channel at daybreak and
reached the Banka Strait only just ahead of the Japanese invasion fleet

which caught the *Vyner Brooke* and the *Li Wo* close behind her. She reached Java and later took part in the evacuation of that island. In company with the *Islander* towing the disabled HMAS *Vendetta* to Australia, she ran into a heavy gale and the *Vendetta's* captain later reported that the last he saw of the *Ping Wo*, she was running before the gale like a surf board.

Prince: An auxiliary minesweeper. Fate unknown.

Pulo Soegi: Described as a small craft. Under the command of Lt Day RNVR, she was sunk by enemy surface vessels at 23.00 hrs near the north end of the Banka Strait. This was close to where the *Fanling* was sunk. She carried 2 officers and 66 men but only 25 survived.

Rahman: A 206 ton Straits Steamship vessel, built in 1926 and converted to a minesweeper by the RN in 1939. She left on 3rd February for Palembang in company with HMS *Gemas* and two Australian corvettes, *Ballarat* and *Toowooma*. They reached the oil port of Palembang on 6th. She later formed part of the Sunda Strait Patrol with the *Wo Kwang*, *Gemas*, *Jeram*, *Sin Aik Lee* and six Dutch vessels. When Java surrendered she sailed for Australia with more escapers but was sunk on 1st March in the Indian Ocean. Survivors were rescued by the yacht *White Swan*.

Rantau or *Rentau*: A sister ship to the *Relau*, the 75 ton palm oil tanker sailed on 12th under the command of S. Baddeley, company employee, and a scratch crew. This included Mansfield and Co.'s Chief Engineer Superintendent Froggart who acted as ship's engineer and Captain McAlister, Singapore Chief Pilot. When they reached Banka Strait during darkness on 14th they found it crowded with vessels, which daylight revealed as the Japanese fleet. Those on board witnessed the capture of their sister ship and later watched the *Tapah* sail into Muntok where it too was seized.

Rawang: A Straits Steamship vessel scuttled during Thursday afternoon, the 12th, in the Inner Roads by Superintendent Engineer, Mr Froggart.

Redang: She was a 531 ton Thai Navigation Company ship, managed by a Danish firm. At' the outbreak of war her Danish skipper, Captain S. Rasmusson, sailed her to Singapore where she was seized by the RN. Taken over by the Ministry of Trade, she was managed by the Straits Steamship Company. On the 12th she embarked 89 passengers including 6 women and 3 children. She was also given a scratch crew of 5 RN engine hands and five naval ratings.

On the 15th, off the Banka Strait, she was attacked by two enemy destroyers. When they opened fire most of the passengers scrambled for cover. Below in one of the cabins two women employees of Mansfield and Company were typing out a passenger list. When the salvo struck the vessel both were killed and the little ship set on fire. As the ship sank the Captain and the RN Ratings managed to get one boat with thirty passengers on board away. They spent the next 24 hours rowing for the shore where they were captured by the Japanese. Amongst the survivors were four women and 2 children, all the other passengers and crew are believed to have died.

Relau: A 75 ton palm oil tanker and a Straits Steamship Company vessel used by the RN to bunker their ships at the Naval Base. When the Base was abandoned on 28th her captain, was ordered by the Naval authorities to leave his loaded vessel at anchor and evacuate to Singapore. The Company was not amused by this and Marine Superintendent F.W. Chamberlain found a new crew and personally went across and brought the vessel around to the Inner Roads.

She spent the next ten days bunkering ships and later ferrying evacuees around the harbour. On the 13th she embarked sixty passengers and left that evening under the command of Captain Chamberlain, with the Company's assistant Chief Engineer looking after the engines. In the next twenty four hours she stopped twice to pick up shipwrecked survivors including 13 Ratings from the *Scorpion* found clinging to a life raft at about 3 pm.

On the 16th she crept through the Banka Strait and was almost through when, as daylight came, her look-outs reported a black shadow ahead. As morning came this revealed itself as an enemy cruiser then an enemy destroyer was reported astern and closing fast. She came alongside and the *Relau* was boarded by armed enemy sailors.

Rhoda: Auxiliary Patrol Vessel. Fate unknown.

RHU: A 254 ton motor vessel converted to a minelayer. She was captured at Singapore and is believed to have become anti-submarine vessel *21 IJN*.

Rompin: This oil fired seaplane tender was aground at Seletar airbase when she was pulled off on the 10th to take part in the evacuation. Under the command of G.R. Spaull it left on 11th towing a large seaplane tender and a yacht, the *White Swan*. Throughout the first night the hawser kept breaking and the tows drifted away in a three knot current. Each time, they were located and brought back under tow. It wasn't until about nine o'clock in the morning that Spaull was able to find a suitable island to hide the boats. There she was overtaken by another escape boat, a small yacht which had engine trouble and Spaull agreed to take her in tow.

Throughout the voyage to Banka her engines gave trouble until eventually she was forced to stop at Muntok for quick repairs to her boilers. Unfortunately when the repairs were complete and an attempt was made to restart her engines – she blew her head.

While the crew were trying to repair the engines a ship's boat from the *Siang Wo*, at anchor nearby, came alongside with a request for her to take the fifteen women they had on board. The *Siang Wo* it seemed, was also having engine trouble. Although Spaull was unable to help, room for two, (Mrs Robinson and Mrs Marsden) was found on the yacht *White Swan*, whose skipper had decided to leave the flotilla and sail the remaining 250 miles to Java.

The tender and the *Rompin* were seized the following day when an enemy force captured the town.

Rosemary: A motor launch which left Pulau Batam on 14th in company with *Changi*, *Hastings Anderson*, *Swift*, *Swallow* and a fifth launch which ran aground. This may have been the *Jane*. The *Rosemary* voyaged to Banka where she was captured on 16th.

Rover, HMS: A 2,030 ton Royal Navy submarine built in Barrow in 1930. She was being repaired at Keppel Harbour when Singapore was about to fall. Finally dockyard fitters made her seaworthy but because of a fault with her electric engines she was unable to submerge. She escaped in the last hours before the surrender, forced to travel on the surface by night and hide during the day. While doing so the look-outs spotted a fishing boat with two naval ratings aboard, both survivors from the *Prince of Wales* and the *Repulse*. They had been acting as 'runners' between the Australians and the Argylls when the surrender was announced. They were picked up and the submarine eventually reached Java.

Ruthania: A Harbour Board vessel. Fate unknown.

St Breok: A 860 ton Saint Class Fleet tug built in 1919 at Hong Kong and Whampoa yards. Her overall length was 143 feet and she was armed with one 12 pdr anti-aircraft gun. She sailed on 12th with 25 passengers and crew on board, two days later she was bombed and sunk in the Sebayor Strait. 24 survivors were rescued by the *ML432* and the other is believed to have been picked up by the *ML310*.

Scorpion: A 700 tons RN gunboat built in 1938 for the Yangtse River Flotilla, with an overall length of 208 feet. She had two 4 inch guns, one 3.7 inch and two 3 pdr.

She sailed on 10th with 150 on board including 58 passengers. Amongst these were 38 communication ratings. For the next three days she suffered continual problems with her engines and only reached the Berhala Strait on 14th.

Her arrival at one end coincided with that of enemy naval units at the other. Out of a monsoon squall emerged a Japanese cruiser and two destroyers. All four ships opened fire simultaneously but within minutes she was hit repeatedly and on fire from bow to stern. Those not injured launched 3 Carley floats, each designed to accommodate twenty people. twenty survivors are believed to have been rescued by the Japanese, thirteen were found next day by the SS *Relau* and the *Mata Hari* picked up six more. Ten are believed to have reached Dabo. 101 men had disappeared.

Scott Harley: A 620 ton Reserve Auxiliary minesweeper built in 1913. Presumed lost on 3rd March 1942. No further information.

Seekingjas: Motor launch, fate unknown.

Shun An: Auxiliary Patrol Vessel, fate unknown.

Siang Wo: A 2,595 ton ex Yangtse River trader taken over by the RN for coastal patrol and minesweeping duties. Her sole armament was a 4 inch gun mounted on the bows and a stern mounted Lewis Gun. The 4 inch gun couldn't be elevated more than 45 degrees and was useless against aircraft. Her company colours had been painted over to RN camouflage in grey green with black stripes.

On 11th she embarked more than 200 passengers including MBC staff, two senior RNR Lieutenant-Commanders, newspaper correspondents and some seventeen women. Under the command of Lt A. Woodley RNR she cast off about 6 pm but unable to find the buoy marking the entrance to the minefield she anchored for the night. At daybreak she became 15th in line through the swept channel and by 11 am was clear of the shipping jam. About noon on 13th near the northern tip of the Banka Strait, and in sight of Muntok lighthouse, she was attacked by enemy aircraft for some two hours.

Shuddering from near misses and a direct hit near the stern she stopped answering to the helm and steamed in circles. With the help of passengers who manned the emergency steering wheel at the stern, Woodley managed to take her into Muntok. When he later checked the damage no trace of the stern Lewis Gun or its gunners was found. Further examination convinced him that she would never last out to Java so the Captain ran her aground on Muntok beach, close to three other beached ships near the lighthouse.

An attempt was made to transfer the fifteen women on board to the *Rompin*, a seaplane tender. She was towing three other boats including the yacht, the *White Swan*. As the *Rompin* was also having engine trouble the women rejoined the ship apart from two who were taken on board the *White Swan*. The last the passengers saw of the yacht, before they were taken into captivity, was her canvas being unfurled as she slowly sailed away through the cliff and tree lined Strait. She had with her Mrs Robinson and Mrs Marsden; the latter has also been referred to as Mrs Mersey.

The Naval Officers on board *Siang Wo*, now took charge and although a passenger wanted to use the Dutch wireless equipment on shore to radio the situation at Banka to Java, so that they could be rescued, the RN officers insisted on radio silence.

When a barge from Muntok arrived to take them off, one RN officer was so drunk he refused to go ashore until a Naval rating found his luggage. This was never found and later, as everyone straggled along Muntok's long jetty carrying their heavy baggage, he walked along without his. In a bad temper he kicked a woman's suitcase over the side and it was swept away.

The naval ratings and the soldiers were sent off to find their own accommodation at the town's YMCA while the officers and civilians booked in at the hotel.

The following evening the Japanese landed, seized the town and occupied the island.

Sumit: An Auxiliary Patrol Vessel, fate unknown.

Sin Aik Lee: This 198 ton Auxiliary minesweeper and a Straits Steamship Company vessel sailed on 7th for Java in company with HMAS *Bendigo* and the *Jeram*. She carried no passengers but her Asian crew were replaced with a leading stoker and three stokers from the HMAS *Woolongong*.

Sin Kheng Seng: Previously owned by the small Kheng Seng Steamship Company she was bought by the Straits Steamship Company and managed by the subsidiary firm of Ho Hong. She left on the 13th under the command of Captain Smith and crewed by Engineer Donnelly and 45 others all crew members of the ill-fated *Empress of Asia*.

Sir Hugh Frazer: A small barge-like vessel used by the army as a ferry for supplying units stationed on nearby islands. Following the surrender of Singapore it evacuated some 200 escapers to Rengat, Sumatra. In addition it embarked a large number from SOE's camp at Pulau Moro and more from the staging posts on the Indragiri.

Stronghold, HMS: This RN destroyer left on 2nd towing the disabled HMAS *Vendetta*. See entry for HMS *Durban*.

Solen: Taken over by the RN as an Examination vessel and was presumed lost at Singapore.

Subadar: The 5,424 ton vessel was sunk off Banka Strait by enemy aircraft on the 13th.

Sui Wo: A 2,672 ton Boom Defence ship built in 1896. As the number of casualties flowing into the Singapore Hospitals reached crisis point, she was equipped with additional berths and stores, and converted to a hospital ship. After embarking hundreds of wounded and medical staff, she sailed on the 9th. She has also been referred to as the *We Sui* and *Wu Sueh*.

Shu Kwang: An Auxiliary Patrol vessel of 788 tons. She was sunk by enemy aircraft on 14th. Some survivors were rescued by the *Tenggaroh* and taken to Tambilahan.

Tapah:A 208 ton Straits Steamship Company vessel built in 1926. She sailed on the 11th with 44 passengers and anchored amongst the traffic jam of shipping around the mouth of the swept channel through the minefield. At daybreak she joined the tail of the queue of ships filing through the minefield, close behind the SS *Relau*.

Once amongst the islands she hid during the day and sailed at night. Close to Banka, while she hugged the coast of Sumatra she sighted survivors on a jungle lined beach trying to attract attention. A boat was sent ashore and discovered they were from the *Giang Bee*. Despite being crowded the captain of the *Tapah* agreed to take almost everyone. The exceptions were fifteen survivors who followed on later in their lifeboat. Shortly afterwards she rescued more survivors this time from the *Redang*. She was captured in the Banka Strait on the 17th.

Tatung: A 1,560 ton steamship captured at Tandjong Batoe.

Talthybius: She was hit whilst tied up alongside the quay during a raid on the 3rd. The waterfront had been pattern bombed causing many fires amongst the nearby godowns. Each day the bombing continued and grew worse until near the end it was almost continuous. The ship's officers and crew, together with firemen, fought an unsuccessful battle to keep the flames from nearby buildings, engulfing the ship. Finally ablaze and unstable from water sprayed over her to contain the fire, she listed over and settled on her side in the harbour on about the 13th.

Tenggaroh: Believed to be the Sultan of Johore's yacht, sailed from Singapore on 13th with army and civilian passengers including one woman. On her voyage to Rengat she picked up survivors from the *Shu Kwang* who were disembarked at Tambilahan. The ship was scuttled at Chanako but is believed to have been salvaged by the Japanese.

Tien Kwang: Built in 1925 this 787 ton vessel was taken over by the RN and became an Auxiliary Patrol vessel. She left on the 13th carrying some 450 key personnel and civilians. These included Public Works employees, nurses and a large contingent of RAF personnel who staffed the secret Radar equipment at Changi.

The following morning she dropped anchor off Pom Pom where she intended to hide for the day. About ten volunteers, mostly RAF, went ashore to cut fronds to camouflage the ship. While they were ashore she was attacked by enemy aircraft; one bomb smashed through its deck to explode in a cabin occupied by four matrons killing all four. Others splashed all around the vessel, destroying boats and rafts and killing people in the water. Two other ships, the *Kung Wo* and the *Kuala* were close by and similarly attacked. In a brief while, some 1,000 passengers from this ship and the *Kuala*, who survived the bombing were floundering in the water. Many were swept away to their deaths, but some did reach the island. When the planes exhausted their bombs they returned to machine gun the swimmers and those on the beach. See entry for *Kuala*.

Trang: This 205 ton vessel was one of the oldest in the Straits Steamship Company's fleet, built in 1912. On the 14th she embarked 80 soldiers and airmen and, under the command of Commander Alexander, cousin to Field Marshal Alexander, she followed *Sin Kheng Seng* and the *Wo Kwang* line astern, through the minefield.

The ship's engines gave Alexander continual trouble until they finally broke down. This caused the ship to drift towards the minefield. Alexander ordered the ship to be scuttled and the seacocks opened. Meanwhile crew and passengers set the ship on fire. When it was well alight he ordered the three ship's boats away. One under the command of Lt Rigden steered for Rengat and was rescued by the *Sir Hugh Frazer*. The other two, commanded by Commander Alexander and Lt Howell, stayed together and reached Dabo where they took over the welfare of the wounded and the evacuation arrangements to the SOE escape route at Rengat.

Vyner Brooke: Like other local vessels the 1670 ton *Vyner Brooke* was taken over by the RN in 1939 and converted to an armed trader/mine-sweeper.

She was launched at Leith in 1927 and became the pride of the Borneo Company fleet. She had accommodation for 35 first class passengers and a Royal Suite for the Brooke's family. The Straits Steamship Company gained control of the firm in the thirties and with it came the *Vyner Brooke*.

She sailed on the 12th under the command of Captain Barton, with 192 passengers including some sixty-four Australian nurses. On the 14th, at 1 pm, she was nine miles north of Banka Strait when she was discovered by enemy aircraft. On board the siren blared and the passengers hurried below. A few who still had them, rammed their steel helmets firmly on their heads. The captain was zig-zagging his ship violently and the first bomb-load exploded harmlessly alongside. Next time the ship wasn't so lucky and a bomb dropped down the funnel and exploded in the engine room causing fires in many places. Another struck the bridge while a third exploded across the open decks.

Someone appeared at the door of the crowded saloon, where women and children clung to the carpeted deck, and called 'abandoned ship.' This caused everyone to rush for the exits. Australian nurses grabbed screaming children and helped the elderly as people fought to clear the burning vessel. On deck three lifeboats had been lowered and rafts thrown overboard. Crew members were also throwing overboard stretchers, deck chairs, hatch covers and anything else that would float. The ship was listing badly when the first lifeboat with Matron Drummond and elderly passengers cleared the vessel. Another boat succeeded in getting away but a third was trapped as the ship began to list and sank taking it with her. The attack and the sinking had lasted fifteen short minutes. Nine nurses from the 2/13th Australian General Hospital, with Matron Paschke of 2/10th drifted away on a raft and were never seen again.

The nurses managed to retain their medical packs containing morphia and field dressing and these were used on the casualties who clung to rafts and drifted around on bits of wreckage. They tried to keep together but the currents swirled them in different directions and although they saw boats in the distance the survivors were ignored.

The boats, large motor launches, were packed with Japanese soldiers heading for Muntok. As these ploughed through flotsam and wreckage slick the soldiers casually watched some survivors bump alongside their boats as they steered through the wreckage towards Banka.

Groups of survivors eventually landed at various parts of the island. Captain Barton had been in the water for 18 hours when he staggered ashore near Muntok. When he walked along the beach he came across his Chief Officer and the Second Engineer and later they found other survivors.

One lifeboat with twenty-one nurses on board was guided ashore in the darkness by a large bonfire, lit by earlier arrivals. Some swimmers were swept into mangrove swamps and despite being tired and exhausted swam clear until they too reached the beach. After resting they followed the waterline and they spotted the bonfire.

The new arrivals brought news of the Japanese landings and after some discussion an officer was nominated to walk into town to surrender and fetch help. While they awaited his return the nurses moved around the group attending to the wounded. Eventually everyone saw an enemy patrol approaching accompanied by the shipwrecked officer. The Japanese officer in command of the patrol of ten soldiers ordered all the men capable of walking to march off along the beach and around the headland. Out of sight of the women and wounded the survivors were used for bayonet practice and killed. When the soldiers returned they ordered the women to run into the sea where they were machine-gunned. Thoroughly enjoying the sport the soldiers, laughing, ran up the beach and ripped open the wounded lying helplessly on the sand where the nurses had left them.

One of the Australian nurses wounded in the massacre feigned death and later struggled ashore to hide in the jungle. Hunger drove her out three days later and she returned to the beached lifeboat to search for food. She was seen by another survivor of the massacre, a British sailor who had been bayoneted and left for dead. He watched her creep across the beach and managed to attract her attention. The two later gave themselves up but kept the news of the massacre a secret to avoid the Japanese killing them to hide the story.

Vulture: An auxiliary minesweeper, fate unknown.

Wanyun: A 674 ton steamship which was immobilised on the 11th and later captured in Singapore.

We Sui: See also *Sui Wo*. This vessel has been referred to as the *We Sui, Wu Sai* and *Sui Wo* but it is believed to be the latter.

Wharry Pu: A launch used around the harbour which escaped with military personnel.

White Swan: Owned by Merton Brown, shipyard manager at Thornycroft Shipyard. She was towed away on 11th by the seaplane tender *Rompin* which also had a second seaplane tender in tow. The following morning while hiding amongst the islands some ten miles south of Singapore they were joined by the *Camiron*. This large yacht was manned by RAF officers crewing her to Java. She too had engine problems and the *Rompin*'s skipper agreed to take her in tow.

The four vessels eventually reached Muntok on 14th where the *Rompin*'s engine broke down for good. Another vessel close by, the *Siang Wo*, also had engine trouble and sent a tender across to the *Rompin* with 15 women on board with the request that she take them on to Batavia. But as the *Rompin*'s captain explained his ship was in a similar state itself so the women returned to their ship. There is a report that the *White Swan* took on board eight women passengers including a Mrs Woosey. Another states in fact she took only two, Mrs Robinson and Mrs Marsden. Possibly all eight joined both the *White Swan* and the *Camiron* who now parted company with *Rompin* and continued their voyage under sail.

The two yachts sailed down the Sumatran side of the strait with Banka but a smudge on the left. On their starboard side, near the mainland, was a small island with towering cliffs rising directly from the sea. As they sailed by a lone figure was seen, amongst the tumble of rocks at the water's edge, waving a stick which they later discovered to be a homemade crutch. This modern day Robinson Crusoe was a pilot of a crashed Wellington bomber, who had been trapped on the island for two days. Without food or water he was ravenous.

Later that day the yachts spotted a sampan from Banka island which sailed out to intercept them. The local fishermen had with them another flyer, who they discovered, was the navigator of the crashed Wellington.

When they arrived at Java, the *White Swan* continued her voyage and set sail for Australia. In the Indian Ocean the crew found survivors from the *Rahman*, sunk by enemy action. After many adventures the crew of the yacht finally reached Australia.

The RAF officers joined the thousands of other airmen at a camp in central Java and were taken prisoner.

Wo Kwang: This 350 ton tug was built in 1927 and was later converted by the RN to an Auxiliary minesweeper. She escaped from Singapore and reached Java on the 17th having evaded the Japanese at Banka Strait. With five other escape ships from Singapore she formed part of the Sunda Strait Patrol.

Wuchang: A 3,204 ton depot ship sailed from Singapore with military personnel. She later became a depot ship for submarines with the Far Eastern Fleet.

Yin Ping: She sailed from Singapore on 13th with 72 passengers, 1 soldier, 3 civilians, 18 RN personnel and 50 from the RAF. Later she met the *Malacca* and transferred across 20 other ranks who eventually reached Rengat.

She was later sunk by gunfire near the Banka Strait leaving only 14 survivors.

APPENDIX II

Memories of *Repulse*
and Singapore

The sinking of HMS Repulse, 10th December, 1941

HMS *Repulse*, HMS *Prince of Wales* and a destroyer screen sailed up the east coast of Malaya seeking the Japanese invasion fleet which was reported to be seen near Kota Bahru and later off Kuantan. One of the stokers on board the *Repulse*, George Avery, remembered that the crew had been closed up at action stations since the ship had been sighted by enemy planes the previous day, 8th December 1941. All the time his 'watch' slept on the hard floor with their gas masks for pillows. His post was in the port condenser room.

The watch went on duty at 8 am and the action started at 11 am. Inside the ship, separating his port condenser room from the one on the starboard side where his friend worked, was a large porthole. When he glanced through he saw the room was full of smoke and heard that the ship had been torpedoed. By 1.30 pm the ship had developed a bad list and was loosing steam putting the boilers out of action. The boilers were also taking in cold water so the Chief Mechanic thought it best that he and his six fellow stokers evacuated the room.

They managed to open the armoured hatch by hand and this led onto a half deck with another manhole door. This was open and they could see the seawater rushing into the ship. 'We went out of the hatch one at a time and when it was my turn the water flung me against a tin fish on the half deck. I grabbed the fin to stop being swept away but the water tore my ring off my finger.' Dragging himself along the torpedo and forcing a way through the rushing torrent in a ship slowly capsizing he eventually reached the deck, which was by now vertical in the sea. 'The ship was on its side with the funnels in the water. With others who followed him up from below, 'we crawled up to the ship's side and walked along it. One of the officers told us to watch out for the screw which was still going around. There had been 82 stokers on watch below and only nine made it to the top. Of my watch only one other survived. The rest must have been swept away inside the ship.

'I dived into the sea and swam away and as I did so I passed three dead sharks, probably concussed through the explosions. I swam to a raft which had Captain Tennant aboard but as there was no room for me I swam off. Eventually after swimming for two miles I was rescued by HMS *Electra*. The ship was so crowded with survivors that we remained on the upper deck covered in fuel oil.'

In the last week of the battle for Singapore George Avery and another seaman acted as runners, taking messages between the Australians and the Argylls. During the Japanese final assault on the 1st Malaya Brigade he and his companion found themselves behind enemy lines. Later in the day they were told by the natives that 'it was all over and we had surrendered.' They escaped in a fishing boat and were picked up by the submarine HMS *Rover*. 'This couldn't dive because of a fault with its electric engines and travelled on the surface, by night, 500 miles to Batavia.'

There he transferred to the depot ship HMS *Ankin*, an old coal burner which could do about eight knots. When the Dutch learnt the Japanese invasion fleet was closing in the ship was ordered to leave for Australia in company with HMAS *Yarra*, a tanker and a supply ship he remembered.*
'All the next day as they sailed slowly through the Strait we were continually straffed by enemy planes and in the distance that night heard the gunfire from the battle of the Java Sea. The following morning we were found by the Japanese fleet, three cruisers and three destroyers. The *Yarra* raced out towards them hiding us behind a smoke screen but it was a hopeless task. Within thirty minutes it was all over but this time, after diving over the side, I managed to get into an open boat with 57 others. This was full of bullet holes and I had the job of bailing out with a big can.'

'Most of the lads were wounded and we used our clothing for bandages. By this time the boat was surrounded by about twenty sharks which kept bumping the boat and trying to tip it up from below. We smashed most of our oars over them to beat them off before we were spotted by a Dutch vessel, the *Zawalli*, that evening. The captain refused to stop after dark to pick up other survivors. Later one of the Dutch officers was overheard to say that should the ship be sunk there were only sufficient rafts and lifeboats for the crew. They mounted two machine guns on the bridge with instructions to shoot any survivors who tried to get to the lifesaving equipment.'

'One of our officers detailed us off into groups and made sure one group was always on duty near the bridge with instructions to seize the machine guns should the ship be attacked. The ship eventually reached Colombo without mishap.'

In Colombo he was put in a working party unloading an ammunition when he was caught in an air-raid. 'A bomb dropped on the aft magazine and blew that half of the ship away. When I jumped off the ship my foot caught in the ship's rail and I crashed into the sea. When I surfaced someone shouted sharks: by this time I was full of fuel oil and eventually dragged out of the water and finished up in hospital to have my stomach pumped out.'

---

* The ships were probably *The British Judge*, a tanker, HMIS *Junna*, HMAS *Yarra*, RFA *Francol* and a wooden minesweeper which had escaped from Singapore, *No 51*.

Concluding his letter George Avery comments: 'I left Singapore with my head in defeat and was fortunate to return on HMS *Ruler* to collect released prisoners of war.'

Singapore

Lieutenant B.L. Jenkins RN was a temporary Sea Transport Officer based in the top floor of the Ocean Building near Clifford Pier.

He remembered that when the 18th Division arrived in mid January, he spent the night telephoning and making arrangements for some 4,000 families to report to Keppel harbour the following day with only light hand luggage. 'That day there was a very bad air-raid and many dockside godowns were burning. Their fires were so fierce that I had difficulty in getting on board one liner until I found a small boat to take me around to the other side of the ship.

'The raids and the fires caused a great deal of confusion which increased when cars began to arrive carrying evacuees. At one time I had to stand on point duty to control the traffic. The local police had by this time disappeared.

'On the 11th the STO, a retired Naval Commander, received instructions from Rear Admiral Malaya to leave for Java on board Naval Units due to arrive that night. These were expected to include the cruiser *Durban* and the *Jupiter*. Their estimated time of arrival was 10 pm. On the way to the docks we passed many fires and in particular I remember a spectacular blaze at Coldbeck McGregor's bonded warehouse where a vast amount of gin and whisky disappeared in vivid blue flames.

'When we arrived at the wharf there was no sign of the ships which eventually arrived at 2 am on the 12th. While we waited with key personnel and specialists, the 9.2 inch coastal defence guns on Pulau Blakang Mati, which had been turned around, fired over our heads towards the Japanese positions in the north and west of the island. Once the ships berthed the embarkation was swift and we departed from Singapore, on the *Jupiter*, just before dawn. Shortly after we cleared the entrance to the harbour we passed between two huge pillars of fire – to starboard were the burning oil tanks on Pulau Bukum while to port Pulau Sambu was a mass of flames and smoke. Astern, away to the north, the blazing oil tanks between the naval base and the causeway provided an impressive backcloth of thick smoke.

'The enemy aircraft found us near Banka Island on the 13th and although we escaped damage the *Jalavihar*, nearby, was hit forward but made Batavia. Shortly afterwards we passed three tankers, deserted and on fire, I never did discover their names. We docked in Batavia on 14th.'

Colonel Warren's Letter to ABDA Command

Hotel D'Orangi
Padang
Sumatra.

Tuesday 24th Feb.

Addressed to Colonel Pried

Dear Colonel

If Killery is still near you will you please pass this to him. I am writing to you as being someone who I am certain is in Java.

I have received two messages from Java — one from Procurator-General (?) dated 15th or so telling me to continue with my plans and send a rep. to Java; the last from you telling me to make for Padang or Sibolga. I arrived at Padang today on a recce of the possibilities of the situation. Gordon Bennett's staff will tell you the situation here.

You will find Capt Broome's report attached. I have two officers still in Malaya and have had no news from them. They left Bagan on 12th Feb. Communications with my Base at Labuan Bilik are such that I cannot get in touch with my rep. there until tomorrow. I had intended sending Broome to Batavia as opportunity offered but as Gordon Bennett's ADC can take his I don't think it is now necessary.

The report may interest you. It raises this point. Can we help the Chinese further i.e. by passing in arms or a W/T set. If so I and some of my party will stay and look after affairs. If we have no arms etc. then I and my party had better leave Sumatra for wherever Killery says.

Padang seems to be organised – as a distributing centre for British personnel. We can look after ourselves and either muck-in with all other military personnel or find our own – perhaps to Java. If Killery has any wish for us to go to Java or Colombo with you – please say which, as I understand things here, British military personnel are being sent to Colombo.

In determining our future disposal I hope K will note what Broome says about the movement of aircraft at sea off the Malayan coast. The report of my remaining two officers may put a different complexion on this. To make the link with Malaya reasonably secure I think a high speed naval vessel is necessary. She could be hidden during the day in the mangrove near Bagan or Labuan Bilik and operate at night. The Dutch must of course be right in the picture. I have told Colonel Overaakers (Comdy Centre, Sumatra) most of my activities – he is most helpful. Japanese patrol craft in future raise difficulties.

Summing up my position I think the following are main points:

1. I have still to get into the picture at Padang.
2. I stay in Sumatra until you or Killery says we can do more good.
3. I want to know where I and party am to go if I have to leave Sumatra i.e. to Java or Colombo.
4. If I am to stay on the north coast and try to keep communications going with Malaya may consideration be given to the provision of a high speed craft – reliable with fuel reserves at Base: also to the provision of W/T set; also to getting Dutch fully into picture in Java.
5. Lieuts. Vanrenan and Graham are still in Malaya (S. Bulah) north of Port Swettenham. I will forward their report earliest opportunity if of value. I must remain until they return or get news of them.
6. I am at present investigating the possibility of joining up with the general evacuation plan from here or of getting a boat and making our getaway if necessary.
7. All is well with us.
8. Please send communications for me to Col. Overaakers — HQ at PRAPAT or TOBAMER.

Yrs sincerely

A.G. Warren

Bibliography

Japan's Imperial Conspiracy, David Bergamini, Heinemann.

Defeat in Malaya, Arthur Swinson, Purnells.

The Royal Australian Navy, G. Herman Gill, Canberra Australian War Memorial.

Australia at War 1939–1945, John Robertson, Heinemann Melbourne.

Chronology of War at Sea Volume 1, Rohwer and Hummelchen, Ian Allen.

Chronology and Index of the Second World War, Royal Institute of International Affairs, Newspaper Archive Development Ltd.

Warships of World War II, H.T. Lenton and J.J. Colledge, Ian Allen.

The Navy at War 1939–1945, Capt. S.W. Roskill R.N., Collins.

Malay Waters, H.M. Tomlinson, Hodder & Stoughton.

The Naked Island, Russell Braddon, Wernie Laurie.

Miracle on the River Kwai, Ernest Gordon, Quality Book Club.

Women beyond the wire, Lavina Warner & John Sandilands, Michael Joseph.

The other side of Tenko, L.L. Barnes. W.H. Allen.

The Boat, Walter Gibson, W.H. Allen.

Singapore to Freedom, Oswald Gilmour, E.J. Burrow.

Last flight from Singapore, Arthur G. Donahue, Macmillan.

The Fall of Singapore, Frank Owen, Michael Joseph Ltd.

You'll Die in Singapore, Charles McCormack, Robert Hale.

It began in Singapore, G.P. Willis and M.P. O'Connor, World Distributors.

Spotlight on Singapore, Denis Russell Roberts, Tandem.

Seventy days to Singapore, Stanley L. Faulk, Robert Hale.

The worst disaster. The fall of Singapore, Raymond Callahan, University of Delaware Press.

Percival and the tragedy of Singapore, Sir John Smyth VC, Macdonald.

SOE Singapore 1941/42, Richard Gough, Kimber.

SOE in the Far East, Charles Cruickshank, Oxford University Press.

Return of the Tiger, Brian Connell, Evan Brothers Ltd.

Ring of Fire, Dick Horton, Leo Cooper Ltd/Secker & Warburg.

Escape from the Rising Sun, Ian Skidmore, Leo Cooper Ltd.

Marines don't hold their horses, Ian Skidmore, W.H. Allen.

Sinister Twilight, Noel Barber, William Collins.

No Time for Geishas, Geoffrey Adams and Hugh Popham, Leo Cooper
    Ltd.
White Coolies, Betty Jeffrey, Angus & Robertson.
Sold for Silver, Janet Lim, Collins.
Bamboo and Bushido, A.G. Allbury, Robert Hale.
Alarm Starboard, Geoffrey Brooke, Patrick Stephens Ltd.

Index